CW01619791

MNAC

MUSEU NACIONAL D'ART DE CATALUNYA

Guide

Board of Trustees of the Museu Nacional d'Art de Catalunya

Generalitat de Catalunya
Ministry of Culture
Barcelona City Council

President
Narcís Serra i Serra

Vice-presidents
Jordi Carulla i Font
Antonio Hidalgo López
Ferran Mascarell i Canalda

Members
Carlos Alberdi Alonso
Aurora Baena Ruíz
Francesc Xavier Boya i Alós
Josep M. Carreté Nadal
Marina Chinchilla Gómez
Josep Ferrer i Sala
Salvador Gabarró Serra
Pere Izquierdo Tugas
Jordi Martí i Grau
Carles Martí i Jufresa
Julián Martínez García
Josep M. Montaner i Martorell
Immaculada Moraleda i Pérez
Miquel Roca Junyent
Jorge Semprún Maura
Gemma Sendra i Planas
Josep Serra Villalba
José Vidal-Beneyto

Secretary
Anna Bernadàs i Mena

Director
M. Teresa Ocaña i Gomà

Administrator
Joan A. Llinares i Gómez

Sponsors
Abertis
Banco Santander Central Hispano
Bassat Ogilvy
Consorci de la Zona Franca de Barcelona
El Periódico de Catalunya
Fomento de Construcciones y Contratas, SA
Freixenet, SA
Fundació Agbar
Fundació Telefónica
Gas Natural SDG
Hewlett-Packard Española, SL
La Vanguardia
Presència
Ràdio Televisió Espanyola a Catalunya
Televisió de Catalunya / Catalunya Ràdio
Yahoo en Català!

© edition
Museu Nacional d'Art de Catalunya
Palau Nacional. Montjuïc Park
08038 Barcelona - www.mnac.es

© Texts: Museu Nacional d'Art de Catalunya

First edition: March 2005
Second edition: July 2006

ISBN: 84-8043-138-5
Legal deposit: B-50.678-04

Edition
Museu Nacional d'Art de Catalunya

Authors
David Balsells (D.B.)
Marta Campo (M.C.)
Jordi Camps i Sòria (J.C.S.)
Eduard Carbonell (E.C.)
Maria Clua i Mercadal (M.C.M.)
Maria Margarita Cuyàs (M.M.C.)
Mercè Doñate (M.D.)
Albert Estrada-Rius (A.E.-R.)
Mariàngels Fondevila (M.F.)
Maria Rosa Manote i Clivilles (M.R.M.C.)
Cristina Mendoza (C.M.)
Montserrat Pagès (M.P.)
Francesc M. Quílez i Corella (F.Q.C.)
Francesc Ruiz i Quesada (F.R.Q.)
Cecília Vidal i Maynou (C.V.M.)
Joan Yeguas (J.Y.)
Gemma Ylla-Català (G.Y.-C.)

Coordination of the texts
Montserrat Gumà

Restoration and preventive conservation
Àngels Comella Gilabert
Joan Bolet

Carmina Admella Baulias
Alejandra Balboa García
Pilar Camón
Núria Canyameres Tomàs
Anna Carreras Tarragó
Pere de Llobet Masachs
Ya-Hui Liu Zhou
Elena López Olivan
Paz Marqués Emo
Vicenç Martí Querol
Antoni Morer Munt
Teresa Novell Carné
Núria Pedragosa Garcia
Joan Pey Oliveras
Carles Pongiluppi Juncà
Núria Prat Grau
Carme Ramells Cabrelles
Emma Sarró Muñoz
Joan Serra Cañellas
Marta Serra Majem
Benoît V. de Tapol
Aurora Velat Sánchez

Photographs
© MNAC-Museu Nacional d'Art de Catalunya. Barcelona. 2004
© The Carmen Thyssen-Bornemisza Collection of Catalan painting on free loan to the Museu Nacional d'Art de Catalunya
© Junta Constructora del Temple Expiatori de la Sagrada Família
© Museo Thyssen Bornemisza. Madrid
© Salvador Dalí, Fundació Gala-Salvador Dalí, VEGAP, 2004
© Joaquim Sunyer, Santiago Rusiñol, Hermen Anglada Camarasa, J. Gutiérrez Solana, J. Torres-García, Xavier Nogués, Pablo Gargallo, Julio González, Ramon Pichot, J. Ortiz Echagüe, Agustí Centelles, VEGAP, Barcelona, 2004

Editorial coordination and production
Núria Giralt
Nèstor Sagimon
and Mireia Almirall

Text revision and translation
Elena Llorens
and Paul Hammond, Andrew Langdon-Davies, Richard Lewis Rees

Photographers
Jordi Calveras
Marta Mérida
Joan Sagristà

Graphic design
Villuendas+Gómez Estudi de disseny

Colour separations
Scan4

Printing
Grup 3

Ground floor

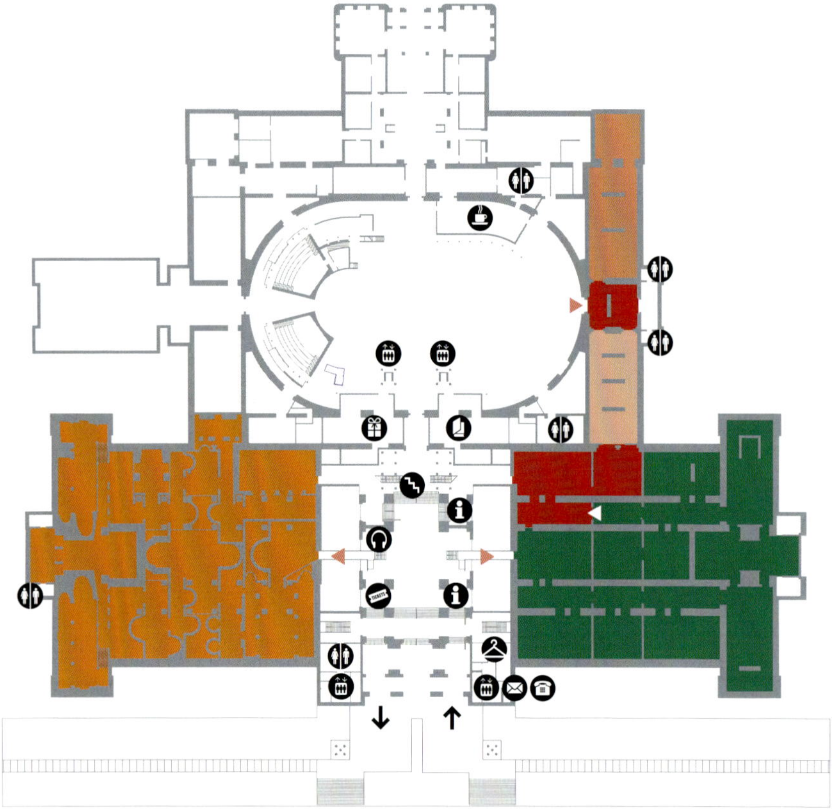

Romanesque art

Gothic art

Renaissance & Baroque art

The Cambó Bequest

The Thyssen-Bornemisza Collection

First floor

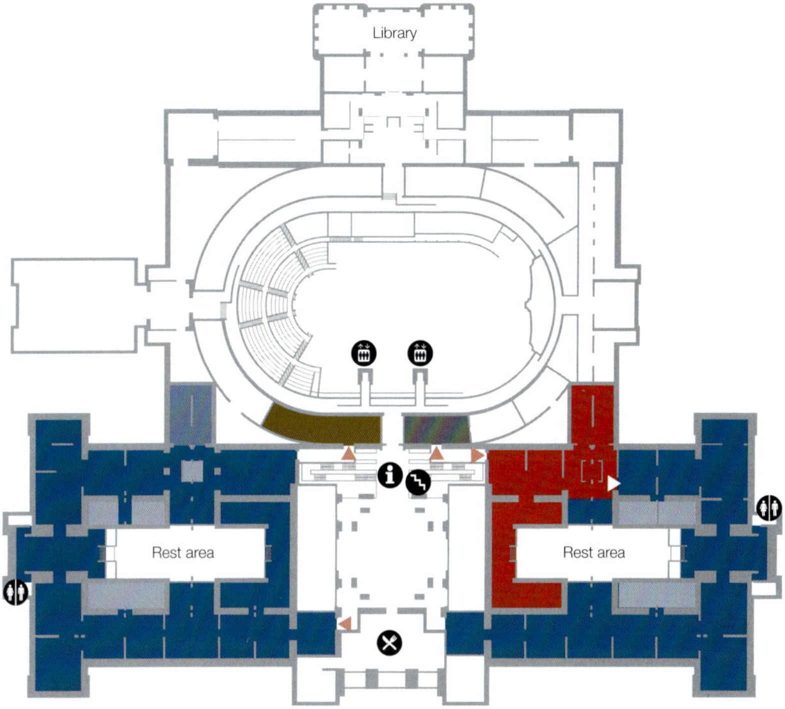

Renaissance & Baroque art

Modern art

The Carmen Thyssen-Bornemisza Collection

Drawings, prints, posters and photography

Photography

Numismatics

Contents

Introduction

The main job of the Museu Nacional d'Art de Catalunya (MNAC) as a museum, apart from preservation, documentation and research, is to generate knowledge, and it is here that the guide you have in your hands becomes a valuable tool for making this knowledge reach the widest possible public. After all, dissemination is another of a museum's chief purposes.

Furthermore, if one of the priorities of a country is also to explain and disseminate its art and compare it, whenever possible, with international art, the role of the MNAC as laid down in the 1990 Museums Law is central. This framework, too, gives a meaning to this guide, whose object is to establish a dialogue between the public and the works of art they contemplate, in an unbroken tour of almost 1,000 years of art in Catalonia, beginning with the presentation of a small, tenth-century altar and ending with the series of sculptures by Julio González from the 1940s, or, in the case of photography, with the work of contemporary photographers. Nevertheless, the goal the Museum has set itself of reaching as large a public as possible means that this tour must find a balance between the demands of the general public and the needs of connoisseurs and art scholars. This twofold demand, which is reflected in this guide, has been and is, for the Museum, a challenge and a stimulus. For this reason, it is a great satisfaction, both to me and to the Museum's team of specialists and professionals who have made it possible, that this guide should become an essential reference for anyone interested in the Catalan art of the last 1,000 years.

In this respect, we must not forget that the MNAC, with its close ties to the history of this country and its people, is the culmination of the recovery and safeguarding of our heritage, a job begun in 1891 with the creation of the Museu Municipal de Belles Arts in the Palau de Belles Arts, which in 1915 was moved to the former arsenal in Ciutadella Park, today the seat of the Catalan Parliament. Thanks to the involvement of the Board of Museums, set up in 1902 and reorganised in 1907, alongside the City Council, Barcelona Provincial Corporation and, later, the Mancomunitat de Catalunya and the Generalitat de Catalunya under the Republic, a plan was launched for the recovery and acquisition of heritage, thanks to which the Museum today has such valuable and representative collections of Romanesque and Gothic art, making the Museu Nacional d'Art de Catalunya an essential point of reference for art scholars. Finally, in 1934, one of the most important landmarks in this whole process was reached when the collections in Ciutadella Park were moved to the Palau Nacional on Montjuïc, built for the large official and cultural events of the 1929 Barcelona International Exhibition. Here, in 1934, the Museu d'Art de Catalunya was inaugurated, with its exhibition of the country's art from Romanesque to the twentieth century.

However, because of the threat posed to the collections by the Civil War, in 1937 they were moved to Paris and then to Olot and Darnius, whence they returned following the end of the armed conflict. But, resuming the thread of history, during General Franco's dictatorship, the unity of Catalan art exhibiting was broken up and in 1945 the collection of nineteenth- and twentieth-century art was split off from the Museu d'Art de Catalunya and housed in the former arsenal in Ciutadella Park, where the Museu d'Art Modern was founded. That same year, the Museu del Gabinet Numismàtic de Catalunya was inaugurated, with its exhibition on the history of coins, paper money and medals, also in Ciutadella Park, where it stayed until 1980.

The distinction between what was considered early art—that is, Romanesque, Gothic and Renaissance and Baroque—and what was called modern art—in other words, that of the nineteenth and twentieth centuries, persisted until 1990, when another important landmark was reached in the gestation of today's Museu Nacional d'Art de Catalunya. This was the passing of the Catalan Museums Law, which once more restored the unity of the collections of the former Museu d'Art de Catalunya, spanning from Romanesque to the 1940s, declared it a national museum and included in the new museum structure the Gabinet de Dibuixos i Gravats, the Gabinet Numismàtic de Catalunya and the Biblioteca General d'Història de l'Art. In a way, then, the MNAC is heir to the spirit of 1934 and includes collections that until now were scattered over various sites. In this quick overview of the history of the Museum, we must not overlook 1996, when the Department of Photography was set up with the wish to include this artistic discipline in the MNAC collections too. This long process is drawing to an end now, 2004, when the Museum's patrimony spans all the arts: sculpture, painting, object art, coins and medals, drawings, prints, posters and photography, and the collections themselves shape a global discourse on Catalan art, from the earliest manifestations of Romanesque to the 1940s, or to the present day in the case of photography, comparing it with international art whenever our collections allow it, as reflected in the pages of the guide it is my pleasure to present to you as director of this great museum.

Both before and after the parenthesis imposed by the Civil War, the Museu d'Art de Catalunya and the Museu d'Art Modern continued their important museum work and added to their collections thanks to acquisitions such as those of the Casellas (1911), Plandiura (1903 and 1932) and Muntadas (1956) collections, amongst other equally significant ones. As a result of the purchases by the Board of Museums, for example, today the Museum can present such outstanding items as the Romanesque woodcarvings of the *Taüll Descent from the Cross* and the *Mondoñedo Crosier*; the Tortosa *Altarpiece of Our Lady of the Angels*, by Pere Serra, and the *Altarpiece of Saint Vincent*, by the Master of Estopiñán—fine examples of Catalan Gothic—El Greco's *Saint Peter and Saint Paul*, an excellent contribution to the collections of Renaissance and Baroque art, and a noteworthy presence of works by Catalan *Modernista* and *Noucentista* artists, added with the acquisition of the Plandiura Collection. I should also mention that, thanks to the acquisition of the Muntadas Collection, the Museum today owns work by important artists like Bernat Martorell, Jaume Huguet, Pedro García de Benabarre and Fernando Gallego, amongst others, all of them central figures in Gothic art, and Ayne Bru, one of the leading names in sixteenth-century Catalan art. On the question of acquisitions, that of the Casellas Collection (1911) deserves a special mention on account of its importance for the collections of the Cabinet of Drawings and Prints, not just because of its artistic value but also because of the change it brought to a collection which until then had been fed by sporadic private contributions. It is also important to mention the Lluís Plandiura collection of posters, which entered the Museum in 1903.

As regards donations, amongst those that stand out are Enric Batlló's (1914), the Cambó Bequest (which entered the Museum between 1949 and 1954 and is important enough to warrant a separate section in this guide), the Espona Bequest (1958), the Domènec Teixidó Bequest (1961), the Bertran Bequest (1970), the Fontana Bequest (1976) and, more recently, the donation by the firm Girbau, SA (1997), which has gifted the series *Life of the Virgin*, by Francesc Pla, known as 'El Vigatà', a good example of the decorations with which the Catalan bourgeoisie of the last quarter of the eighteenth century embellished the rooms of their private homes. Under this heading we can, for example, speak of the arrival of the *Virgin from Ger* and the *Châsse of Saint Stephen*, two basic items in the MNAC's Romanesque collection, without forgetting the presence of such important names in the history of art as Zurbarán, El Greco and Stanzione. These speak for the greatness of the Museum and are all represented in the Espona Bequest. We must not forget the arrival at the Museum of one of the most emblematic works in the collection of Romanesque art, the *Batlló Majesty*, a donation by Enric Batlló, who also donated Pere Joan's *Saviour*, a quite remarkable Catalan Gothic carving in stone. But the bequest of the Fontana Collection is no less important, as it has given the Museum an excellent selection of Gothic work by the Lleida, Aragon and Valencian schools. A case apart is the donation to the Museum in 1909, by Ramon Casas himself, of his portraits in charcoal, a genuine iconographic gallery of the artist's contemporaries, the donation by Roberta González in 1974 of works by her father, the great avant-garde artist Julio González, and that of work by artists such as Carles Fontserè, Oriol Maspons, Toni Catany, Pere Formiguera and Colita, amongst others, all of which have helped to shape the collections of the Department of Photography during this initial period.

And we must not forget important permanent loans such as those by the Reial Acadèmia de Bones Lletres (1879) and the Reial Acadèmia de Belles Arts de Sant Jordi (loaned in 1902 and added in 1906), the Gil Collection (loaned in 1922 and partly acquired in 1944) and the Bosch i Catarineu Collection (entered the Museum in 1935 and was acquired in 1950) and several from the Museo del Prado. On this point, for example, we might single out the presence of an emblematic Gothic work, Gonçal Peris Sarrià's *Altarpiece of Saint Barbara of Puertomingalbo*, which came to the Museum from the Bosch i Catarineu Collection. More recently, we must not underestimate the permanent loans by the Generalitat de Catalunya and the Fondo Fotográfico de la Universidad de Navarra, which have been an important addition to the collections of the MNAC's Department of Photography.

As regards artistic collections from the nineteenth and twentieth centuries, the general exhibitions of fine arts organised by Barcelona City Council between 1891 and 1911, the official exhibitions (also organised by the City Council) of the twenties and the spring exhibitions of the following decade take on special significance. These complete the thread of the Museum's exhibitions thanks to the purchase of works by Catalan and foreign artists, some of which have taken Catalan art to its moments of maximum splendour. On this subject, though, the arrival of two oils by Mariano Fortuny, *The Spanish Wedding* and *The Print Collector*, deserves a special mention, as it was made possible by private donations to a subscription organised by the Board of Museums, which managed to rouse the interest of the public in the city's museums.

Recent permanent loans from the Thyssen-Bornemisza Collection and the Carmen Thyssen-Bornemisza Collection, evidence of the MNAC's wish to try and extend, enlarge and complete its museological discourse, deserve a special mention in view of the important material they contain. The first of these provides a global view of European art from Gothic to Rococo, and in the second we can savour an exquisite collection of Catalan painting by the most representative artists of the nineteenth and twentieth centuries.

However, in the context of its duty as a museum to preserve, research and disseminate the heritage in the broadest sense, the MNAC differs from other museums in two main aspects which, when all is said and done, make it the backbone of the rest of the country's art museums and cultural institutions. First of all, it provides a series of technical facilities outside the strict scope of the museum. In this respect, for example, the MNAC supervises the restoration of architectural sculpture and work in painting, sculpture and other artistic techniques, as well as advising other museums on questions referring to security, museography and preventive conservation. Through its technical services, the MNAC provides support and assistance to museums and cultural institutions requesting it, for which it carries out studies and analyses aimed at assessment and diagnosis, with proposals for improvements or for the initial installation in the sphere of safeguarding heritage, installations and people, preparation of museological and museographical projects, design of organisations and the establishment and running of museum structures.

But at the same time the MNAC has become an important research centre built around the Art History Library, the General Archive and the laboratories. To mention just a few examples, the MNAC's Department of Restoration and Preventive Conservation has earned itself a leading position as a centre for research into new techniques and materials and their application in the world of preservation and restoration of works of art. At the same time, we must not forget that the Library is an important documentation and study centre and a point of reference for art historians, particularly of Catalan art, thanks to the exchanges and the partnerships it maintains with other libraries, universities and museums, both here and abroad.

Because of all this, although the Museu Nacional d'Art de Catalunya, by virtue of its collections, already has a place amongst the best museums in Europe, once open to the public it must also earn itself a leading position on the international scene for its activities in the fields of research, documentation, restoration, dissemination.., the challenge facing us now. Two thousand and four is therefore the close of one period and the start of a new one: that of the Museum's consolidation in Catalonia and Spain and that of its integration in international museum circles. While its national status makes it one of our main cultural institutions and a point of reference for the rest of the country's museums, it is at the same time beginning its international promotion, thereby contributing to the understanding and promotion of the Catalan artistic world on a global level.

As I have said, the priority considered by a country of explaining its art and comparing it with international art is approached at the MNAC via an all-round project which, in my opinion, will allow us to enter Europe coherently. Museums can obviously contribute rich collections on individual artists, but then the final discourse is a sum of partial, unconnected discourses. On the other hand, the MNAC, as well as the great artists, has an ample discourse on offer explaining the history of art and a heritage from one particular place in Europe. Personally, I think this is a good way of entering Europe, because I feel that the contribution made to the European artistic heritage by a country's art, with its periods of splendour and decadence, with its individuals, but with a genuinely coherent discourse, dotted whenever possible with international references and counterpoints, helps us and future generations of Europeans to get to know an artistic past at the same time as it leads to the enjoyment of art and, all together, to raise the cultural level in this country and in Europe.

But precisely because museums generate knowledge in that they preserve works of art, document them and research them, thus allowing us to advance in our understanding of history and of art history, they must also establish bridges for cultural dialogue. On this point, guides like this one are valid and useful instruments because they disseminate collections on the basis of investigation, but without forgetting scientific rigour, because scientificism, didactics and publicising go together and complement one another. Only in this way will we enter fully into the concept of the twenty-first-century museum, a research centre and a generator of knowledge that must be able to reach as much of today's public as possible, anyone today who wants to enjoy art, regardless of when it was created. Museums must learn to communicate with this public, but without forgetting the demands of art historians and researchers. After all, in an increasingly globalised world, we must try to find common ground for everyone. Why shouldn't this common ground be our cultural heritage? In this respect, museums must enter the twenty-first century fully and with renewed meaning. I therefore repeat my conviction that, wherever you come from, the book you have in your hands is the instrument that will help you feel at home with us, as it is the starting point from which you can get to know and understand the various works in the permanent exhibition. At the same time, you will be able to place them in the context of a global discourse, that of European art. This to me, as director of the MNAC, with the duty to lead the museum down these new paths in the face of the challenges unfolding before us, is a great satisfaction.

Eduard Carbonell i Esteller
Director of the MNAC

Romanesque art

The collection of Romanesque art

The collection of Romanesque art is undoubtedly one of the Museum's most emblematic, above all by virtue of its series of exceptional groups of mural painting. The collection comprises Catalan artworks from the eleventh, twelfth and thirteenth centuries, which may be compared to others from the rest of Spain and abroad. Besides mural painting, mention should be made of the examples of panel painting and wood carving, many of which are paradigmatic pieces in their respective media, as well as remarkable holdings of stone sculpture and metalwork.

Much of the collection was put together between the late nineteenth century and the first third of the twentieth century. Interest in evidence of Romanesque artifacts grew out of the desire to recover and study the Catalan medieval past, particularly on the part of cultural movements such as the 'Renaixença', whose aim was to get to know the country, and to define and assert the Catalans' right to their own identity. This endeavour went hand-in-hand with attempts to safeguard the architectural and artistic heritage. As the process unfolded, one factor in particular had a determining effect on the nature of the Romanesque art collection, and particularly on that of the murals: as a result of their being studied, published and seen by art dealers, interest in them gradually increased during the initial decades of the twentieth century, and this in turn led to attempts to export them, an operation in which Italian experts were called upon to remove the frescoes from their original sites. The Board of Museums was quick to react and halt the operation, and shortly afterwards it was decided to transfer the paintings to Barcelona and to install them in the Museum. This took place between 1919 and 1923, and the details of the entire operation of removal, transfer and installation, which have been published on several occasions, now form part of the Museum's history.

Today the selection and arrangement of the works follows a chronological and stylistic discourse, determined above all by the murals, although examples of panel painting are occasionally included. In that respect, some of the most significant trends of the period are represented, such as the strand of French filiation—*Sant Joan in Boí*—and the Italianate—*Sant Quirze de Pedret*—from around the year 1100. Dating from a later period are the most important works in the collection, namely the paintings from *Sant Climent in Taüll*, especially those of the main apse, and the ones from *Santa Maria in Taüll*. Outstanding among later sets of works are those belonging to the art of the year 1200 or so, notably several Catalan groups of mural and panel painting (*Frontal from Avià*) as well as a Castilian group (*San Pedro in Arlanza*) and one from Aragon (*Sigena*). This latter was one of the wonders of medieval Hispanic painting until it was severely damaged by fire in 1936, during the Spanish Civil War.

In between, a series of sections and parts of sections allow us to explain several significant aspects of the Romanesque, particularly techniques and iconography. Outstanding among the panel paintings, mainly intended as altar furniture, are the *Frontal from La Seu d'Urgell or of the Apostles*, and the ones from *Cardet* and *Avià*. For its part, the collection of wood carving offers a broad, comprehensive view of the Romanesque, with works of extraordinary quality representing different typologies, such as the *Virgin from Ger*, the *Batlló Majesty* and the two carvings of the Erill la Vall *Descent from the Cross*, a truly exemplary work from the Romanesque period. Finally, the collection also features outstanding examples of sculpture in stone, such as the *Capitals from Sant Francesc*, and of enamel work, such as the *Mondoñedo Crosier*.

The altar from Sant Serni de Tavèrnoles stands out on account of its size, the composition and the subject depicted, a series of bishop saints.

The dimensions of this item are larger than is usual in known altar frontals. This suggested the possibility that it was a sarcophagus or an altarpiece, but the size and importance of the monastery it came from allowed large liturgical celebrations that would have required an altar of these proportions. The work depicts nine bishop saints, of which the central figure is possibly St Sernin, patron of the monastery the item comes from and bishop and martyr in Toulouse. This subject is very uncommon in panel painting, which used to concentrate the decoration around a central figure and arrange the scenes or figures in registers. On the sides, which were obviously painted by a different artist, are the bishops Martin and Bricius, identified by inscriptions.

The little we know about this altar has made stylistic analysis of the frontal our main source of information and there are various interpretations of it. The stylisation of the figures and the ornamental effect of the almost seriated rhythm of the personages have associated it with the resources used in mural painting, while such aspects as the precision of the line in defining the drapery have linked it to the decoration characteristic of miniaturists. However, the work could have belonged to a workshop connected with La Seu d'Urgell, for which reason it has been installed in the apse of La Seu d'Urgell (see pp. 22 and 23). G.Y.-C.

The frontal, the item covering the front of the altar, stands out for the quality of its bright colours and because it illustrates some of the characteristics of composition in Romanesque art, such as bilateral symmetry, abstraction of the background, with no reference to space or context, and the unnatural geometrical treatment of form to be observed in the folds of the clothing. It also shows certain conventions of representation, such as so-called hierarchical perspective, which consists in representing the chief character in a larger size.

The composition is presided by the *Maiestas Domini*, or Christ in Majesty, represented in a double mandorla in the Carolingian tradition. According to the Bible sources inspiring the vision, the Lord's throne is the arc of Heaven and he has the Earth as his footstool. His face is framed by a cruciform halo and his expression is severe. He is holding the Book of Revelation in his left hand and blessing with his right. The Apostles figure in the lateral compartments, arranged in tiered pyramids, an original compositional formula, although it was already known in the art of the Early Empire and also appears in the famous eleventh-century Romanesque bibles of Rodes and Ripoll. The disciples are all addressing the Saviour, either with their eyes or with the inclination of their heads, and are carrying books or scrolls. Peter, furthermore, is holding the keys. Opposite him, on the other side, is Paul, with his characteristic bald head. Both the image of Christ and the quality of the yellow and red used and even the bordering on the frame are very similar to those on the frontal from Sant Martí d'Ix (MNAC/MAC 15802), which probably came from the same workshop. M.P.

Altar from Tavèrnoles

Twelfth century

MNAC/MAC 15786, the altar frontal
MNAC/MAC 64003 and 64006, the altar sides

Frontal from La Seu d'Urgell or of the Apostles

First half of the twelfth century

MNAC/MAC 15803

The decoration on this apse is a noteworthy sample from the MNAC's unique collection of Romanesque mural painting, most of which comes from the diocese of Urgell.

In the apse there was a large representation of the Theophany, or manifestation of the Lord, inspired in the Gospel and the Book of Revelation. Christ appeared in all his splendour, upright and imposing in the mandorla of his glory, with the Earth as his footstool, in keeping with the Biblical interpretation. He was surrounded by the Tetramorph, or symbols of the Evangelists, of which John's eagle and Luke's bull are preserved almost whole. The vision evoked in this image is both the Ascent of Christ and his triumphant return at the end of time. An attractive Greek fret in the classical tradition separates this register from the one below, in which are the Virgin and the Apostles, centred in the figures of Peter, with the keys, and Mary, with a crown in her hand, a curious iconographic detail referring to the Kingdom of Heaven. Also portrayed are Andrew, with the cross, a beardless John the Evangelist and Paul, the Apostle of the Gentiles, who represent the Church militant attending the manifestation of God. Attractive floral borders decorated the windows. Stylistically, these paintings show a synthesis of different influences from Lombardy, Occitaine and Peitieu. M.P.

Apse from La Seu d'Urgell

First half of the twelfth century

MNAC/MAC 15867

This capital is a very outstanding example of Hispano-Muslim art production in the period of the caliphs and belongs to one of its most brilliant phases, that of the Caliph Al-Hakam II (961-76), as can be seen from the inscription on the abacus referring to him and to his minister Ga'far, who died in 970. This allows us to date the capital fairly exactly to between 961 and 970. Many works from this period in Al-Andalus can be dated from the inscriptions. This particular capital comes from the work of remodelling the Alcazar in Cordoba.

As happens with many capitals from this period in Al-Andalus, the item's general structure shows links with the late Roman tradition, with a pattern deriving from the classic Corinthian type: two levels of acanthus leaves on the cylindrical part and the volutes on the upper corners. The relief is obtained by trepanning, while some of the details are bevelled. Further characteristics of these Andalusian works are the absence of necking and the fact that the decorative sense is provided by the contrast between light and dark and a tendency towards a geometricisation of shapes.

This production contrasts with that of the late Middle Ages in Catalonia, as we see in some of the items included in the same section where this capital is exhibited. We must not forget that in many ways the Islamic world was a source of contacts and enrichment for Christian areas, amongst them the Catalan counties of the tenth and eleventh centuries. J.C.S.

These two items are highly representative of eleventh-century sculpture in Catalonia and of one of the most significant trends of this period. Furthermore, they come from one of the most outstanding buildings of the architecture of the eleventh century, the church of Sant Pere in the castle of Àger, an important strategic power centre with a view to the conquest of the Catalan counties towards the south in the face of Islamic domination.

The impost is decorated with an undulating stem on which are inscribed two registers of semi-palmettes. This impost, as regards both the decoration and the facture, has been associated with other similar items, such as the imposts from Barcelona Cathedral, two of which are also exhibited in the Museum's Romanesque art gallery (MNAC/MAC 14397 and 14398). The decoration on the capital consists of palmettes surrounded by pointed arches and arranged in two rows of registers. This type of decorative motif was very common during this period in Catalonia. The bevelling procedure by which the effects of light and shade outlining the motifs are achieved is also characteristic.

The decoration in Sant Pere d'Àger consisted basically of plant and geometrical motifs. This can be seen in the remains preserved *in situ* and also in the items kept at the Museu de Lleida Diocesà i Comarcal. Other ensembles, however, had figural decoration, such as the lintels from Saint-Genis-des-Fontaines and Saint-André-de-Sorède, in Roussillon, and also in Sant Pere de Rodes. J.C.S.

Andalusian capital from the period of the caliphs

961-70 / AH 350-60 (according to the inscription from the period of the Caliph Al-Hakam II)

MNAC/MAC 122001

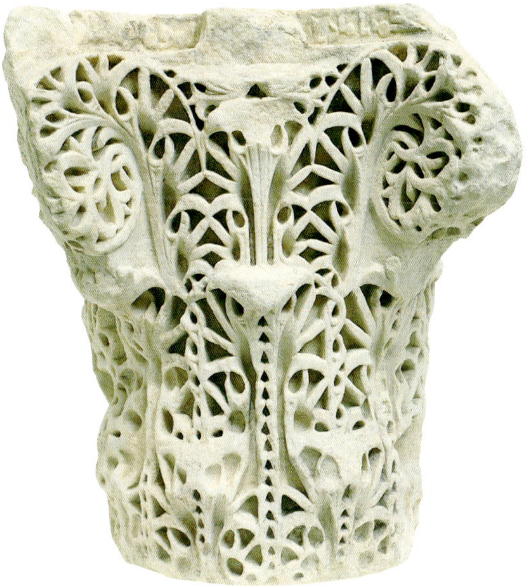

Capital and impost from Àger

Eleventh century

MNAC/MAC 24002 and 49368

Paintings from Boí

c. 1100 the interior and
twelfth century the façade

MNAC/MAC 15796, 15822,
15862, 15951-15956, 200423-
200441 and 200817

The paintings from Sant Joan in Boí make up what is considered one of the finest groups in Catalan Romanesque painting. Their chronology, around 1100, has been established indirectly on the basis of the architecture of the building and from comparison with the paintings in other churches in the valley of Boí: Sant Climent and Santa Maria in Taüll. Their study has led to comparison with those of Saint Martin de Vicq (Nohant-Vicq, Indre, central France) from the second half of the twelfth century, in which has been found not so much a certain interdependence but the use of common, possibly Carolingian European models.

Of the whole, what remains is basically the painting from the aisles and the arches separating the nave and the aisles, enough to reveal a rich iconographic programme with ample references to the story of the Redemption. Exemplary scenes are depicted from the lives of saints, of which the most important fragment is the

Lapidation of Saint Stephen, a vast repertory of animals of a moralistic nature (mainly on the intradoses of the arches) and a scene with minstrels, something very unusual, which in this case must be taken as being in praise of the Lord. There was also a representation of the Day of Judgement from which the surviving fragments of Paradise, Hell and the apocalyptic dragon came.

The paintings from Boí must be considered an example of an underlying French influence in Catalonia which was different from the Italian influence that was to dominate the Romanesque pictorial scenario in Catalonia after the paintings of the Pedret Circle. E.C.

At the end of the eleventh century, the Romanesque mural painting of northern Italy arrived in Catalonia with a spread similar to that of Lombardic Romanesque architecture. The work of Italian painters, then, accompanied the architecture and soon had important repercussions.

The clearest example of this Lombardy-related painting is the Sant Quirze de Pedret ensemble, which stylistically comes close to the paintings of Sant Pere in Àger (pp. 36 and 37), Santa Maria in Àneu (pp. 32 and 33) and Sant Pere in El Burgal (pp. 34 and 35), and to those of Saint-Lizier in Couserans (France), preserved *in situ*.

The MNAC keeps the two side apses from Sant Quirze de Pedret and the Museu Diocesà i Comarcal in Solsona keeps the decoration of the central apse. Taken together they present an important apocalyptic series in which the subject of the Church is related to the coming of the Day of Judgement in a way that is not frequent, centering on the parable of the wise and foolish Virgins in the southern apsidiole.

According to this parable, to be found in the Gospel according to Matthew (25, 1-3) and depicted on the intrados of the arch, only those prepared will be able to enter the house of the Lord—that is, the Kingdom of Heaven. The wise virgins, who with forethought had brought oil for their lamps, are shown sitting at the bridegroom's table wearing a crown, the symbol of eternal life. The foolish virgins, on the other hand, who have no oil for their lamps, are shown standing and without crowns. On the vault of the apse is a Virgin in majesty, as a *Virgo prudentissima*, and on the right of the entrance, is a personification of the Church also wearing a crown.

The remains of paint in the lateral apse have been interpreted as the gathered Apostles presided by Peter, the head of the Church of Rome, which underlines the importance of the doctrine of the Church and of the Gregorian reform. E.C.

Side Apses from Pedret
End of the eleventh century
MNAC/MAC 15973 and 22991-22992

Santa Maria in Àneu was the most important church in the Àneu Valley and belonged to the cathedral chapter of Urgell. From the stylistic circle of Pedret, of Lombardic influence, the decoration of the apse reveals the existence of an elaborate iconographic and theological programme setting off the prophetic hopes of the Old Testament—that is, hope in the coming of a Messiah who was to redeem humanity—against fulfillment of the prophecies—that is, the coming of the Messiah announced by the prophets.

At the bottom is the announcement, the biblical prophecy, represented by means of combined images of the visions of Isaiah and Ezequiel. In keeping with the first, two magnificent seraphim with three pairs of wings each purify the mouth of the prophets with glowing embers which they are holding with tongs. Next to them are the prophets, represented with their hands together in an attitude of reverence. At the same time, the seraphim intone the Trisagion, or song of praise to the Lord, represented by the letters SCS, SCS, SCS, which mean 'holy, holy, holy'. From this moment, the word of the prophets will be the word of God. Beneath the central window are the wheels of fire of Yahweh's chariot, described in Ezequiel's vision, which symbolise the presence of the Lord. On the vault was the Virgin and Child, representing the accomplishment of the prophecies, in the scene from Epiphany, with two archangels, Michael and Gabriel, patrons of sinners, in a representation very similar to that in the apse from Santa Maria in Cap d'Aran (The Cloisters, New York). A third archangel, Raphael, is represented on the right of the semi-cylinder, perhaps as the introducer of the two donor clergymen who appear on the left of the apse. M.P.

Apse from Àneu
End of the eleventh century
MNAC/MAC 15874

The very noteworthy style of the paintings from the Burgal apse is linked to the Pedret Circle, of Lombardic influence. The programme of images, with its marked Eucharistic and ecclesiological sense (referring to the Eucharist and the Church), contained a Theophany or vision of the divinity on the vault, which was presided by the figure of the *Maiestas Domini* or Christ in Majesty, which to judge from the surviving remains must have been monumental. It was flanked by the figures of two prophets in a reverent attitude of beseeching and by two archangels carrying signs with inscriptions on which they advocated for sinners. These have been partly preserved. In the lower register is a representation of the Church militant, with imposing, grim-looking apostles and saints sitting in a semicircle and centred by the figures of Mary, with the chalice, and John the Baptist, with the Lamb, the symbol of the death and resurrection of Christ, of great Eucharistic significance. Beside them are Peter, with the keys, Paul, with a scroll and a volume, and John the Evangelist, on the right, plus another apostle on the left. An attractive Greek fret separates this area from the painted drapery there was at the bottom of the apse.

What especially distinguishes this apse is the figure of the richly dressed female donor holding a lighted candle. She appears superimposed on the drapery, as though approaching the holy images. She is wearing a luxurious dress decorated with precious stones and from the remains of an inscription can be identified as the Countess Llúcia, wife of Artau I of Pallars Sobirà. The paintings probably date from the time of their children Artau II and Ot, who was soon to be bishop of Urgell. In the church, *in situ*, close to the apse, is the portrait of other characters, presumably also members of the count's family. M.P.

Apse from El Burgal
End of the eleventh century
MNAC/MAC 113138

The church of Sant Pere in Àger, founded by Arnau Mir of Tost, who conquered the valley of Àger from the Saracens, was the see of a regular canonry exempt from ordinary jurisdictions (in other words, it did not depend on the Bishop of Urgell), with enormous estates from the donations by the founder and his descendants. In keeping with its importance, the church, now in ruins, was very monumental.

Of the paintings that once decorated it, only scattered fragments remain of the main and southern apses, of which the most outstanding and complete is that of the two apostles, Thaddeus and James, from the first arcosolium in the central apse. The two monumental apostles of Àger are presented in a face-on, hieratic position, with scrolls or volumes in their hands, which they are holding in alternating positions, at the same time as the colour of their nimbuses and their clothing also differs. The beardless one on the left is Thaddeus and the one on the right, with a beard, is James, as the inscriptions indicate. The pictorial style belongs to the Lombardic-influenced Pedret Circle and shows a close relationship with that in the paintings in the cathedral of Saint-Lizier in Couserans (*in situ*, France). As in Saint-Lizier, in each of the niches in the apse of Sant Pere in Àger there must have been a pair of apostles. All together they must have made up the Apostolic College, whose representation was fully meaningful in Augustinian chapter houses like that of Àger, who, in keeping with the Gregorian reform, wanted to strengthen the independence of the Church as an institution in the face of secular power. M.P.

The panel of the *Baldachin from Tost*, which covered the altar to give it more importance, corresponds to the type of liturgical furnishing that was attached by beams to the apse wall. Another type of Romanesque baldachin is the one that has the form of a shrine, which could also be of wood, like the one from Toses (MNAC/MAC 4523-4525), or else stone, like the one that used to be at the monastery of Ripoll and of which the finely carved bases have been preserved.

The Tost panel has a representation of the Lord in Majesty, with a crucifer halo and enthroned in the mandorla, which at one time must have been golden, with the book in his left hand with a Biblical citation, EGO SVM LUX MVNDI, which proclaims him as the light of the world. With his right hand, he makes the sign of blessing. Around him are the four symbols of the Evangelists or the Tetramorph, each of which, instead of the book of the Gospel of earlier examples, has a sign or phylactery with his name. On John's eagle and Luke's bull can be observed, in particular, the subordination of the figure to its frame—that is, to the available space, even when this involves strange or unnatural distortion of the forms. Here, the way the configuration of these two symbols is dealt with is especially noteworthy. In addition, the pictorial style shows some figurative features of a more naturalistic type, such as the figure and face of Matthew's angel, which comes closer to the new spirit of Gothic. This convergence of the resources of two pictorial languages shows the artistic influences and tensions of a time of change. As regards the colours, recent restoration has made it possible to recover the original very bright blue and red. M.P.

Apostles from Àger
c. 1100
MNAC/MAC 65467

Baldachin from Tost
c. 1200
MNAC/MAC 3905

Carved images in wood were one of the basic elements of a Romanesque church and were located mainly around the altar. They were placed in prominent positions, but could also be used as reliquaries and sometimes took part in certain liturgical events such as processions.

The *Virgin from Ger* is one of the most important examples of wood carving from the twelfth century in Catalonia, on account of the type it represents as well as its brilliant technique. To these features must be added its good state of general preservation. Iconographically, it corresponds to the concept of Mary as the *Sedes Sapientiae*—that is, the seat of wisdom—and symbolises the Church. This is why the figure of the Child appears front-on and rigid, without any sign relating Him to Mary. It is worth pointing out the softness of Mary's facial features and of the folds of the clothing.

From early twentieth-century photographs we know that this image was retouched and adapted for a new concept of the subject. The Child was moved and placed on Mary's left knee. This fact is of great interest as it reminds us that some of these works were used outside the period when they were first created and were adapted to the new demands of religious worship and thought. J.C.S.

The *Frontal from Cardet*, along with the one from Rigatell (see pp. 68 and 69), is one of the best and most representative works from the Ribagorza workshop, so called as the source of a series of works of similar style and technique. The technique features the use in backgrounds and on frames of stucco reliefs, which were once coated with fine layers of metal and yellow varnish (known as *colradura*) to give them the appearance of precious metal. The pictorial style is highly narrative and uses a lot of bright colours that, in their day, with the gilding that has since been lost, must have been even brighter. These sightly works must have been in great demand, something we can deduce from the number of specimens preserved.

The frontal is presided by the Virgin and Child, enthroned inside an almond-shaped mandorla surrounded by the Tetramorph, the four symbolic beings that proclaimed the Gospel. In the side compartments, separated by thin columns, are scenes from Christ's childhood, beginning with the Annunciation by the angel to Mary and the Visitation by the latter to St Elizabeth. It continues with the Nativity and, behind Joseph, the Annunciation to the Shepherds, a highly descriptive scene full of detail, with landscape elements characteristic of the time. The Magi with their offerings, in the Epiphany, address the central figures. The last compartment depicts two scenes, without any architectural separation: the Slaughter of the Innocents, which is difficult to recognise as the soldiers' spears and the slaughtered children have been lost, and the Flight into Egypt. M.P.

Virgin from Ger

Second half of the twelfth century

MNAC/MAC 65503

Frontal from Cardet

Second half of the thirteenth century

MNAC/MAC 3903

Paintings from Sant Climent in Taüll

c. 1123

MNAC/MAC 15966

The paintings in the central apse of Sant Climent in Taüll are the most emblematic in the Museum's collection of Romanesque art and make up one of the most representative and one of the finest works of Romanesque art.

The central theme of the apse is a Theophany, or vision of God, at the end of time, based mainly on the text of Revelation. In the middle, Christ in Majesty inscribed in a mandorla, seated on the arc of Heaven and with the Earth at his feet, blesses with his right hand, while his left holds a book with the inscription EGO SUM LUX MUNDI ('I am the light of the world'). On either side are the Alpha and the Omega, symbols that God is the beginning and the end of all things. He is surrounded by the four Evangelists. Saints, apostles and the Virgin Mary occupy the semi-cylinder and several scenes from the Old and New Testaments are depicted on the arches

over the entrance to the apse. One scene that stands out is of Lazarus the beggar at the door of the rich man Epulon's house, on the intrados of the arch, and at the top, the hand of God and the *Agnus Dei* (the Lamb of God), symbolising the death and resurrection of Christ (Rev 5, 6-14).

The style combines the geometricisation of forms and the general symmetry of the composition with the decorativism in the details and ornamental elements. The volume of the pronounced drapery is geometrical, emphasised by coloured lines and glazing, contrasting with the flat tones of the background. In addition, the symmetry, frontality, hieratic nature and the very representation of God could derive from Byzantine art, possibly via Italy. The bands of colour in the backgrounds, present in many Catalan Romanesque paintings, could remind us of what is known as Mozarabic illumination in tenth-century Hispanic manuscripts.

The exceptional artistic nature and the high quality of these paintings have been corroborated by the study of the pigments, which are of better quality and preparation than in other Catalan churches. Some imported pigments have even been found. Through the use of superimposed layers, the painter obtains more intense chromatic effects. Thus blue, obtained from aerinite, is applied over a layer of black, and cinnabar is applied over haematite to get red.

Painted on one of the columns of the nave is the church's inscription of consecration by bishop Ramon de Roda from Ribagorza on 10 December 1123. This reference is fundamental for dating the paintings, of which there are still remains *in situ*. E.C.

The censer is a small brazier used to burn incense during certain liturgical ceremonies. Its use is documented since ancient times and in the Romanesque period it is frequently represented. In the Museum, for example, it can be seen in the mural paintings from Esterri de Cardós (MNAC/MAC 15970), Sorpe (MNAC/MAC 113144) and Sant Esteve in Andorra (MNAC/MAC 35706-35711).

In the Romanesque period it took various forms, one of which was spherical, of which this item is an obvious example. It consists of two semi-spherical pieces, of which the upper one has tracery, decorated with plant elements and pairs of opposed birds in circles. This theme is very common and belongs to repertories reflecting the memory of the Byzantine or Islamic world through productions from the world of textiles or ivory. The item was hung from chains attached at four points, which also mark the quadripartite distribution of the item's decoration.

Some of the most important centres for the production of precious metals and enamel in Western Europe during the Romanesque period were Liege, Cologne, Limoges and Silos. We can also assume there were workshops for more local consumption which followed the procedures and models used in the more important centres. In this framework, the spherical censer had been fairly unanimously considered a good example of a Catalan item reflecting local production prior to the great spread of products from Limoges, introduced on a large scale in various parts of Europe, including Catalonia. J.C.S.

Reliquary caskets were one of the objects that were used for keeping relics in churches. This particular example, dedicated to St Stephen, is one of the numerous examples of this type that came out of the workshops of Limoges. For a variety of reasons, Limoges became one of the great production centres for objects for worship and liturgy in metal or enamel.

The worship of relics grew up from the earliest days of Christianity and became very strong during the early Middle Ages. The relics could be not only bodily remains attributed to holy figures, but also supposed fragments of their clothing or instruments of their martyrdom. They could also be mementos of pilgrimages, especially to the Holy Land, and, of course, fragments of the Cross on which Christ was supposedly crucified.

The *Châsse of Saint Stephen* is an item which, as often happens in these cases, has an architectural structure consisting of a parallelepiped box with a gable lid. In this case, though, it is of modest dimensions and the general composition is very synthetic. The front contains scenes from the life of St Stephen: the martyr's detention on the lid and his lapidation on the vertical face. The gilded tone of the figures contrasts skilfully with the fields of colour, in which the blues stand out, especially that of the background. We do not know what church this casket came from, but it is likely that it was intended for an altar or a church dedicated to this saint, an important object of worship in Limoges. J.C.S.

Censer
Catalonia, second quarter of the twelfth century
MNAC/MAC 4581

Châsse of Saint Stephen
Limoges, *c.* 1210-20
MNAC/MAC 65526

This item is a sample of the considerable production of the stone-carving workshops at the abbey of Santa Maria in Ripoll. Unlike works like the ones from Àger, it represents a far more developed point in Romanesque sculpture, at a date after 1150. It is decorated with a head, with half-human and half-monstrous features, wearing a helmet and apparently with a ram coming out of its maw. The symbolism, though difficult to pin down, shows up the negative aspect of the head and gives it a demoniacal meaning, heightened by the pointed ears and the ferocious nature that generally characterise it. However, motifs of this sort were very common in Romanesque art and appeared in a number of variants.

Stylistically, its descriptive nature is clearly demonstrated by the way the smallest details have been worked with a certain geometricisation, which makes the item stylistically closer to other objects from Ripoll, especially some parts of the monastery church's great doorway, one of the masterpieces of Romanesque carving in Catalonia.

It is difficult to tell what this voussoir was originally intended for, as it was found in the monastery, underground. We can only think it must have formed part of an arch over a door in the site at Ripoll, along with other preserved remains. The workshops active in Ripoll are characterised by their contacts with the great centres of Languedoc, especially Toulouse, and also by their analogies with certain works from northern Italy. J.C.S.

These five capitals come from one of the great sites in Besalú, the church of Santa Maria, in which there are still remains *in situ*.

Three of the capitals are of plant themes, with a decorative scheme and motifs derived from the classic Corinthian. The deep, vigorous carving to be observed on it, combined with the use of trepanning, makes one realise how extraordinarily widespread these technical and formal solutions were in the Romanesque carving of the Mediterranean Languedoc and Provence and is a fine example of the persistence of the sculpture of Roman antiquity, as can also be seen in the *Capitals from the Camarasa Pillar* (see pp. 48 and 49).

The other two capitals are from the exterior of the apse and show figuration. The composition consists of figures holding on to the stalks of the volutes and flanked by birds, very possibly eagles. The crudeness of the carving, consisting of dry, angular, highly simplified forms, suggests that the workshop that made the items was not particularly used to working with figurative elements, though the opposite was true as regards plant repertories.

The decoration of the church preserved *in situ* generally presents the same subject matter as the capitals in the Museum, which are marked by their austerity. The same goes for the remains preserved on one wall of the building known as El Conventet, beside the monastery of Pedralbes, in Barcelona. The church of Santa Maria in Besalú depended on the Augustinian chapter of Saint-Ruf in Avignon (Provence), so that its sculpture seems to adapt to the reference point of this great centre, also marked by austerity. J.C.S.

Permanent loan from the Generalitat de Catalunya, Gòdia dation, 1994

Voussoir from Ripoll

Second half of the twelfth century

MNAC/MAC 12264

Capitals from Santa Maria in Besalú

Between 1137 and 1167/71

MNAC 200685-200689

The elements from Camarasa help explain architectural, monumental sculpture as one of the great contributions in the Romanesque period. Indeed, sculptural decoration in stone or similar materials became widespread and developed in full integration with the architectural elements of the building, emphasising its most important points and areas. Romanesque also saw the birth of figurative and historiated subject matter, which in some cases was spectacular in the way it covered surfaces.

On the *Capitals from the Camarasa Pillar* the historiated subject matter is combined with plant and, in particular, Corinthian themes. On the left is represented the scene of the Original Sin, with Adam and Eve on either side of the tree with the serpent, the symbol of the Devil. This subject reflected the idea of man's fall into sin. On the right is represented the sacrifice of Isaac, which foreshadowed the death of Christ and is a reference to the Eucharist, celebrated on the altar, which is why we find this scene so often represented in the vicinity of the presbytery, as in this case. It is important to bear in mind that this cycle was completed with other themes historiated on other pillars in the crossing, which are still partly preserved in the original church. As regards the capitals, which bring to mind those of a Corinthian type, it should be mentioned that they provide a very significant example of the survival of formulae from Antiquity during the Romanesque period.

Nevertheless, the Camarasa series belongs to a late moment in Romanesque, at the beginning of the thirteenth century, and is part of a trend that can be observed on some of the most important monuments of the time in Barcelona. J.C.S.

The capitals were discovered as a result of the excavations carried out for the construction of a house in Plaça del Duc de Medinaceli, in Barcelona. They have always been connected with the cloister of Sant Nicolau, a pilgrims' hospital where the convent of Sant Francesc was established after 1232. Both hospital and convent have now disappeared.

The first of the capitals presents figures that appear amongst a series of leaves, a common subject generically during the Romanesque period. It stands out for the agility of the forms and the masses, with a certain classical air, especially in the heads. The second capital shows a series of clergymen holding different liturgical objects. The third capital is badly damaged and is decorated with plant motifs.

From the stylistic point of view, this series of capitals is related to the work of the artistic circle of Master Mateo, a name that appears on the *Portico of Glory* of Santiago de Compostela Cathedral, one of the key works of Hispanic medieval carving. What is especially remarkable is the similarity between the first capital and some of the work produced in the site in Santiago and others in the contemporary Galician sphere. In this respect, the capitals of Sant Francesc are an exceptional reflection of Santiago production in Catalonia and particularly in Barcelona in the thirteenth century. We must not forget that the Museum keeps various examples from other sites in Barcelona of the same period, as for example remains of the cloister of the monastery of Sant Pere de les Puel·les. However, the capitals in question belong to a very late moment in Romanesque and show solutions that come close to Gothic art. J.C.S.

Capitals from the Camarasa Pillar
First third of the thirteenth century

MNAC/MAC 17601-17605

Capitals from Sant Francesc
c. 1200-20

MNAC/MAC 14202, 14203 and 14206

The Santa Maria de Taüll ensemble is one of the most complete series of Romanesque pictures kept in the Museum. Originally, the church interior was totally decorated and despite not being preserved intact what we have is enough for us to know with some certainty what themes were represented and how they were distributed inside the church and to distinguish the different artists.

In the most important part of the church, the apse, the Virgin Mary is portrayed as the Child's throne in a scene from the Adoration of the Magi. It is the representation of the first acknowledgement of Christ's divinity by all nations and of the different ages of man. Inside the semi-cylinder are representations of apostles as witnesses of this divine manifestation and on the arches preceding the apse is the Hand of God, the figure of Abel (an allegory of Christ's sacrifice and the Eucharist), and the *Agnus Dei*. In the previous section there are remains of what must have been a *Maiestas Domini* with the Tetramorph, of which anthropo-zoomorphic figures have survived that would have represented two Evangelists, a seraph and the archangel Gabriel. There are also representations of animals inscribed in circles beneath the figures of the Apostles, which generically resemble the subjects on Oriental textiles.

On the side walls of the church there were often scenes from the Bible or of saints, distributed in different registers. Here, next to the side apse, we find, for example, Herod with the Three Wise Men, who, in a synthesis of two different episodes, visit Herod and adore the Child. On the columns of the nave and the intradoses of the arches there are pictures of saints and prophets representative of the Church, amongst them St Clement and St Nicholas. On the west wall was the usual representation of the Day of Judgement and a version of the fight between David and Goliath (Psalms 17, 4-54), which represents the struggle of good against evil.

Paintings from Santa Maria in Taüll

c. 1123 the apses and later the aisles

MNAC/MAC 15836

The consecration of the church by the Bishop of Roda and Barbastro on 11 December 1123 provides the key for dating the paintings at the east end. The artist, associated with Castilian sites like Santa Cruz de Maderuelo (Museo del Prado), is the best in this ensemble. His style shows a clear dependence on that of the central apse of Sant Climent in Taüll (see pp. 40-3), especially in the modelling of the forms and the geometricisation of clothing.

The artist responsible for the rest of the paintings in the church is later, more rustic and has less technical resources. He has been called the Master of the Last Judgement and is connected with the paintings of the apsidiole of Sant Climent in Taüll. E.C.

Most of the altar frontals known to us from the Romanesque period in Catalonia consist of a panel, painted in tempera, which in some cases is complemented with stucco relief elements. But alongside this more widespread form there were other technical possibilities, such as fresco painting or carved stone or marble or, as in this case, carved polychrome wood. Remember that some decoration and details, using gilded effects, resembled or imitated more luxurious items covered with precious metals.

The *Frontal from Santa Maria in Taüll* is part of a series of works discovered at the beginning of the twentieth century in the churches of the valley of Boí and is one of the items of highest quality from the Ribagorza workshops. These works are characterised by the cleanness of their forms, a certain vigour and a schematism that has led them to be compared to monumental sculptural groups of the second half of the twelfth century.

The composition and iconography are very common in this sort of item. In the central register is Christ in Majesty, inscribed in the mandorla, surrounded by the symbols of the Evangelists, whose marks remain. On either side are arranged the figures of the Apostles on two levels under the arches. The figures are carved in pine wood and preserve important traces of polychromy. J.C.S.

The monumental sculptural groups in wood of the Descent from the Cross are an important chapter in Romanesque carving in Catalonia on account of the high artistic quality of the works preserved and of the unique features of their iconography. A very significant proportion comes from the valley of Boí. One aspect that sets these Catalan series of carvings apart from other renderings of this theme is the presence of seven figures: in the centre was the figure of Christ, sustained by Joseph of Arimathea (on his right, the left for the observer) and Nicodemus on his right; on either side are Mary and St John, and at the ends the figures of the two thieves, Dymas and Gestas.

The theme of the Descent brings a greater narrative and dramatic sense to the treatment of the two episodes of the Calvary and may be related to the liturgical plays of the time. But the presence of these groups in Catalonia during the twelfth and thirteenth centuries, as some have tried to show, could also respond to the struggle against the heresy of Catharism. As the subject could have a Eucharistic meaning, it could be used as a reply to the negation by the Cathars of the death of Christ and of the Eucharist itself.

The *Erill la Vall Descent* is the most complete of all the groups known to us from the Catalan western Pyrenees, but it is broken up between the Museu Episcopal de Vic and the MNAC. Our Museum exhibits the carvings of Mary and of St John. As a whole it is a masterpiece of Romanesque carving in Catalonia, to the extent that other works have been arranged around it, such as the *Descent from Santa Maria in Taüll* (MNAC/MAC 3925), what remains of the one from Durro (MNAC/MAC 15895), as well as works of other typologies (altar frontals, crucifixes). J.C.S.

Frontal from Santa Maria in Taüll
Second half of the twelfth century
MNAC/MAC 3904

Virgin and Saint John of the Erill la Vall Descent from the Cross
Twelfth century
MNAC/MAC 3917 and 3918

Within the Romanesque wood carving of Catalonia, this is an exceptional item as it can be precisely dated, something that only happens in two other works. In a restoration undertaken in 1952 a cavity was discovered behind the figure of Christ which contained various relics wrapped in Hispano-Muslim fabrics and some parchments. One of these parchments contained an inscription in which could be read the date the work was consecrated, 1147, from which it takes its name. Another parchment mentioned the acknowledgement of the relics in 1521, which shows the item was still in use after the Middle Ages and remodelled at that moment. To some extent, the piece is valuable for the dating of similar works and also reminds us that some carvings were also used as reliquaries.

Unlike the Maiestàs (or Christ triumphant), *The Christ from 1147* is an example of the Suffering Christ (Christus Patiens), depicted half naked, dressed only in a short loincloth or *perizonium* and with his arms noticeably bent. Although it is a reference to the redemptive death of Christ, it dwells more on the aspect of suffering, on the death of Christ the man. The hard facial features help to stress this aspect, as does the treatment of the anatomy. Nevertheless, we must bear in mind that the work has lost practically all its polychrome, so that its present appearance is very different from the original. The Catalan area has numerous examples of this typology, and of Romanesque in general. Amongst the main precedents is the *Christ from Gero*, kept in Cologne and dated between 960 and 980. J.C.S.

The representation of Christ nailed to the Cross, the crucifix, corresponds to a typology of which many examples from the Romanesque period have been preserved. We find it in two variants: that of the more humanised Christ suffering and that of the Christ in Majesty, represented victorious and triumphant in the face of death.

The *Batlló Majesty* is an emblematic example of the Christ triumphant model, in which he is dressed in a long-sleeved tunic (*manicata*) fastened at the waist with a cingule. It preserves the polychrome, with a rich decoration of circles inscribing floral motifs that brings to mind Oriental textiles. The head is bowed and the eyes open with a relatively serene expression and the face is bearded, the long hair falls over his shoulders and the arms are well extended horizontally. At the top of the cross is the inscription IHS NAZARENVS REX IVDEORUM ('Jesus of Nazareth king of the Jews'), as in other examples. The back preserves remains of the Lamb of God, as happened with most crosses and as we see in the *Bagergue Cross*, also exhibited in the Romanesque art gallery (MNAC/MAC 3937).

Its quality, with the skilful schematisation of the features of the figure, on the basis of planes and angles, puts the *Batlló Majesty* at the head of a group of carvings from the eastern Catalan Pyrenees which also stands out for the *Beget Majesty*, still kept in its original church. The carving under discussion might come from the same area, as it was purchased by Enric Batlló from an antiquarian in Olot (La Garrotxa). The *Volto Santo* in Lucca (Tuscany, Italy), another famous item of wood carving from the European Middle Ages, is often considered a prototype for this model. J.C.S.

The Christ from 1147
Consecrated in 1147 (according to a parchment found on the back)

MNAC/MAC 15950

Batlló Majesty
Mid-twelfth century

MNAC/MAC 15937

The Museum keeps a noteworthy collection of paintings from the parish church of Sant Pere in Sorpe which are completed by fragments at the Museu Diocesà d'Urgell. The apse of the church was demolished in the eighteenth century, so that the paintings preserved are those from the triumphal arches, the walls of the nave and the arches. The programme of images is difficult to reconstruct as it is incomplete, but its scenes show a surprising iconographic wealth and stylistic filiation.

On the walls of the nave are juxtaposed scenes from the Old and New Testaments. On the right can be made out the Original Sin, while on the left wall, on two registers, is the story of the Redemption, with subjects such as the Annunciation and the Birth of Christ at the top and the Crucifixion in the lower register. This is one of the best-preserved parts and the one showing most artistic quality, to which must be added iconographic details based on apocryphal texts. Some motifs go back a long way in Byzantine art, such as the Virgin of the Annunciation with the spindle in her hands or the Bathing of the Child in the Nativity scene. Others, though, are present in the Carolingian tradition and have parallels in sites in Lombardy, with the presence of a girl watching the Annunciation.

The triumphal arches that preceded the apse have representations of various saints worshipped in the Church of Milan, something that suggests links with this centre and the world of Lombardy. There is also an excellent picture of the Virgin with Child sitting between a leafy tree and a dry one, which could symbolise the Church and the Synagogue, respectively. This image of Mary, taken as a link between the laws of the Old and New Testaments, has been compared stylistically with the one from the central apse of Santa Maria in Taüll (see pp. 50-3). The scene beneath shows the miraculous catch of fish on the Sea of Tiberias (John 21, 1-9) and can be interpreted as an image of the Church. In addition, on the intradoses of the arches communicating with the aisles there are some signs of the Zodiac—to be precise, Gemini, Cancer and Sagittarius. G.Y.-C.

Paintings from Sorpe
Mid-twelfth century
MNAC/MAC 113144

The paintings in this apse are attributed to the stylistic circle of the Master of Santa Coloma in Andorra, so called on account of the decoration in the church of this name (in the Staatliche Museen zu Berlin). Other Andorran paintings linked to him are the ones from Sant Romà de les Bons (MNAC/MAC 15783 and 15787). Although various influences can be made out in this style and it shows elements inherited or assimilated from Taüll, the most remarkable is the one from El Burgal (see pp. 34 and 35), from the Pedret Circle. Whereas in Santa Coloma there is a certain monumentality, the pictorial art of Engolasters is more ingenuous and graceful.

The apse of this church dedicated to St Michael is presided by a vision of the Lord in Majesty, portrayed in the mandorla, sitting on the arc of the Heavens, with the Book of Life open in one hand and making the sign of blessing with the other. The Alpha and the Omega, representing the beginning and the end, appear strangely hanging one from the other. Around them is arranged the Tetramorph, though incomplete, since instead of Matthew's angel there is the archangel St Michael, the patron of the church, at the moment of slaying the apocalyptic dragon. John's eagle appears magnificent on the right and below some flying angels carry a bull and lion, symbols of Mark and Luke (portrayed very small), in circles. Lower down are represented the Apostles. They are small figures that seem to be moving. We can recognise Peter, with the keys, and on the other side of the window, with his characteristic bald head, is Paul. Next to him, according to the inscription, is Andrew. At the mouth of the apse there are imitation capitals and on the key of the arch the figure of the Lamb of God, carried by wingless angels. Beneath it, various saints in squares. M.P.

The *Frontal from Baltarga* is one of the works in which the stylistic influence of the strongly Byzantinising 1200 art in Catalonia shows most clearly, especially in the intense and penetrating treatment and expression of the faces, comparable only to those on the *Frontal from Orellà* in El Conflent (*in situ*). It has also been related to the now lost *Frontal from Saint-Genis-des-Fontaines*, which was signed by a Magister Alexandre. The Baltarga frontal also stands out for the rotundity of the volumes, which have a sculptural value, noticeable in the rendering of the bodies of Christ and the Apostles.

As regards the iconography of the work, in the centre of the frontal is the Lord in Majesty, seated on an upholstered throne, making the sign of blessing and with the Earth as his footstool. Around him, outside the mandorla, are the symbols of the Tetramorph and in the lateral compartments, the Apostles and the Virgin, sitting in twos in this order: St John the Evangelist and the Virgin, St Andrew and St James and finally St Philip and St Thomas. A fourth compartment presents the passion and martyrdom of the patron saint of the church the work came from, Andrew, crucified on a Latin cross and not the Greek cross more common in the West.

The frontal also stands out for its clear, successful and high-quality chromatic opposition. M.P.

Apse from Engolasters
c. 1160
MNAC/MAC 15972

Frontal from Baltarga
c. 1200
MNAC/MAC 15804

This frontal is highly characteristic of the so-called art of 1200, which, though with variations and to different degrees, spread throughout the Christian West and is characterised by the powerful influence from the most recent Byzantine art, that of the time of the Comnens emperors.

The art of 1200 is characterised by the more sculptural modelling of the bodies, which on the *Frontal from Avià* can be appreciated above all in the angel of the Annunciation and in the figures of the Magi, who are arriving to adore the Child. It can also be seen in the treatment given to the faces, with large eyes and aquiline noses. This stylistic influence was often accompanied by the inclusion of new iconographic themes, of both Byzantine and Western origin. The novelty of this frontal lies in the gesture and pose of the Child, who is obviously blessing the first scenes of the story of the Redemption: the Annunciation and the Visitation. The tenderness shown by the Mother, despite her frontal position, is also one of the novelties of the time, along with the trefoiled arch on slender columns that frame her like a baldachin. As regards the other scenes, it is important to point out that in the Nativity, the Virgin Mary reclines half-length on a straw mattress, an iconography of Byzantine origin, and that the presence of the ox and the mule is part of a tradition included in the apocryphal gospels. Joseph's perplexed expression also stands out. The last scene is the Presentation at the Temple, depicted at the moment the elder Simeon, having recognised the Messiah, returns the Child to His mother's arms. M.P.

Frontal from Avià

c. 1170-90

MNAC/MAC 15784

It is not known where this beam originally came from, or whether it formed part of a baldachin, which it would have helped to support, or else whether it could have been used to support some liturgical image or object, perhaps placed horizontally like the one in the Toses apse.

It contains seven episodes from the Passion of Christ, arranged side by side in frames. These are, from left to right: the Arrest, the Flagellation, the Road to Calvary, the Crucifixion (partly damaged due to a later reuse of the beam), the Descent from the Cross, the Lament over the body of Christ in the highly dramatic scene of the Holy Burial (of Byzantine influence), and finally the Resurrection, in which an angel of the Lord is seated over the empty grave, on one side of which must have been the Holy Women.

A minutely detailed work, the *Beam of the Passion* shows a close relation with manuscript illustration, in particular with the style of the second illustrator, the one of most quality, of the royal cartulary called *Liber Feudorum Maior* (Archivo de la Corona de Aragon), dated between 1172 and 1196. The isolated figures, like the crowded groups of people, on the beam and in the codex, are identically represented. It has also been related, though less directly, to the *Beatus of Las Huelgas* (Pierpoint Morgan Library, New York), from this Cistercian abbey under royal patronage. M.P.

This type of vase in the form of a dove which was used as a recipient for the host was often hung near the altar. In these cases, its shape also brought to mind the presence of the Holy Spirit in the Eucharist.

Its use is known to go back to the first centuries of Christianity. It is mentioned in writings from the third century and although there are written accounts of Eucharistic doves made with precious metals, the only surviving examples are made from simpler materials. From the beginning of the thirteenth century, these items were also one of the characteristic products of Limoges production.

The piece under discussion is one of the most outstanding of its type. The body is made from various sheets of copper, amongst which the wings stand out on account of their colour. Here they are arranged in groups of three or four different colours, contrasting with the gilded effect of the rest. J.C.S.

Beam of the Passion
c. 1200-20
MNAC/MAC 15833

Eucharistic Dove
Limoges, first half of the thirteenth century
MNAC/MAC 65534

The crosier is the staff carried by bishops and abbots as a sign of authority. The end was often profusely decorated and was made from luxury materials such as ivory or precious metals.

Amongst the formulas most often used to decorate the top is one in the form of a volute, with a scroll that forms the frame for various decorative resources. One of the commonest themes is that of the archangel Michael slaying the dragon, a theme which has to be interpreted as the victory of good over evil and which can be observed in the *Mondoñedo Crosier*. The subject of the reptile crops up again on other parts of this item, such as the node and the shaft.

This is one of the most outstanding pieces in the collection, both in terms of quality and because we know its provenance and certain details of its past. We must bear in mind, first of all, that this is one of the few Romanesque items in this technique in the Hispanic world whose history is known. Stylistically, it is an item produced in Limoges close to 1200. There are accounts that in the thirteenth century this crosier was in the sacristy of the former cathedral of Ribadeo (Lugo, Galicia) and that it had been found, along with a pair of sandals, in a sarcophagus attributed to the bishop of this Galician see, Pelayo de Cebeyra (1199-1218). Towards the mid-nineteenth century this item was to be found in Mondoñedo, another Galician cathedral see which has given the item its name. Later it entered the collection of Lluís Plandiura, purchased by the Museum in 1932. J.C.S.

In response to the demands of worship and of the liturgy there were some items in churches, such as ciboriums, that could reach a certain degree of luxury with gold or silver overlays or with the addition of precious stones. Many works, though, were made with more affordable metals such as gilded and often enamelled copper. Limoges, in central France, was one of the main centres for enamel items during the Romanesque period and its products can be found in many parts of Europe. The enamel procedure that predominated during the Romanesque was that known as *champlevé*, which consists in laying down the coloured glass paste in engraved hollows a few millimetres thick on the surface of the metal sheet.

The *Ciborium from La Cerdanya* is a quality item, an example of the scope of the renovating tendencies of 1200 and one of the oldest examples of the arrival in Catalonia of products from Limoges. Its most outstanding aspect is the decoration with half-length figures arranged in pairs in a network of rhombuses and curvilinear triangles. This and the decoration of the interior come very close to the Limoges ciborium made by the master Alpais kept at the Musée du Louvre in Paris. J.C.S.

Mondoñedo Crosier
Limoges, *c.* 1200

MNAC/MAC 4544

Ciborium from La Cerdanya
Limoges, *c.* 1195-1200

MNAC/MAC 12106

The archangels are the only angels with names, for which reason they have a rich iconography, especially Michael, Gabriel and Raphael, who are attributed with specific exploits and missions of importance in the story of the Salvation. This frontal reproduces four episodes in which these archangels and their deeds are the absolute protagonists, especially Michael, the prince of the heavenly hosts.

In the first of the four compartments are Raphael and Gabriel, who, as the liturgical prayer says, are carrying a dead person's soul (represented naked and sexless in a white sheet) off to Heaven. In the neighbouring compartment Michael, armed with a spear and a shield, fights with the dragon, the incarnation of the Devil, whom according to the account in Revelation he will vanquish. In the other compartments is the weighing of souls by Michael, with a black devil trying to cheat, and the Miracle on Mount Gargano, in which the Archangel appears to a hunter in the form of a bull. The hunter's arrow changes course and returns to pierce his eye, demonstrating the miraculous nature of the episode and the wish of the Archangel to have a shrine raised to him on that spot. This representation stands out for the hill in the form of a Corinthian capital. The outer border and the stucco bands of framing, which must once have been gilded, imitated precious metals.

This is a characteristic work of the period, with a detailed language and a taste for anecdote, with a pictorial style related to the mural paintings of Sant Pau de Casserres, *in situ*, and with the altar from Lluçà (Museu Episcopal de Vic). M.P.

One of the most outstanding and most representative works from the Ribagorza workshop, along with the *Frontal from Cardet* (see pp. 38 and 39), is the one from the shrine of Rigatell, which in some bibliographies is referred to with the mistaken name of Betesa, which was the former municipality it belonged to.

With the characteristic stucco background, which was once gilded, and a pictorial style close to Gothic, the frontal is presided over by the Virgin and Child. Mary is presented seated on a tall upholstered seat, crowned and beneath a baldachin, as she suckles the Child, who makes the sign of blessing with his right hand and holds the Book in the other. In the lateral compartments there are four scenes referring to the first episodes of the story of the Salvation. At the top on the left is a representation of the Annunciation, with the archangel Gabriel, and written in the nimbus of the Virgin Mary is the angelic greeting: AVE MARIA GRATIA PLENA. Next is the Nativity, with Mary lying on a straw mattress and the Child, of whom only the silhouette is visible, in the manger, with the ox and the mule from the apocryphal gospels. The scene also includes the apparition of the angel of the Lord to a doubting Joseph to tell him that the fruit Mary has conceived is the Holy Spirit's, an episode from the Gospel according to Matthew. Lower down, the Magi are arriving to adore the Child and finally, at the bottom right, the Annunciation to the Shepherds, which is the worst eroded scene of the whole series. Nevertheless, although quite a lot of paint is missing, the stucco shows the outlines of trees and animals, a sheep and a dog. The scene stands out for the clothing of the shepherds and their gestures of joy. M.P.

Frontal of the Archangels
c. 1220-50
MNAC/MAC 3913

Frontal from Rigatell
Second half of the thirteenth century
MNAC/MAC 35701

The paintings from San Pedro in Arlanza are a valuable example of the mural painting of about 1200 in Castile. It should be remembered that Arlanza was one of the most important monasteries of the early Middle Ages in Castile. It was related to Count Fernán González and later protected by the Castilian kings and queens.

The fragments preserved come from a palatine hall situated in the Torre del Tesoro [Tower of the Treasure] and formed part of a repertory organised around a central register containing representations of fantastic animals placed symmetrically beside the windows. Amongst others, the Museum keeps a panel with a griffin, a hybrid creature with the body of a lion and the head and wings of an eagle, in an attitude of watchfulness. This was often the role in which these creatures appeared, even in the world of ancient Mesopotamia, next to entrances to buildings or rooms. In Arlanza the figure takes on great monumentality, and in keeping with their location they can be interpreted as guardians of an important, representative part of the monastery.

The repertory of Arlanza also had structures of a military nature that represented the arms of the House of Castile, like the one kept at the Museum. The other subjects decorating this room were of a zoomorphic, plant or geometrical type, as we can see in another fragment presenting a winged dragon and a border. The style of the paintings from Arlanza is related to other Hispanic works of 1200, amongst them manuscript illustration, something that can be seen in the refinement and precision of the motifs. G.Y.-C.

Paintings from San Pedro in Arlanza

c. 1210

MNAC/MAC 40142, 40144 and 40145

The monastery of hospitaller nuns of Santa María in Sigena was founded by Queen Sança, wife of Alfonso I of Catalonia (II of Aragon), who retired there once widowed. The nunnery was also to house her grave and that of her son, King Peter I of Catalonia (II of Aragon). This royal patronage explains the high artistic standard of the frescos. The brownish tone they have today is the result of the alteration of the original colours in the fire in the nunnery in 1936, at the beginning of the Civil War. Even so, we can still appreciate the marked Byzantinising influence and the high quality of the pictures, which can be attributed to painters who had previously worked in Sicily alongside Greek artists and on the illumination of the Winchester Bible.

The iconographic programme of the chapter house included three main cycles. That of the Old Testament, with such scenes as the Original Sin, the Labours of Adam and Eve, the Death of Abel, the Construction of Noah's Ark, the Sacrifice of Isaac, the Crossing of the Red Sea and others, was represented on the diaphragm arches supporting the coffered ceiling, at the top of which is a real and imaginary bestiary and exuberant vegetation. On the perimeter walls was the New Testament, which started on the north wall with the Annunciation and the Nativity, while Jesus's public life was represented on the east wall. All of this part was lost in the fire. This cycle culminated in the Flagellation, the Crucifixion and the Resurrection on the south wall. The third cycle was the Genealogy of Christ, which, with the portraits of the generations, occupied the intradoses of the arches. M.P.

Chapter House of Sigena

c. 1190-4

MNAC/MAC 68703-68709

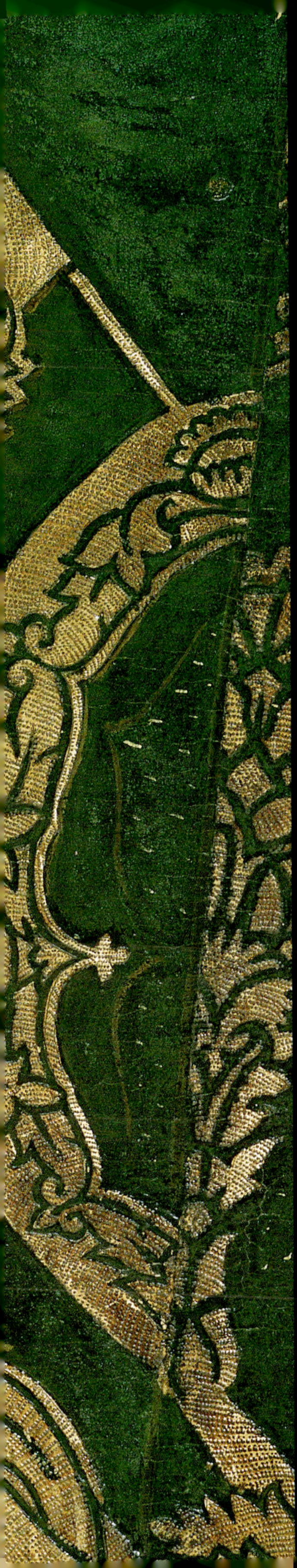

Gothic art

The collection of Gothic art

The MNAC collection of Gothic art displays the output of both Catalonia itself and those territories with cultural links to Catalonia during the Lower Middle Ages (from the late thirteenth until the fifteenth centuries).

This period, one of the most brilliant in the entire history of Catalan art, coincided with the country's maximum territorial expansion and the consolidation of its central position in the political, economic and cultural spheres within the context of Mediterranean Europe of the time.

The Catalan nucleus of the collection allows visitors to observe the emergence, development and culmination of the Gothic style, along with the reinterpretation in the Kingdom of Aragon of its different manifestations: the linear or Franco-Gothic, the Italianate Gothic, the 'courtly' or International Gothic and its Flemish-influenced counterpart. Both the kinship between the Catalan Gothic and the different European strands of the period on the one hand, and its own unique qualities, which came to the forefront from the courtly style onwards, on the other, are clearly appreciable in the work of major figures of international repute such as the Catalans Bernat Martorell and Jaume Huguet, and Bartolomé Bermejo, who was active in Catalonia during a period in his career.

Among the most important typological items in the collection are the painted altarpieces, that is, the liturgical furniture par excellence of the period or, in their absence, the panels that have been preserved. And in the formal field, the richness and ornamental profusion of the figurative arts as a whole, which include murals, goldsmithing, enamelwork, sculpture in stone, wood and ivory and, above all, painting on panel, first in tempera and later in oils.

The chronological and stylistic arrangement of the permanent exhibition, in which different genres and techniques stand side-by-side, allows visitors to compare and contrast Catalan art with the creative output of other territories during the same period. Moreover, and by virtue of their unquestionable artistic importance, certain nuclei of particular thematic interest are presented in monographic format. For example, civic art burgeoned to such a phenomenal extent during the Gothic period that it deserves specific attention in its own right. Turning to a different sphere, devotion to the Virgin and the funerary genre took visual form in works of such extraordinary variety and conceptual richness that they too are presented monographically.

Episodes from the conquest of Majorca by James I in 1229 were painted in the form of a frieze below one of the ceilings of Palau Caldes, also known as Palau Aguilar, on Carrer de Montcada, Barcelona. The fact that the Caldes family was related to that of King Alfonso the Liberal (d. 1291), conqueror of Minorca, re-conqueror of Majorca and grandson of James I, would explain the subject matter of the paintings, which together constitute a magnificent example of the historical genre.

The cycle begins with the scene of *The Assembly of Barcelona* (MNAC/MAC 71449), held in December 1228, at which it was decided to proceed with the conquest. The most significant episodes, however, are the *Battle of Portopí*, the *Encampment of James I* and the *Assault on the City of Majorca* (MNAC/MAC 71447).

Master of the Conquest of Majorca
Battle of Portopí
1285-90
MNAC/MAC 71448

This circular scalloped basin without handles features a low, moulded base with a zig-zag band in the middle between two fillets. Although few silver vessels have survived from the European Gothic, we learn from royal and municipal inventories that they were common in the fourteenth and fifteenth centuries. This particular type, however, is not documented until relatively late. Among the items included in the inventory of dishes and silverware the city of Barcelona presented as a gift to Isabella the Catholic are 'bassines dargent daurades dins e defora...gallonades' ['silver basins gilded on the inside and outside...scalloped'].

The Saragossa hallmark, thanks to which we are able to date the piece from the last third of the fifteenth century, is at the top outer edge of the bowl.

The eagle in the middle of the reverse side of the basin may either have a heraldic meaning or serve merely ornamental purposes. M.R.M.C.

The protagonists of the feat may be identified thanks to the heraldic repertory on the military clothing, the tents and other elements. Included among them are the Count of Roussillon, who was also the king's uncle, Nunyo Sans, Ponç Hug d'Empúries, Guillem de Montcada, Ramon de Centelles, Gilabert de Cruïlles, the Bishop of Barcelona, Berenguer de Palou, and the King James I.

Major characteristics of the work are its narrative quality and its fidelity to more or less contemporary historical chronicles: *El Llibre dels Feits* or *Crònica del Rei Jaume I el Conqueridor*. Note also the dynamism and vivacity of the colour. The raised viewpoint allowed the painter to superimpose scenes, thereby depicting simultaneous events, which are linked together by an undulating landscape background. M.R.M.C.

Scalloped Bowl
Manufactured in Saragossa
c. 1470-1500
MNAC/MAC 114078

The Soriguerola panel is the most important painting by an anonymous artist to whom several works—the product either of his own hand or of his workshop—have been attributed.

The panel attests to the progressive evolution of the former Romanesque structure of altar frontals during the Gothic period. Given its substantial length, it is unlikely that the work would have served the purpose of a frontal; it would more probably have been placed as a panel above the altar. Of all the scenes, the only one that apparently bears no relation to St Michael is that of the Last Supper. Regarding this, besides the possible link between the work and the altar as a place for Eucharistic sacrifice, we must not overlook the important connection that Francesc Eiximenis established years later between the Archangel St Michael and the Last Supper in his *Llibre dels Àngels*.

A vertical border divides the panel into two parts. The top left section features three scenes, of which only two have been preserved: the Miracle on Mount Gargano and the account of the event to the Bishop of Siponte. The Last Supper occupies the entire bottom register.

Master of Soriguerola
Panel of Saint Michael
End of the thirteenth century
MNAC/MAC 3901

Preserved in the MNAC are five carvings of seated figures, undoubtedly related to each other by virtue of their style and the fact that they were all executed around 1300 at the very latest. An image of St John the Baptist (at the church of Santa Maria in Arties) forms part of the same stylistic group.

The characteristics that allow us to relate them are the physiognomic traits, which are clearly similar, and the folds in some parts of the clothing. Furthermore, certain details of attire and gesture confirm their links with French art.

This holy deacon is one of the finest of the works. Despite the hieratic stiffness of the figure, it marks a step beyond the archaic qualities of the previous period by virtue of its observation from the natural, the refined simplicity, the harmony of the facial features and the sense of monumentality it denotes.

Another sculpture from the group, which represents a female saint (MNAC/MAC 64015), provides highly useful information regarding its origins, since on the base there is a scroll with the following inscription: HOC OPUS FUIT FACTUM APUD SANCTUM BERTRANDUM CONVENARUM MAGISTRUM UBUS (?) DORAMAIMUS.

As regards the assignment to master Doramaimus, it must be borne in mind that the inscription was repainted some time ago over an illegible name, which makes the transcription at least questionable. On the other hand, however, the general information the inscription provides about the location of the workshop where this carving, and by extension all the others, were made, Saint-Bertrand-de-Comminges, does seem to be reliable and it is of great interest. M.R.M.C.

The panel's right-hand side features the Weighing of Souls or Psychostasis, in which two demons attempt to confuse St Michael while an angel delivers the soul of the chosen one to St Peter. Next come six figures, which we might identify as the blessed. The hand of a demon, depicted in hell in the bottom register, relates the demonic world with the scene of the Psychostasis, while St Peter seems to link this composition to the world of heaven. The narrative concludes with St Michael's fight against the apocalyptic dragon. F.R.Q.

Saint-Bertrand-de-Comminges Workshop
Deacon Saint
c. 1300
MNAC/MAC 3925

In this painting and in the *Panel of the Holy Trinity and of Corpus Christi* (MNAC/MAC 9920), both from Vallbona de les Monges, we observe the continuity of the French-linked language and the tenuous reflection of coexistence with the new stylistic trends from the Italian Peninsula. It is clear evidence of the fact that the linear style and the Italianate style need not be at odds with each other. Indeed, on occasions they form part of the same artistic language.

The panels, which have on occasions been attributed to sculptor Guillem Seguer, may have belonged to the same altar. In this case, the *Panel of the Virgin* would have been the frontal and the *Panel of the Holy Trinity and of Corpus Christi* the altarpiece.

The broad Eucharistic iconography of the panels includes several clearly anti-Jewish scenes. It must be remembered, in this context, that the Eucharist contains the sacrifice of Christ and that on the altar the Mass revives the sacrifice on the Cross. The heretic, in his attempt to desecrate the Holy Form, causes the blood of Christ to be shed. In these renderings, the Jews, responsible for the death of Christ, repeat the offence in their intention to slay the Saviour and, as a consequence, annul the salvation of the believer through the Eucharist as well as to eliminate the permanent presence of Christ from among Christians. The purpose of some of the anti-Jewish images on the panels of Vallbona de les Monges is to show a Jewish people whose aim is to disrupt the message of eternal salvation that Jesus announced by instituting the Eucharist. F.R.Q.

This sculpture forms part of a larger group composed of three more apostles and constitutes the only example preserved in the MNAC of a group of the Apostles in the genre of monumental sculpture. This was a common theme in the decoration of the jambs of the great doorways of Gothic churches. The other sculptures from the same group—*St Peter, St James the Greater*, and *St Bartholomew*—are preserved in the Copenhagen Kunstindustrimuseum.

In the monument to which the sculptures originally belonged, the collegiate church of Gandía, the twelve apostles were accompanied by two bishops. Although the church doorway no longer survives, from the total number of sculptures it presented we might surmise that it bore similarities to the Apostles Doorway of the archpriest's church in Morella or, further north, to the main doorway of Huesca Cathedral.

The seven sculptures hitherto located date from around 1387 and are the work of Joan and Pere Llobet. According to the records, they were paid thirty florins for these pieces.

The quality of the figure of St Paul is unquestionable, by virtue especially of its monumentality and of the highly skilful simplification of planes. A relationship has been established between this piece and the anonymous sepulchre of Ramon Serra the Elder, in the chapel of St Philip and St James at the church of Santa Maria in Cervera, which scholars attribute to the sculptor and goldsmith Pere Moragues. M.R.M.C.

Attributed to Guillem Seguer
(documented between 1341 and 1348)
Panel of the Virgin
Mid-fourteenth century
MNAC/MAC 9919

Joan Llobet
(active between 1386 and 1391)
Saint Paul
c. 1386
MNAC/MAC 15792

This *Head of Christ* is associated with a rendering of the Holy Burial, better known in Catalonia as the Holy Sepulchre group, located in a chapel of the church of the convent of Sant Agustí Vell, Barcelona. The convent, according to ancient records, was built by the guilds of wool manufacturers and dyers and dedicated to the Corpus Christi in 1352.

The fracture in the neck suggests that the head belonged to the complete body of a Christ recumbent and that, consequently, it formed part of a group consisting of a number of no-longer surviving sculptures that together would have configured the Holy Sepulchre, highly characteristic of Catalan sculpture from the thirteen hundreds.

This hypothesis is supported by the similarities between this fragment and the head of a splendid Christ recumbent preserved intact at the former collegiate church of Sant Feliu, Girona. The resemblance lies in the subject matter of both works, their naturalistic treatment, and stylistic aspects. The Head in the MNAC features certain material resources such as the addition of bramble twigs that serve to intensify the dramatic effect of the thorny-crowned head.

A number of scholars are inclined to attribute both this Head and the Christ recumbent in Girona to Jaume Cascalls, although according to surviving contracts the latter work is by the Norman master Aloi of Montbrai (1350), a sculptor active in Catalonia as from the second quarter of the fourteenth century and, like Cascalls, closely associated with King Peter the Ceremonious (1319-87). In this context, however, we should take into account that both sculptors were professionally associated for a certain length of time. M.R.M.C.

The style of this sculpture dates back to the era of Peter the Ceremonious (1319-87), a monarch whose deeply-rooted dynastic sense led him to commission the construction of the Royal Pantheon of the House of Aragon-Barcelona at the monastery of Santa Maria de Poblet, to which the village of La Figuera was closely linked.

For stylistic reasons, the work has been attributed to Jaume Cascalls, one of the most renowned masters at the service of the monarch, and it has been related to the sculpture known as *St Charlemagne* (Museu de la Catedral, Girona). Indeed, it has even been surmised that both sculptures may be portraits of King Peter, a supposition supported by the attribute of the crown that characterises the St Anthony from La Figuera, together with the staff in the form of a tau, believed to have been made from an old sword. Nevertheless, the iconographical source of the crown attribute, which was far from common in the Catalan plastic arts of that time, is to be found in the psalm of the offertory in the St Anthony's Day Mass, which leaves no doubt as to the identity of the image. M.R.M.C.

Attributed to Jaume Cascalls
(active between 1345 and 1377/9)
Head of Christ
c. 1352
MNAC/MAC 34879

Attributed to Jaume Cascalls
(active between 1345 and 1377/9)
Saint Anthony the Abbot
c. 1350
MNAC/MAC 24085 and 24086

This juvenile male image in alabaster presents the attribute of a damaged phylactery, where it is still possible to read the inscription AVE G, which corresponds to the beginning of the salutation 'Ave gratia' from the episode of the Annunciation. The remains of this legend, therefore, provide the key to identification of the Archangel Gabriel.

The other traditional attribute of the messenger, the sceptre or crosier representing divine power, surmounted by the lily that symbolises the purity of Mary, has been lost, along with the angel's left hand and the image of the Virgin.

The figure's half-open mouth and the posture of the head evoke the sacred dialogue between Gabriel and Mary. The Archangel has no wings, due to the fact that after it was made the sculpture was hollowed out from behind in order to reduce its weight.

The fact that for stylistic reasons this high-quality sculpture is attributed to the sculptor Bartomeu de Robió, who executed the fourteenth-century high altarpiece of the Seu Vella [Old Cathedral] in Lleida and was the director of works of this see, supports the hypothesis that the sculpture came from Lleida. M.R.M.C.

The central compartment of this altarpiece features St Vincent and the Calvary and twelve scenes from the life of this deacon saint, whilst the side compartments feature the renderings of the Holy Women at the Sepulchre and the *Noli me Tangere*.

At the saint's feet are the praying figures of a Dominican and a soldier. The fact that the person who first commissioned the piece appears there suggests that the triptych was conceived initially for a centre in Huesca linked in some way to the Dominicans.

The altarpiece is the work possibly of an Italian painter active in Huesca, since the style and iconography denote strong links with Italy and reveal the artist's knowledge of Florentine painting subsequent to Giotto's. Despite lack of documentation regarding the name of the artist, the links with Italy, the presence in Saragossa of the painter Rómulo da Firenze from 1367 to 1372 and, above all, the execution in 1367 of an altarpiece for the convent of Friars Preachers in Huesca have led some researchers to contend that Rómulo da Firenze might have been responsible for this altarpiece of St Vincent from Estopiñán. Even so, and without questioning the feasibility of the attribution to Rómulo da Firenze, the punching work seems to suggest a date around the mid-fourteenth century.

Outstanding features of this work include the imposing figure of the saint and the magnificent punching work on a gilt background, on which the name of the saint, S. VINCENCIUS, appears. F.R.Q.

Attributed to Bartomeu de Robió
(documented in Lleida between 1359 and 1376)
Archangel Gabriel from an Annunciation
Second half of the fourteenth century
MNAC/MAC 9875

Master of Estopiñán
Triptych of Saint Vincent
c. 1350-70
MNAC/MAC 3940

This splendid fourteenth-century sculpture is a fine example of the relationship between Aragon and French art: the ring-shaped clasp that holds the mantle or the crown that the Virgin wears above her veil, with ivy leaves, are unlike what was common in the country. On the other hand, the expression of the face and the shape of the eyes present points in common with works from France.

Links have been pointed out between the work of Arén and the Virgin that presides over the sculptural decoration on the tympanum over the main door of Huesca Cathedral, attributed to the teams working under the guidance of Guillermo Inglés around 1328. Furthermore, strong links exist between this latter work and the 'Puerta Preciosa' of Pamplona Cathedral and, further south, with the important schools of the cathedrals of Burgos and Leon, where the intensity of the French influence is well known. M.R.M.C.

Of this major Marian altarpiece, the left-hand panel is preserved in the MNAC while a scene from the top of the right-hand compartment, depicting the Nativity, is at the Harvard University Fogg Art Museum (Cambridge, Massachusetts).

The MNAC panel presents the Annunciation at the top and the Magi at the bottom. Two stiles, one on either side, include several renderings of the Cistercian calendar of saints' days, which strongly suggests that the altarpiece was originally conceived for a monastic centre of the Cistercian order, although it has also been associated with the collegiate church of Sant Vicenç in Cardona.

The artistic personality of the anonymous painter of the panels at the MNAC and the Fogg Art Museum, which has been linked to the painting of Arnau Bassa, is also present in a triptych featuring scenes of the Virgin preserved at the Walters Art Museum in Baltimore. This work was attributed to a painter christened with the name Master of Baltimore, whose intervention may also be appreciated in some of the miniatures and *marginalia* of the *Queen Mary of Navarre's Book of Hours*, now preserved at the Biblioteca Nazionale Marciana, Venice, a codex illuminated by Ferrer Bassa and his workshop.

Nevertheless, the Italianate influences present in the painting of the Master of Baltimore do not entirely coincide with those observable in the work of the Bassas. Points of reference to be taken into account in the study of the Master of Baltimore's painting are the cultural exchanges between Avignon and Genoa and the connections between these centres and Barcelona; the Sienese painting and the connection between Pisa and Majorca, and once again their derivation towards the Catalan capital. F.R.Q.

French School
Virgin of Perafita
Second half of the fourteenth century
MNAC/MAC 24092

Master of Baltimore
Annunciation and Epiphany
c. 1347-60
MNAC/MAC 15855

This work is clear evidence of the evolution of the altarpiece as from the second third of the fourteenth century. The main panel depicts the Virgin, flanked by St Catherine and St Mary Magdalene. The figure of the person who commissioned the piece is at the feet of the Virgin, and is identified by the inscription on his habit: FRA: FONTANER: D: GLRA: COMNADOR: D: SIXENA.

This legend is an important point of reference in the history of the altarpiece, since no document has survived recording either its commissioning or its funding. Fra [Friar] Fontaner de Glera was prior of Sigena at some date after 1363; consequently, either Jaume or Pere Serra, probably the latter, might have executed the Sigena altarpiece between 1363 and 1375, since Francesc Serra died in 1362.

The twelve scenes on the side compartments are linked to the Marian *goigs* [couplets extolling the Virgin or the Saints] and are surmounted by the Calvary. On the predella, four Eucharistic miracles are arranged around the central image of the Last Supper. The paintings devoted to the said miracles contain an explicit reference to medieval society's disapproval of the Jews and their having been the cause of 'divine wrath', which took the form of successive outbreaks of the plague and famine. F.R.Q.

Master of Sigena, probably Pere Serra
(active in Barcelona between 1357 and 1405/8)

Altarpiece of the Virgin
c. 1363-75

MNAC/MAC 15916

The central panel of *Our Lady of the Angels* and the two sections of the predella of this altarpiece have been attributed to Pere Serra on the basis of the documented works by this artist. In this context, the links between the Virgin at the MNAC and the Queen of Heaven from the *Altarpiece of the Holy Ghost* at the church of Santa Maria de l'Aurora, Manresa, seem to corroborate the hypothesis that Pere Serra was responsible for the work at Tortosa.

The records indicate that this exceptional *Virgin* was commissioned by the Tortosa notary Bernat Macip, who also funded the construction of the apse chapel in Tortosa Cathedral where his family coat of arms may be seen, which is located to the right of the apse central oratory. Although we do not know the date of the commission, the stylistic traits of the Marian altarpiece would place it around the year 1385. Furthermore, we do know that in the latter part of the sixteenth century the remains of the altarpiece, together with others that occupied the apse chapels of Tortosa Cathedral, were transferred to the convent of Santa Clara by order of Bishop Gaspar Punter.

The image of the Virgin surrounded by angels attests to the prevailing Italianate style that the Bassas and Ramon Destorrents formulated just before the pictorial canons of the International Gothic were introduced. In this composition, six musician angels witness the tender glances exchanged between the Mother and Child, who does not let go of the slender thread to which the bird is tied. F.R.Q.

Preserved in the MNAC are two major works by the painter known as the Master of Villahermosa, this altarpiece from Xelva and the panel depicting the *Virgin Suckling the Child* from Albarracín. This artist's name is linked to three altarpieces preserved at the parish church of Villahermosa del Río (Castellón): one featuring the Eucharist, another the Last Judgement and the third the Virgin, works that attest to the artist's training in Barcelona and the evolution of his style.

Given that the artist spent his formative years in the Catalan capital and subsequently worked in Valencia, two hypotheses have been put forward regarding his identity: Llorenç Saragossa on the one hand and, on the other, the son of the eldest of the Serra brothers, Francesc Serra II.

The most prestigious painter in Barcelona early in the thirteen-seventies seems to have been Llorenç Saragossa, to judge from the fact that in a letter dated 1373 Peter the Ceremonious (1319-87) described him as 'lo millor pintor que en aquesta ciutat sia' ['the best painter of all in this city']. One year later, in November 1374, Saragossa pledged that he would settle in Valencia, as indeed he did, since he lived there until his death in either 1405 or 1406. As regards Francesc Serra II, we know that he moved to Valencia in around 1379. However, the lack of documented works by either painter makes it impossible to confirm which of the two was responsible for the catalogue of works assigned to the Master of Villahermosa. F.R.Q.

Pere Serra
(active in Barcelona
between 1357 and 1405/8)
Our Lady of the Angels
c. 1385
MNAC/MAC 3950

Master of Villahermosa
Altarpiece of the Virgin Suckling the Child, Saint Clare and Saint Anthony the Abbot
Last quarter of the fourteenth century
MNAC/MAC 64027

This altarpiece, one of the best pieces in the Museum's Gothic collection, has also been attributed to the Valencian painter Gonçal Peris, who may have been assisted in this case by Jaume Mateu.

The central compartment depicts the saint crowned with her characteristic attributes: the tower, which alludes to her imprisonment, and the palm, representative of her martyrdom. On the sides, and following an earlier, by then partially forgotten, tradition, each compartment recounts two different episodes from the life of the saint. Thus, the first panel shows the priest Valentine baptising the young princess and the moment when, as a consequence of this baptism, her father, King Dioscurus,

Attributed to Gonçal Peris Sarrià
(documented in Valencia between 1380 and 1451)
Altarpiece of Saint Barbara
c. 1410-25
MNAC/MAC 35672

ordered her to be imprisoned in a tower. In this scene, St Barbara tells the building supervisor to increase the number of windows to three. This is not only an allusion to the Holy Trinity but also the motive for which the saint is regarded as patron of the building trades. The confrontation between the young princess and her father, her flight and the transformation of the shepherd and his flock into marble statues as punishment for their betrayal are the passages from the life of the saint featured in the second register. The two remaining compartments narrate four episodes relating to the passion and death of the virtuous girl. Divine punishment and the figuration of her soul received by an angel complete the hagiographic narrative. F.R.Q.

This sculpture is one of the most exquisitely elegant Gothic images of the standing Virgin and Child to be found in Catalonia. Its most outstanding aesthetic qualities are the serene, idealised face and the figure's slender proportions. The slant—or *hanchement*—of the figure also contributes to the balance of the composition, thanks to the gentleness of the curvature, unlike other sculptures of the period that address the same theme.

Although it is generally stated that this image is from Sallent de Sanaüja, nothing is known of its original site or the context in which it was conceived. It was apparently executed during the second half of the fourteenth century, by which time Catalan Gothic sculpture had reached a synthesis of the French and Italian influences and created a school with its own, consolidated language.

Dating from the same period and with a set of very similar characteristics—even in the stylistic field—is the *Virgin* from Boixadors (Anoia), preserved in the Museu Episopal de Vic and believed to be by the same artist. M.R.M.C.

This painting formed part of the ceiling decoration of the former Sala del Consell in the Casa de la Ciutat [City Hall] of Valencia and formed part of a set of fifteen portraits of the sovereigns of the House of Aragon, of which three more are in the MNAC, while the whereabouts of the remaining eleven are unknown. The panels at the MNAC are related to James I the Conqueror (1208-76), Alfonso II the Liberal (1265-91) (MNAC/MAC 9775), Peter III the Ceremonious (1319-87) (MNAC/MAC 9776) and Alfonso IV the Magnanimous (1396-1458) (MNAC/MAC 9777).

A document dated 3 September 1427 records the fact that painters Gonçal Peris Sarrià, Jaume Mateu and Joan Moreno were paid 9,191 solidus and 9 deniers for gilding the mouldings and for fifteen 'tabulas pictas' for the Sala del Consell in Valencia City Hall. One year later, on 6 May 1428, these same artists together with Bartomeu Avella received 3,042 solidus and 6 deniers as the rest of a larger sum.

The fact that Gherardo Starnina, Pere Nicolau and Marsal Sas were active in Valencia provides us with an idea of the high artistic standards that prevailed in the city around 1400, standards that, far from lowering during the first half of the fifteenth century, were enriched by the work of painters who trained at those studios, including Gonçal Peris, Gonçal Peris Sarrià, Jaume Mateu (Nicolau's nephew) and Miquel Alcanyís.

The stylistic affinities between the main painters, the importance of their studios and the fact that they hired teams of artists for the execution of specific works create serious difficulties when it comes to deciding on who was actually responsible for each of these panels. F.R.Q.

Virgin
Second half of the fourteenth century
MNAC/MAC 4359

Jaume Mateu
(documented in Valencia between 1402 and 1452) and
Gonçal Peris Sarrià
(documented in Valencia between 1380 and 1451)
Supposed Portrait of James I
1427
MNAC/MAC 9774

The artist depicts St Sebastian dressed in the elegant fashion of the time and takes the stylistic traits of the International Gothic almost to the limit. Crowning the panel is a *Calvary*, featuring a number of foreshortened horses.

The St Sebastian altarpiece, which on 9 August 1417 Pere de Condamines commissioned Joan Mates to paint for the Pia Almoina, Barcelona, belongs to the artist's last output and denotes the extent to which Mates had evolved away from his beginnings with Pere Serra, who remained loyal to the Italianising canons.

After the death of Pere Serra, Mates set up his own workshop, where he executed a number of documented works besides this altarpiece, the *Altarpiece of Saint Ambrose and Saint Martin* for Barcelona Cathedral (1411-14) and the one for Vila-rodona (1422), which no longer survives.

In Mates's artistic evolution towards the International Gothic, we must take into account other artists closer to Valencian centres such as Pere Nicolau and the Master of Cinctorres, as well as the schools of northern France and the lower Rhine, influences that Mates may have received from Guerau Gener, an artist active in the Barcelona and Valencia areas. Thanks to this cultural exchange, Mates was able to develop a style much esteemed at the time, especially by the nobility and the clergy, as we learn from the substantial number of works he was commissioned to execute for Barcelona Cathedral. F.R.Q.

Permanent loan from Joan Ainaud and Frederic-Pau Verrié, 1947

The only documented work by Mur is the *Altarpiece of Saint Peter* from Vinaixa, currently preserved in the Museu Diocesà in Tarragona, which was commissioned in 1420 and forms the fundamental basis on which Ramon de Mur has been identified as the former Master of Guimerà.

This pictorial reference is sufficient to attribute other works to him, such as the Guimerà altarpiece (Museu Episcopal de Vic), executed between 1402 and 1412, and this Cervera panel, which would have been the central compartment of a Marian altarpiece. The scene depicts the Virgin, crowned and seated on a substantially architectural throne, with the Child and eight angels who complete the tender maternal tableau.

Beyond Ramon de Mur's contacts with the painter Mateu Ortoneda, his creative output is fruit of the dialogue between Valencian and Catalan painting and, more specifically, between the painting of Castellón, represented by the Master of Cinctorres and the Master of Xèrica, and that of Tarragona. Furthermore, there were strong affinities between the work of Ramon de Mur and that of the Master of Retascón, evident in the striking expressionism of his works and the way he addresses architecture.

Despite the fact that Ramon de Mur most probably hailed from Tarragona, his known paintings were executed in Tàrrega and Montblanc, cities in which he would have received commissions from neighbouring towns such as Guimerà, Santa Coloma de Queralt, Vinaixa, Cervera and Granyena de Segarra. F.R.Q.

Joan Mates
(Vilafranca del Penedès,
c. 1370 – Barcelona, 1431)
Saint Sebastian and Calvary
1417-25
MNAC/MAC 42340

Ramon de Mur
(active in Tarragona and Lleida
between 1412 and 1435)
Virgin Suckling the Child
c. 1415-25
MNAC/MAC 15818

This panel with its corresponding stile formed part as the main compartment of an altarpiece dedicated to St John the Baptist and St Stephen. The painting, coming from Puigcerdà, has been linked to that city's church of Sant Domènec, which seems feasible in view of the relics of St John the Baptist preserved there and the two Dominican dedications on the stile: a Pope belonging to the order, who might be either Innocent V or Benedict XI, both beatified later, and St Catherine of Siena, who was canonised in 1461.

The presence of new Flemish trends and the mixed media of tempera and oil on the panel of *Saint John the Baptist and Saint Stephen* denotes the acceptance in Catalonia of the innovations that emerged in Flanders, introduced here by Lluís Dalmau, who executed the *Altarpiece of the Virgin of the Councillors* (see pp. 110-11), which he completed in 1445.

The stylistic affinities between this work and a number of panels from the *Altarpiece of Saint Michael* in Castelló d'Empúries led to its attribution to an anonymous painter named the Master of Castelló d'Empúries. Later, it was decided that this artist was in fact Joan Antigó and Honorat Borrassà, and it was revealed that the piece had been executed in 1448.

The fact that Joan Antigó assumed responsibility for the Borrassàs' Girona workshop leads to the assumption that Honorat would have trained under him. Indeed, their relationship was further consolidated by the marriage between Caterina Borrassà, Honorat's sister, and Antigó. F.R.Q.

The Barcelona Cathedral choir includes, besides the episcopal chair for Bishop Planella, attributed to Pere de Sant Joan, an artist from Picardy, a set of stalls consisting of a double row of collapsible seats for canons and a pulpit.

The higher of the two rows was carved at the end of the fourteenth century under the supervision of Pere Sanglada. This work marked the introduction into Barcelona of the innovations of the International Gothic, with which Sanglada became familiar during a trip to Flanders to purchase oak timber.

Of all the spaces in the choir stalls suitable for decoration, the Misericord and the area around it is the most extensive, and given the fact that it is half concealed from view, is the most suitable for rich profane iconography. Indeed, the collapsible nature of the seats and the fact that the Misericord is visible only when the seat is upright favour the cultivation of this kind of subject matter. The decoration is arranged symmetrically, surrounding the Misericord itself, which acts as a small seat for canons when they are required to stand in order to pray.

This kind of composition may be observed in the two excellent misericords preserved at the MNAC. It has been suggested that this one depicts two men measuring their strength against each other flanked by two skilfully carved male figures, while the other (MNAC/MAC 45161) shows a fiesta amusement consisting of tying a bull and subsequently dragging it along. M.R.M.C.

Attributed to Joan Antigó
(Girona, *c.* 1409-53) and
Honorat Borrassà
(Girona, *c.* 1424-57)
Saint John the Baptist and Saint Stephen
c. 1445-53
MNAC/MAC 15845

Pere Sanglada
(documented after 1386 and who died in Barcelona in 1408)
Misericord depicting men gauging their strength
Between 1394 and 1399
MNAC/MAC 45160

These two panels, together with that of *The Resurrection of Christ* (MNAC/MAC 40906), formerly occupied one of the lateral compartments of the former Gothic altarpiece at the monastery of Santes Creus. The other three side compartments, most of the predella and the three sculptures that formed part of the altarpiece, the Virgin in the middle flanked by St Benedict and St Bernard, are preserved in one of the chapels of Tarragona Cathedral and at the city's Museu Diocesà. In the seventeenth century the main altar of the monastery of Santes Creus was replaced by a Baroque one, and the original Gothic altarpiece was transferred to the parish church of Guàrdia de Prats. The more modest dimensions of the new site meant that the altarpiece had to be partially disassembled and later, in 1890, the three MNAC panels were sold. Of these, the Museum acquired *The Resurrection of Christ* from a Madrid antique dealer in 1945. In 1976, the widow of Pere Fontana i Almeda donated the other two to the MNAC.

This altarpiece, in which painting and sculpture are combined, was originally commissioned from the painter Pere Serra in January 1403. However, the artist died before he was able to complete it. We know that the person entrusted with finishing the work was painter Guerau Gener, but on his death it was eventually concluded by Borrassà.

Some of the faces reflect the strong Germanic and Italianising influences that prevailed in Valencian painting of the period, which characterised the work of Guerau Gener more than that of Lluís Borrassà. F.R.Q.

Gift of 'Doña Pilar Rabal Rabal en memoria de su esposo Pedro Fontana Almeda. Barcelona, 1976'

Guerau Gener
(active in Barcelona and Valencia between 1390 and 1409/10) and

Lluís Borrassà
(Girona, *c.* 1360 – Barcelona, 1424/5)

Nativity and Saint John the Evangelist

1407-11

MNAC/MAC 114740 and 114739

This painting has been attributed to the Master of Albatàrrec by virtue of its stylistic and compositional affinities with the central panel of the *Altarpiece of the Saviour* at the parish church of Albatàrrec.

Given that a number of panels dedicated to the Virgin preserved at the Museu de Lleida Diocesà i Comarcal are signed by Jaume Ferrer, it has been suggested that the anonymous Master of Albatàrrec was in fact this painter. Nonetheless, and bearing in mind that another painter of the same name was also active in Lleida, some scholars have christened the former Jaume Ferrer I and the latter Jaume Ferrer II. The main doubt when it comes to evaluating this supposition is whether or not to accept the link between the catalogue of works assigned to the Master of Albatàrrec and the four Marian panels, since these latter paintings, signed by Jaume Ferrer, who years later executed the *Altarpiece of Saint Jerome, Saint Sebastian and Saint Martin of Tours* (see p. 106), might date from the painter's youth.

As we ponder the feasibility of this assignation, we must bear in mind that the Master of Albatàrrec's output was limited to the first quarter of the fifteenth century, a time from which no documentary records exist of the activity of any artist by the name of Jaume Ferrer. Consequently, and until we have more information regarding Jaume Ferrer I, it would be more prudent to continue attributing this painting of the Saviour to the Master of Albatàrrec. F.R.Q.

This panel, by Blasco de Grañén, formerly known as the Master of Lanaja, depicts St Michael's fight with the devil. The angel, wearing the silvery armour of the period, runs his sword through the head of the diabolical beast. The angel's physiognomy and his curly hair denote Blasco de Grañén's indebtedness to the painting of Valencia. An example of this relationship would be the links between this work and a *Panel of Saint Michael* preserved at Los Angeles County Museum of Art.

The dimensions of the panel under discussion suggest that it may have been one of the side compartments of an altarpiece dedicated to three saints, although it might also have been the central one of a small altarpiece dedicated to St Michael only. A St Thomas, a fragment from a panel showing St Michael's fight against the devils and an image of Doubting Thomas have been linked to the panel of St Michael. Recently, the panel has also been associated with a *Virgin* from the Beck Collection, New York, as the possible central compartment of the altarpiece.

The importance of Blasco de Grañén in Aragonese painting may be gauged in terms not only of the quality of his work but also of the fact that he established a school. Jaume Romeu, Pascual Ortoneda, Antonio Ruill, Juan Arnaldín and Pedro García de Benabarre, among others, reveal artistic affinities with Grañén's painting, while Jaime Arnaldín, Petrico Fernández and probably his nephew, Martín de Soria, all trained at his workshop. F.R.Q.

Gift of 'Doña Pilar Rabal Rabal en memoria de su esposo Pedro Fontana Almeda. Barcelona, 1976'

Attributed to the Master of Albatàrrec
The Saviour
c. 1420-30
MNAC/MAC 4505

Blasco de Grañén
(documented in Saragossa between 1422 and 1459)
Saint Michael the Archangel
c. 1435-45
MNAC/MAC 114741

These three panels, together with the Calvary, formed part of an altarpiece dedicated to the three saints with which a predella featuring episodes from the life of St Jerome, now part of a private collection in Saragossa, has also been associated.

The links between the work preserved at the MNAC and the altarpiece of the Paeria in Lleida, also by Jaume Ferrer, are both stylistic and compositional. Even so, this type of altarpiece, which assigns greater importance to the main figures than to hagiographic narrative, is rare in Catalonia, being more characteristic of Valencia and Majorca and, as from that time, of Aragon, as we learn from a substantial number of works.

From the *Verdú Altarpiece* onwards, a work partially preserved at the Museu Episcopal de Vic and executed between 1432 and 1434, Jaume Ferrer's painting style evolved along lines that suggest the influence of Blasco de Grañén's workshop and, more particularly, of Bernat Martorell, with whom Ferrer collaborated on the enlargement of the former high altarpiece at the Seu Vella [Old Catedral] in Lleida. F.R.Q.

Gift of 'Doña Pilar Rabal Rabal en memoria de su esposo Pedro Fontana Almeda. Barcelona, 1976'

Jaume Ferrer

(active in Lleida between 1430 and 1461)

Saint Jerome, Saint Martin of Tours, Saint Sebastian and Calvary

c. 1445-55

MNAC/MAC 114743, 114744, 114745 and 114742

The *Altarpiece of Saint Vincent* is preserved intact and is an example of the most common type of pictorial support from the period in Catalonia, although, due to its small dimensions, it only includes two scenes on either side of the image of the saint to which it is dedicated. The top panel, instead of the usual Calvary, depicts the Virgin of Mercy sheltering saints Benedict and Bernard beneath her mantle.

The delicate central figure of St Vincent, pictured before the cross of one of his martyrdoms and with the palm that alludes to them, and the Book, presents appreciable loss of glazing in the dalmatic. On the left, from top to bottom, we see the Judgement of St Vincent and St Valerius and St Vincent on the rack; on the right, St Vincent's torture on the grid and his peaceful death in bed, before Dacian and his torturers. The five splendid compartments of the predella feature different passages from the Passion of Christ.

The altarpiece dust-shield features the anagram JHS and the coat of arms of the monastery of Poblet. It is for this reason that the work has occasionally been associated with the chapel dedicated to St Vincent in Poblet. Nonetheless, given the provenance of the altarpiece, the hermitage of La Santa Creu in Menàrguens, it is likely that the work was originally conceived for this town since, on the one hand, Menàrguens depends on the monastery of Poblet and, on the other, its parish church is dedicated to St Vincent.

As regards its dating, the commission for the painted altarpiece might be linked to Martorell's sojourn in Lleida in 1441. F.R.Q.

This is one of the two panels surmounting an altarpiece dedicated to St Lucy, the central image and four compartments featuring hagiographic scenes of which belong to a private Paris collection, formerly part of the Martin Le Roy Collection in the same city, while the other top panel is preserved in a private Barcelona collection.

This altarpiece would have been commissioned when Martorell was completing his *Altarpiece of Saint George* (conserved in Chicago), one of the best periods in Martorell's painting, which bears his personal imprint. In this context, we should note that Martorell's output during the fourteen thirties reveals the influence of Florentine and Nordic models. To judge from documentary evidence that links Martorell with painters Ambrogio Salarii and Dello Delli, and from the affinities between the work of Martorell and that of Delli, we assume that the two artists came into personal contact. Besides the influence of Delli, we must also take into account that of Julià Nofre, a Florentine sculptor active in Barcelona Cathedral between 1431 and 1435.

The person who commissioned the altarpiece may have been Pere de Palou, canon and precentor of Barcelona Cathedral and deputy of the General. This figure is related to Bernat Martorell in the payment of the altarpiece of Monzón, executed in 1437, his family coat of arms being very similar to the one that features on this panel. F.R.Q.

Permanent loan from the Generalitat de Catalunya, 1995

Bernat Martorell
(Sant Celoni, *c.* 1400 – Barcelona, 1452)
Altarpiece of Saint Vincent
c. 1438-40
MNAC/MAC 15797

Bernat Martorell
(Sant Celoni, *c.* 1400 – Barcelona, 1452)
Martyrdom of Saint Lucy
c. 1435-40
MNAC 200795

On 6 June 1443, the Consell de Cent of Barcelona [Consultative Assembly of Barcelona's municipal government] agreed to commission an altarpiece for the chapel of the City Hall. To this end, they appointed a committee of twelve dignitaries. Three months later, on 4 September 1443, the committee met with the five councillors of that year and decided that the altarpiece be painted by 'lo millor e pus apte pintor qui encercar e trobar se posgués' ['the best and most skilled painter that could be sought and found']. Thus, on 29 October Lluís Dalmau was entrusted with the task and one month later, on 26 November, Francí Gomar was hired to produce the framework of carpentry.

A splendid throne, resting on four lions and featuring the figures of several prophets, frames the Virgin and Child. On the base of the seat, an inscription tells us that the work was completed in 1445: SUB ANNO MCCCCXLV PER LUDOVICUM DALMAU FUI DEPICTUM. On either side we see the five councillors, kneeling in an attitude of prayer, who commissioned the work, together with St Eulàlia and St Andrew bearing the cross that alludes to their martyrdom.

This painting is one of the first to introduce the concept of portraiture, since the contract stipulated that the donors should appear as they really were. On the other hand, the technique employed—tempera and oil paint—is a point of reference in the introduction of this technique into Catalan panel painting. These factors and the stylistic postulates of the panel reveal the Flemish influence (especially that of Jan van Eyck) on Dalmau's painting. F.R.Q.

Lluís Dalmau
(active in Valencia and Barcelona between 1428 and 1461)
Virgin of the Councillors
1443-5
MNAC/MAC 15938

The formal characteristics of this image are fairly representative of northern European art of the fifteenth century, the influence of which spread throughout most of Europe during the second half of the century. In this context, the meticulous treatment of the curls in the beard and the angular facial features stand out. The folds of the attire are heavy and severely cut, to the extent that they have a somewhat metallic appearance. The fact that the piece is carved out of linden wood leads to the supposition that its provenance is southern Germany, where this tree species was widely used in art.

The sculpture presents the usual attributes of the holy bishop of Myra: the staff, from which the volute is missing, and the three balls of gold alluding to an episode in his hagiographic legend according to which Nicholas of Bari provided three poor girls with a dowry so that they may be honourably married and preserved from sinning. M.R.M.C.

This painting, which may have been the central compartment of an altarpiece dedicated to the Virgin, is one of Pedro García de Benabarre's most successful works. The composition is centered by the enthroned image of the Virgin and Child, surrounded by two musician angels and a further two angelic beings who offer them grapes and pears, fruit that alludes to the blood and sacrifice of Christ on the Cross (grapes) and to hope of Salvation (pears). Mary also holds pears in her hand in the *Panel of the Apocalyptic Virgin and Saint Vincent Ferrer*, from which we infer a message of hope. This latter composition, preserved at the Museum (MNAC/MAC 114748), was also painted by Pedro García de Benabarre.

Pedro García de Benabarre would have trained under the Aragonese painter Blasco de Grañén, together with whom he is documented in Saragossa between 1445 and 1447. The records show that two years later he was already receiving his own commissions. It seems that he moved to Benabarre in around 1452 and he remained there until 1455, when he settled in Barcelona, having been summoned there by Bernat Martorell's widow and son.

The legend that appears at the foot of the Virgin's seat informs us of the name of the artist: PERE GARCIA DE BENAVARRE MA PINTAT ANY 14. The absence of the date in which the work was executed has led to several hypotheses: while most scholars contend that it was painted around 1470, others tend to date it from before the painter's move to Barcelona. F.R.Q.

German School
Saint Nicholas
Fifteenth century
MNAC/MAC 65507

Pedro García de Benabarre
(documented in Aragon and Catalonia between 1445 and 1483)
Virgin and Four Angels
c. 1470 (?)
MNAC/MAC 15817

The panel depicts the figures of St George, dressed in armour and carrying an axe and a sword, and of the princess, with a diadem in her hands, crowned by a cruciferous pennon, and holding a shield with remains of a cross featuring a cursive inscription in Arabic. The coat of arms of the Cabrera family appears on the reverse side of the panel.

Behind the images of St George and the princess we observe a portico that opens onto a landscape with cypresses. This links the MNAC panel with two paintings that were preserved at the Kaiser Friedrich Museum, Berlin, until 1945. Their current whereabouts are unknown.

The left-hand Berlin panel features the figure of a knight being presented by St John the Baptist, probably Bernat Joan de Cabrera, while its right-hand counterpart depicts a lady presented by St Louis of Toulouse, who might be Violant de Prades. The reverse sides of both missing panels depict two figures in grisaille, one of which is incomplete. The knight panel features the figure of St Peter the Apostle and the lower part of that of St John the Evangelist, while the lady panel features St Paul and the lower part of a torso that might be either St John the Baptist or St James the Greater.

One of the iconographical peculiarities of the Cabreras altarpiece is the presence of the cypress as the only tree. The fact that since Antiquity the cypress had been regarded as the tree of the dead and a token of hope for the afterlife suggests that the altarpiece has a certain funerary quality, a plausible hypothesis supported by the presence of the donors. F.R.Q.

Jaume Huguet
(Valls, *c.* 1412 – Barcelona, 1492)
Saint George and the Princess
c. 1459-75
MNAC/MAC 15868

Of the set of compositions comprising the high altarpiece of the church of Sant Agustí Vell, Barcelona, preserved at the MNAC, six related episodes from the life of the saint. Those of the Last Supper and the Road to Calvary, preserved in the Museu Marès, formed part of the predella.

From the date when the altarpiece was commissioned to be painted and completed in four years (1463) to the date of its actual completion (1486) a period of twenty-three years passed, which suggests that more than one artist was involved in its execution.

Regarding the original arrangement of the piece, we know that a sculpture of St Augustine stood on the lower part of the central section and, above it, an image of the Virgin. The altarpiece was almost twelve metres long and included two side compartments each on either side of the central one.

Most of the preserved paintings depict St Augustine dressed as a bishop, except for two scenes. The first of these features the saint and his mother, St Monica, listening to a sermon delivered by St Ambrose in Milan, while the second shows the conversion of St Augustine to Christianity. The best of all the paintings of the *Altarpiece of Saint Augustine*, the one we are commenting here, begins the hagiographic cycle of the saint as bishop and is followed by St Augustine's dispute with Fortunatus and the other heretics, by the vision of the Infant Jesus and, finally, by the scene in which St Augustine washes the feet of Jesus the pilgrim. F.R.Q.

Jaume Huguet
(Valls, *c.* 1412 – Barcelona, 1492)
Consecration of Saint Augustine
c. 1466-75
MNAC/MAC 24140

This painting formed part of the *Altarpiece of Saint Stephen of Granollers,* of which, besides three scenes from the predella, six compartments are preserved relating the life of the protomartyr saint, the Calvary, and four figures of prophets that formed part of the dust-shield. These latter were painted by Joan Gascó.

According to the *Golden Legend* Princess Eudoxia, the daughter of Emperor Theodosius, had travelled to Constantinople to free herself from the devil who possessed her. She would not be cured, however, until the mortal remains of St Stephen were taken to Rome. Thus this compartment must have been the one that concluded the story of St Stephen on the Granollers altarpiece, since it confirms that the body of the protomartyr was transferred from Constantinople to Rome, where it was laid to rest alongside that of his companion St Lawrence. The insignia in the middle of the one-legged pilgrim's hat, the two crossed keys of St Peter, allude to this pilgrim's journey to the Holy City, prompted by the hope of cure.

In the presence of the stupefied Emperor Theodosius and his wife, both crowned and dressed in sumptuous attire, St Stephen approves the exorcism of Princess Eudoxia and expels the devil from her body.

The possible date when the *Altarpiece of Saint Stephen of Granollers* was commissioned, around 1492, and the fact that Pau Vergós died in 1495 suggests that the artist himself intervened relatively little in the piece, most of the work having been executed by his workshop, since the altarpiece was finished in 1500. F.R.Q.

The style of this work, specifically the attire of the Virgin, allows us to deduce both its date (around 1500) and the Flemish influence under which the anonymous artist carved it.

Regarding the latter question, we must not overlook the prestige the art of the Low Countries had come to enjoy towards the end of the Middle Ages, to the extent that Flemish works in different media—sculpted and painted altarpieces, textiles, miniatures and so on—were imported all over Europe and Flemish artists summoned to work to places far from their homeland. This latter phenomenon had a decisive effect on the process of assimilation of Flemish figurative culture, which in places such as the Crown of Castile reached great intensity and gave rise to what has been termed Hispano-Flemish art. The internationalisation of the style explains why close affinities may be detected in works executed far from each other.

It is assumed that this sculpture is Castilian in origin, the product, more specifically, of the busy studios that Gil de Siloé established in Burgos. Indeed, the fluctuations in style characteristic of this artist's output are often explained by the great number of commissions he received for the cathedral of Burgos and the Miraflores charterhouse, which forced him to employ many craftsmen at his workshop. This work in particular shows clear affinities with master Siloé's artistic milieu. M.R.M.C.

The Vergós workshop
Princess Eudoxia Before the Tomb of Saint Stephen
c. 1495-1500
MNAC/MAC 24146

Gil de Siloé Circle
Virgin
c. 1500
MNAC/MAC 64028

This panel, along with that of the *Resurrection* (MNAC/MAC 15871), constitute two magnificent examples of the work of the Cordovan painter Bartolomé Bermejo. They formed part of a predella, two further compartments of which now belong to a private Barcelona collection. Some scholars contend that the four compositions, *Christ in Limbo, Entry into Paradise, Resurrection* and *Ascension* were centered by either a tabernacle or the panel of the *Pietà*, now preserved at the Museo del Castillo de Peralada.

The iconographical narrative of these paintings must be placed in a Eucharistic programme of salvation of souls, which might have links with this piece. Regarding the dimensions of the works, the panels at the MNAC lost one of the five timber strips of the support, as we can see in that of the *Resurrection*, in which the cross that Christ carries is severed. Thus, the four paintings would have shared the same dimensions and, given their considerable size, we assume that the compartments of the predella of the high altarpiece of the church of Santo Domingo de Silos at Daroca (Saragossa) would have numbered precisely four, two on either side of the tabernacle. This information, the source of which is the contract that Bermejo signed in 1474, is further ratified in the covenant dated November 1477, which stipulates that Bermejo 'haya de acabar e dar acabado todo el banco del dito retaulo que tiene començado a fazer' ['must finish the entire predella of the said altarpiece he has already started to paint'] in May 1478. F.R.Q.

Bartolomé Bermejo
(Cordoba, *c.* 1440 – Barcelona, *c.* 1501)
Christ in Limbo
c. 1475
MNAC/MAC 15872

On the basis of an unconventional iconographical interpretation, the painter Fernando Gallego recreates the traditional theme of the Adoration of the Magi. Into this common scene the painter introduced a number of figurative quotations that while leaving the overall content unchanged, contribute to its enrichment. In particular, one of the Magi, Balthasar, is depicted with a black face.

In general terms, Gallego reveals unequivocal affinities with the figurative culture of northern Europe, particularly in the use of a visual repertoire that reveals a combination of different influences. The result is a highly eclectic idiom that denotes familiarity with the work of many contemporary artists, specifically Rogier van der Weyden, Petrus Christus, Conrad Witz, Dierick and Thierry Bouts and the Master of Uttenheim, and the occasional influence of some of the solutions adopted by the painter and engraver Martin Schongauer (1450-91). Even so, the more or less explicit presence of these figurative borrowings in no way detracts from the original way in which Gallego addresses the theme of the Epiphany.

This work in particular constitutes a highly significant and qualitatively very respectable episode in the artistic career of a painter who, from the city of Salamanca, the main centre of his activity, became one of the most outstanding representatives of Castilian painting during the last third of the fifteenth century. F.Q.C.

The panel depicting *Saint Jerome Penitent* constitutes a major contribution to Catalan art of the late fifteenth century. Particularly notable is the recreation of a landscape setting with highly successful naturalistic features. The presence of this landscape, a wide panorama, is a practically unique element comparable only to the one that Bartolomé Bermejo painted around the same time for his Desplà *Pietà* panel in Barcelona Cathedral.

Painters' main iconographical source at the time was the *Specchio di Vera Penitenza* by Jacopo Passavanti, who contributed to establishing a type of penitent that became widespread as the fifteenth century unfolded. The figure of Jerome, who inflicts penitence upon himself in the solitude of the desert, is a transcription to image of the famous passage from the letter written around 384 to Eustachius, in which the learned Doctor of the Church describes his life in the desert of Chalcis. The artist, however, in accordance with common practice at the time, does not adhere strictly to the hagiographic narrative and transfers the act of penitence to a scenario far from the Syrian desert. In this way, by recreating a landscape much closer to the believer's environment, he intensifies the devotional meaning of the religious image. F.Q.C.

Fernando Gallego
(documented in Salamanca between 1468 and 1507)
Epiphany
c. 1480-90
MNAC/MAC 64084

Attributed to the Master of La Seu d'Urgell
Saint Jerome Penitent
c. 1495
MNAC/MAC 15821

Of all the fragments that constituted the decoration of the doors of the organ at La Seu d'Urgell Cathedral, the scene of the Presentation of Jesus at the Temple is remarkable for its quality and originality.

This theme became popular in the iconography of the period and served to pinpoint the important role that Providence had assigned to the Church in its redeeming mission. Indeed, the entire iconographic programme revolves around the theme of the Church as a community of believers. In this context we should note that the Jewish rite of Presentation or Purification, following the dictates of the law of Moses, took place, once the regulation forty days after the birth of Jesus had passed, in a synagogue. From this perspective we understand the graphic resource employed by the painter, who tends to evoke a space that serves as a sumptuous backdrop to the evangelical narrative. On the other hand, the arbitrary way in which the architectural style of the building is interpreted is well suited to the pictorial uses of the Flemish world, so that the final result is an eclectic combination of elements—columns, capitals decorated with plant motifs and so forth—that neither responds to a specific architectural style nor follows prevailing contemporary models.

It was also Judaic law that obliged the mother of the new-born child to sacrifice a lamb or, in the case of women of humble origin, to make an offering of two pigeons, one for her child and the other for her sins, as we observe in this particular panel. F.Q.C.

This panel, which depicts the apparition of the Virgin and Child before St Francis at the church of La Porziuncola in Assisi, is the one after which the anonymous artist who painted it is named, an artist who might have been court painter Jacomart. The Barcelona work has affinities especially with the panel of the *Virgin of Canon Van der Paele* at the Groeningemuseum, Bruges (1436), and mainly with the *Giustiniani Triptych* (1437), preserved at the Gemäldegalerie Alte Meister, Dresden, both by Jan van Eyck. In this context we should note the images and symbolic backdrop around the throne of the Virgin of La Porziuncola, which denote the painter's familiarity with the work of Van Eyck, especially the *Giustiniani Triptych*, a work commissioned by the Genovese Giustiniani family. Furthermore, Alfonso V the Magnanimous (1396-1458) purchased a triptych by Van Eyck from the Genovese Giovanbattista Lomellino in 1444, the year in which Jacomart was in Naples. It is highly probable, therefore, that Jacomart acted in an advisory capacity in the acquisition of the triptych of Genoa, where he would have had the opportunity to admire the *Giustiniani Triptych*.

Moreover, the small *Eternal Father* panel, which may have been painted by Joan Reixac, must be taken into account. Indeed, the montage of the two pieces at Albocàsser might respond to Reixac's having continued a work that Jacomart was unable to complete, as in the case of the *Altarpiece of Saint Michael* in Burjassot. F.R.Q.

Attributed to the Master of La Seu d'Urgell
Presentation of Jesus at the Temple
c. 1495
MNAC/MAC 5711 and 5714

Joan Reixac
(Barcelona [?], *c.* 1411 – Valencia, 1486/92)
The Eternal Father

Master of the Porziuncola: Jaume Baço, alias Jacomart (?)
(Valencia, *c.* 1411 – Valencia, 1461)
Apparition of the Virgin Before Saint Francis
c. 1450
MNAC/MAC 64055 and 64103

The ensemble presided over by St Ursula includes the scenes of the Crucifixion and the Virgin surrounded by angels, with St Bernard of Clairvaux who introduces the donor to her, all in the central compartment, while the side compartments feature six scenes from the life, martyrdom and miracles of St Ursula and her fellow virgins. The predella and the dust-shield feature the images of saints interspersed with the Mur family coats of arms.

The death of Jacomart in 1461 meant that Joan Reixac assumed a leading role in Valencian artistic circles, which lasted until the fourteen eighties in the case of the master and until the early sixteenth century in that of the members of his studio who helped him satisfy the numerous commissions he received. Martí Torner, Pere Terrencs, Joan Barceló and the Master of Presepio achieved a synthesis of many of the Flemish stylistic trends that Joan Reixac cultivated in Valencia.

It is in the art produced by Reixac after Jacomart's death that we must place his output of the fourteen sixties, an oeuvre of high quality as we observe in works such as the *Altarpiece of Saint Ursula*, an icon signed by the painter in 1468 and destined for Poblet, although its provenance is Cubells, and the *Altarpiece of the Epiphany* (MNAC/MAC 50621), funded in 1469 by Guillem Joan 'of the family of the Joans'. F.R.Q.

Joan Reixac
(Barcelona [?], *c.* 1411 –
Valencia, 1486/92)
Altarpiece of Saint Ursula and the Eleven Thousand Virgins
1468
MNAC/MAC 15927

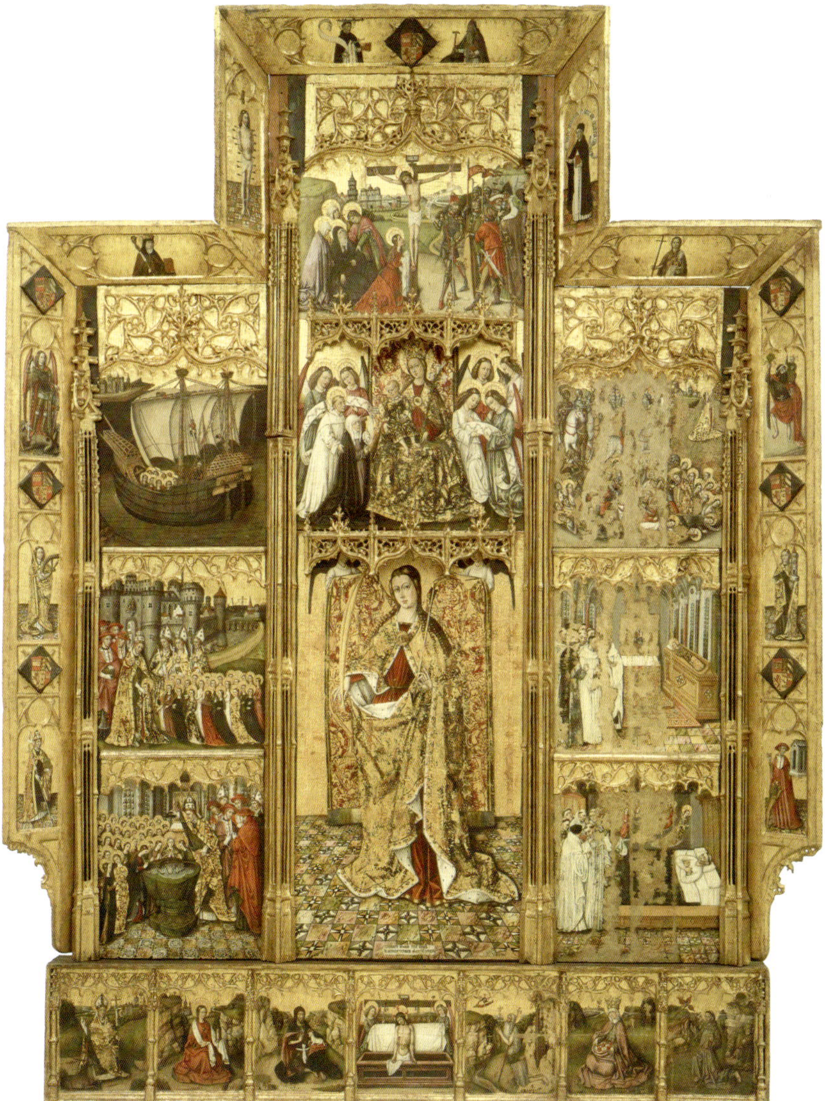

This altarpiece was commissioned from Miguel Ximénez early in 1494 by the members of the Confraternity of St John of the monastery of Sigena. In the middle, the figure of St John the Baptist, wearing a camel-hair tunic and a large purple mantle, points with his finger towards the figure of the *Agnus Dei* or Lamb of God.

The celebration, on the same day, of the festivities of St Fabian and St Sebastian led to the occasional practice of dedicating the same altarpiece to both. St Fabian is depicted as a bishop with the rake of his martyrdom while St Sebastian, dressed as a knight of the period, bears his attributes of the arrow and the sword.

A number of works, including the signed altarpiece of St Michael and St Catherine at the church of Santa María in Ejea de los Caballeros (Saragossa), the high altarpiece of the church of Blesa (Teruel), executed between 1481 and 1487 in collaboration with Martín Bernat, and these panels from Sigena, clearly define the artistic personality of Miguel Ximénez, who was greatly influenced by Bartolomé Bermejo and by the engravings of Martin Schongauer (1450-91). On May 11 1484, Ximénez was appointed court painter to Ferdinand the Catholic.

The fact that this work and the panel of St John the Baptist, executed by Martín Bernat for the church dedicated to the saint in Zaidín and currently preserved at the Museu de Lleida Diocesà i Comarcal, date from the same period provides us with an opportunity to note the similarities and differences between the work of the two painters. F.R.Q.

The year 1412 saw the foundation of the hospital of Sant Sever for poor clergymen on Carrer de la Palla, Barcelona. In 1937 three sculptures were discovered from the original building, sculptures that had been enclosed between walls. The central one, the whereabouts of which are unknown, featured Bishop St Severus, flanked on either side by clergymen in an attitude of prayer, now preserved at the MNAC, which reveal the naturalistic evolution of fifteenth-century sculpture. These figures have been attributed to Girona sculptor Pere Oller, who received his training while working on the choir of Barcelona Cathedral under orders from Pere Sanglada, an advocate of the International Gothic style. Having won fame and prestige, Oller received major commissions such as the high altarpiece for Vic Cathedral in 1420. He also worked in Barcelona Cathedral. In 1416 he was designated by Alfonso IV the Magnanimous (1396-1458) to sculpt the tomb of his late father, Ferdinand I of Antequera, in the Royal Pantheon of the Cistercian monastery of Santa Maria de Poblet. One of the most characteristic qualities of Pere Oller's style is his technical virtuosity. M.R.M.C.

Miguel Ximénez
(born in Pareja, Guadalajara, and documented in Saragossa between 1462 and 1505)
Saint John the Baptist, Saint Fabian and Saint Sebastian
1494
MNAC/MAC 15858

Attributed to Pere Oller
(documented between 1395 and 1444)
Clergymen Praying
First quarter of the fifteenth century
MNAC/MAC 66168 and 66169

The presence of the figure of the donor finds one of its most unusual expressions in the Villadiego polyptych, a magnificent testimony to a pictorial language revealing the typological and formal dependence on the models that were being gestated at the time in northern Europe. This influence is particularly appreciable in the modelling of long, slender figures that bring to mind figurative archetypes reminiscent of the art of Dierick Bouts. In any case, the anonymous Master of Villadiego embodies the introduction into Castile of a figurative culture of northern origin that came to prevail during the last decades of the fifteenth century until it crystallised in what is termed the 'Hispano-Flemish style'. The extraordinary pictorial quality of the entire group suggests that the artist was almost certainly Flemish in origin.

Pentagonal in ground plan, this liturgical furnishing consists of four panels, two on either side of the carving of St John the Evangelist, the altarpiece's titular saint, those on the left featuring St John the Baptist and St Bonaventure and those on the right St Sebastian and St James the Greater, with the figure of the donor dressed as a pilgrim. It is precisely the link between this anonymous kneeling figure and the effigy of the saint that suggests that this was a votive donation made by a pilgrim on the Road to Santiago. F.Q.C.

Permanent loan from the Generalitat de Catalunya, 1994

The iconography of the Mass of St Gregory was one of the most popular themes of fifteenth-century European painting. In fact, this was an episode in the life of Pope Gregory based on apocryphal sources, a legendary account that appeared in the fourteenth century that tells of the pontiff's religious crisis as he was holding mass, a personal doubt as to the presence of Christ and his transubstantiation in the sacrificial rite of the Eucharist. What is surprising in this case, however, is the absence of architectural references, common to all the images of the period, whose purpose was to provide a frame for the scene evoking the solemn setting of the church of the Holy Cross in Jerusalem, the sacred place where, according to tradition, Christ appeared miraculously before Pope Gregory while the latter was saying mass. It was also very common to find this kind of iconography in a funerary context, as a visual rendering of the doctrine of the redemption of souls, salvation to which the image—*vera effigie*—of the donor portrayed by Diego de la Cruz aspired.

The work reveals the influence of the models and compositional formulae of Rogier van der Weyden, who tended to accentuate the dramatic effects of the *imago pietatis* (image of piety), to which the melancholy, almost languid facial expressions make a highly effective contribution. F.Q.C.

Permanent loan from the Generalitat de Catalunya, 1994

Flemish School
Polyptych of Saint John the Evangelist
c. 1480-90
MNAC 200683 and 200684

Attributed to Diego de la Cruz
(active between 1482 and 1500)
Mass of Saint Gregory
Between 1475 and 1480
MNAC 200701

The *Altarpiece of the Virgin, Saint Augustine and Saint Nicholas of Tolentino*, which Antoine de Lonhy painted between 1460 and 1462, is preserved partly at the MNAC and partly at the Museo del Castillo de Peralada. While the main body may be admired at the MNAC, at Peralada two compartments are kept that would probably have constituted the predella.

On this particular panel a donor and an escutcheon with the initials BN feature at the feet of the Virgin. The initials are probably those of the founder of the Augustinian monastery of Domus Dei at Miralles, Bernat Nicolau. This personage, who was also one of the founders of the monastery of Sant Jeroni de la Murtra, Badalona, in 1413, is known to have been buried in Miralles. The funerary character of some of the scenes would therefore be linked to the tomb of the merchant.

From the stylistic viewpoint, in recent years a number of major studies have been conducted on the figure of Antoine de Lonhy, who executed the stained-glass rose window of the basilica of Santa Maria del Mar, Barcelona, thanks to which we may now reach a better understanding of his work. Furthermore, the identification of the Master of Saluces and the Master of the Turin Trinity as Lonhy is of vital importance, since it allows us to trace the artistic evolution of this painter beyond his Barcelona works, executed between 1460 and 1462. F.R.Q.

This outstanding piece within the output of European Gothic silversmithing, worked in gilt, enamelled silver, corresponds to a common typology in the Crown of Aragon and to the most widespread models of the Old Continent, since it presents elements of diverse provenance: of a Franco-Burgundian nature by virtue of the enamel figurations, of Italian origin by virtue of the technique applied to these elements and of Central European roots by virtue of the typology of the chalice.

It was made at a Valencian silversmith's workshop, as we learn from the identifying mark bearing the abbreviated Latin name VALEN, in a rectangle, engraved on the frontal lobe on the reverse side, and the circular symbol of the crown of the Kingdom adorned with a trilobate floral decoration. The mixtilinear foot, subdivided into six lobes, is decorated with transparent enamel plates, in the Italian fashion, depicting Christ Crucified, the Virgin of Sorrows and St John the Evangelist. In the middle of the vertical axis, the coats of arms in lozenge of Queen María de Luna (1357-1406), the wife of Martin the Humane (1372-1410), are represented, featuring the chequered half moon and the stripes of Aragon. The cobalt blue enamel, against a gridiron background, and the transparent emerald green apparel are highly characteristic of Valencian enamel work from around 1400.

The chalice preserved at the MNAC has affinities with the *Chalice of the Count of Majorca*—at the Musée du Louvre—and with that of the Archbishop of Saragossa Lope Fernández de Luna—at the parish church of Longares—and with that of Bishop Galceran de Vilanova—at the Museu Diocesà de la Seu d'Urgell—all the work of Barcelona silversmiths. M.R.M.C.

Antoine de Lonhy
(active between 1446 and 1480/90)
Altarpiece of the Virgin, Saint Augustine and Saint Nicholas of Tolentino
1461-2
MNAC/MAC 5088

Chalice of Queen María de Luna
Manufactured in Valencia
Between 1396 and 1406
MNAC/MAC 40425

In 1323 King James II (1267-1327) commissioned sculptor Johannes of Tournai to execute a sepulchre for the mortal remains of his second wife, Queen Mary of Cyprus (d. 1322). All that remains of the sepulchre is the recumbent figure, which would have formed part of the cover, dressed in the Franciscan habit although bearing the crown and the sceptre that symbolise her status. The characteristics and style of this delicate, elegant work reflect the Franco-Flemish origins of the artists whom the records show were involved in its execution: Johannes of Tournai, one of the many masters from abroad who settled in Catalonia at the beginning of the Gothic period and brought with them the entire technical and stylistic knowledge they had culled from their homelands, and Jacques of France, whom we assume collaborated with architect Jaume de Faveran (1321-30) in work on Girona Cathedral at the same time that the latter directed work on Narbonne Cathedral.

One of the innovations that Johannes of Tournai introduced, as we observe in other funerary works of his such as the sepulchres of Hug de Cardona (MNAC/MAC 200412) and of St Narcissus at the Girona church of Sant Feliu, are the finishing touches with decorative complements in the form of coloured glazed backgrounds, often blue, or of other materials, such as coloured stones, which we assume enriched the crown and the ring of the effigy of Mary of Cyprus, in imitation of true gems. M.R.M.C.

Permanent loan from the Reial Acadèmia de Bones Lletres de Barcelona to the Museu Provincial d'Antiguitats de Barcelona, 1876

Pere Moragues was one of the most prominent Catalan artists of the second half of the fourteenth century. An architect, sculptor and silversmith, he secured a numerous clientele, including King Peter III the Ceremonious (1319-87), who appointed him as his personal domestic. The most outstanding works by Moragues include the *Reliquary of the Corporals of Daroca* (1384), the image of the Virgin of La Mercè, Barcelona (*c.* 1361) and the tomb of the archbishop of Saragossa Lope Fernández de Luna, on which he worked late in the thirteen seventies.

The artist's refined style is reflected in the delicate sculpting of this recumbent figure. Furthermore, in his funerary work Moragues marked a step forward in the development of naturalism and prepared the ground for the International Gothic that was to burgeon at the end of the century.

Everything seems to indicate that the provenance of this figure is the monastery of Sant Cugat del Vallès, and the subject is almost certainly Abbot Arnau Ramon de Biure, who was assassinated at the monastery church on Christmas Night 1351, while he was saying mass. The figure is dressed as an officiant and he wears a skullcap instead of the mitre. The crosier has disappeared. The figure's attire therefore supports the hypothesis that it represents Abbot Biure. M.R.M.C.

Johannes of Tournai
(first half of the fourteenth century) and

Jacques of France
(documented in the first half of the fourteenth century)

Recumbent Figure of Queen Mary of Cyprus (d. 1322)
c. 1323

MNAC/MAC 9877

Attributed to Pere Moragues
(Barcelona, *c.* 1330 and documented until 1388)

Recumbent Figure of a Clergyman
(Abbot Arnau de Biure [?], d. 1351)
c. 1385

MNAC/MAC 9923

Between the late thirteenth and the second quarter of the fourteenth centuries the Roussillon and the Cerdanya witnessed the emergence of a funerary typology so successful that it spread to regions such as the Ripollès, the Alt Empordà and the Garrotxa. It consisted of relatively small marble gravestones the purpose of which was to cover ossuaries. The central space was reserved for the funeral exequies or the deposition of the deceased in the tomb, while the epitaph and the heraldic devices were arranged around the perimeter. Other widely cultivated themes include the Crucifixion, the Descent from the Cross, the Virgin and Child and the Last Judgement.

One excellent example of the type is that of Margarida Cadell (d. 1308), which has been associated with the style of an artist subjected to French influence. It was found in a cupboard, behind the altarpiece of the chapel of Saint Francis at the church of Santa Maria, Puigcerdà. Points to note here are a certain interest in space—the inverted perspective of the sarcophagus—and the lady's Franciscan habit, which symbolises her renunciation of earthly things, an attitude to death that the Franciscans strongly advocated.

Margarida Cadell and her family's predilection for the mendicant orders, shared by numerous members of the Cerdanya nobility in emulation of James II of Majorca (1243-1311) and his family, is confirmed by the fact that her husband, Guillem Cadell, donated 400 Barcelona solidus to the construction of the preachers' monastery and stipulated that if he died in Puigcerdà he was to be buried in the Dominican cemetery. M.R.M.C.

These images of mourners constitute a visual rendering of the moment of grief, or *planctus*, from one of the scenes from the hermitage of San Andrés de Mahamud, Burgos, which together with the paintings more strictly religious in theme decorated the tomb of Sancho Sánchez Carrillo. The recumbent figure of this knight is preserved at the Cincinnati Art Museum, Ohio, and in Mahamud.

Along with the four panels of mourners, a further two feature the escutcheons of Sancho Sánchez Carrillo and two more the Crucifixion, Christ in Majesty with the Tetramorph, the Annunciation, the Birth of Christ, the Dormition and the Coronation of the Virgin.

Research conducted by Fernando Gutiérrez Baños has unearthed the original deeds of the hermitage of San Andrés de Mahamud, dated 9 February 1295. This document authorises Don Sancho Sánchez Carrillo and his wife, Doña Juana, to be buried in this sacred precinct.

Stylistically speaking, the Mahamud panels belong to the Castilian linear Gothic, influenced by contemporary English miniatures. F.R.Q.

Gravestone of Margarida Cadell (d. 1308)

First quarter of the fourteenth century

MNAC/MAC 4366

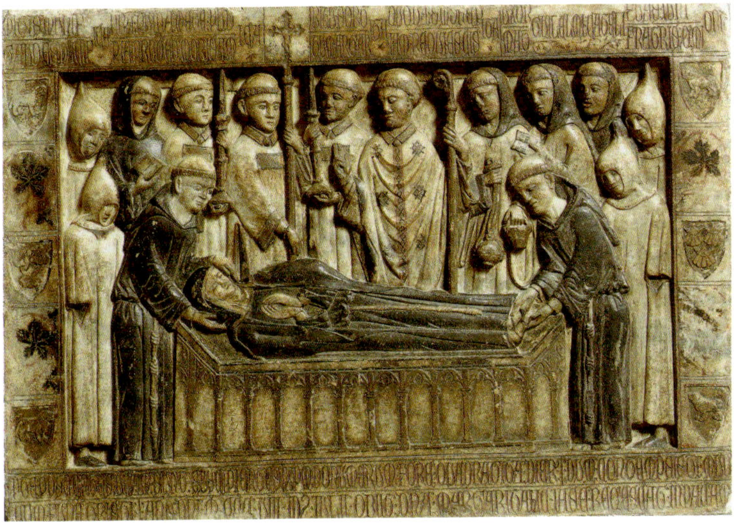

Mourners

Late thirteenth century (*c.* 1295)

MNAC/MAC 4372

Behind the Palau Episcopal in Barcelona, in the area of the church and square of Sant Felip Neri, until 1872 stood the remains of an old cemetery belonging to the cathedral, known as Montjuïc del Bisbe. Years before the cemetery chapel had been demolished, a chapel first documented in the late fifteenth century and the assumed provenance of this *Mary Magdalene*. Despite the differences in terms of material and style, this sculpture has been linked to two further standing female figures (MNAC/MAC 9841 and 9855) from the same place. One of them holds a pot of ointment, as this one does, and it is supposed that together they would have represented either the Holy Women visiting the Holy Sepulchre or else a group of the Holy Sepulchre.

The quality and state of preservation of this *Mary Magdalene* are better than those of the other two. This particular image is flat behind, which suggests that it might originally have belonged to an architectural structure or an altarpiece. It is feasible to contend that the Montjuïc del Bisbe group was a combination of pieces of differing origins and by different artists involved in work on Barcelona Cathedral. M.R.M.C.

The attribution of this Holy Generation to the painter and sculptor Michael Pacher is perfectly feasible bearing in mind questions such as the assumed provenance of the piece, namely a monastery in Munich, and above all the style.

The iconography of the groups known as the Holy Generation or St Anne-triple responds to the widespread intention at the time to assign St Anne a preponderant role, since she is regarded as the initiator of the mysteries of virginal conception. As fruit of the Embrace with St Joachim at the Golden Gate, Mary was born free of original sin, which would explain the idea of the miraculous gestation of Jesus Christ, since Mary herself was the outcome of immaculate conception.

Besides this example of the rendering of St Anne standing, the theme has been expressed in other iconographical ways, more deeply rooted in Catalonia and denoting with greater clarity the genealogical concatenation of the figures. One is the vertical superimposition of the three images—St Anne, the Virgin and the Child—with a figure seated one on the other successively, following the same axis and in ascending order in terms of size, or else the arrangement of the three figures superimposed on different axes in accordance with a pyramidal composition resembling juxtaposition, as we observe in the sculpture addressing the same theme attributed to Adrian van Wësel (MNAC/MAC 131055). M.R.M.C.

Mary Magdalene
Second third of
the fourteenth century
MNAC/MAC 9797

Attributed to Michael Pacher
(documented between 1435 and 1498)
The Holy Generation
Fifteenth century
MNAC/MAC 17661

The ivory works documented in the inventories of the period and which enrich museum collections all over the world are highly varied in terms of typology, since they embrace diptychs, triptychs and devotional images for personal boudoirs. From this we therefore assume that ivory work was common practice in Parisian workshops, although it would have been one among several sculptural specialities. We must also bear in mind that due to the rarity and costliness of the material, these pieces would have been luxury items that only the rich could afford.

Approximately between 1320 and 1330, Paris workshops seemed to have been very busy, the main product being images of the Virgin and Child, with unmistakable common traits of which this particular sculpture is a synthesis: finesse, high average quality despite the 'mass produced' nature of the pieces, exaltation of tenderness in the relationship between the two protagonists through the Child's look or gesture, who places his hand on his Mother's breast, similar postures of Mother and Child, and idealised facial features. M.R.M.C.

The composition, the seat of honour that serves as a frame and the arrangement of the figures in this carving are taken almost literally from an engraving by Martin Schongauer (1450-91) that addresses the same theme of the Coronation and forms part of a series on the life of the Saviour. The prestige of the master engraver from Colmar was immense in his own day and has persisted over the ages. Indeed, his graphic work was the most widely imitated until Albrecht Dürer (1471-1528) appeared on the scene. Consequently, Schongauer exerted a deep influence on his immediate circles and those further afield in terms of technique, style, composition and iconography. It need not surprise us, therefore, that his oeuvre was an essential point of reference for late Gothic works in numerous European countries.

In terms of style, the configuration of the figures in the scene of the Coronation responds to the typologies most widespread among late fifteenth-century Flemish and German masters. M.R.M.C.

Virgin
Manufactured in Paris
First half of the fourteenth century
MNAC/MAC 5223

Central European School
Coronation of the Virgin
End of the fifteenth century
MNAC/MAC 5270

Renaissance & Baroque art

The collection of Renaissance & Baroque art

The Museu Nacional d'Art de Catalunya is renowned above all as a museum of Romanesque art or, in any case, as a museum of medieval and *Modernista* art by virtue of its extraordinary collections from these periods. Although this prestige is thoroughly justified, we must not overlook the fact that the Museum also houses a valuable holding of Renaissance and Baroque art. Unlike other major national museums in Europe, which were created on the basis of a central nucleus, such as the collections accrued by royal families or the nobility, the MNAC collections were built up as a recovery process of the local heritage of Catalonia and were enlarged thanks to gifts and acquisitions from private collections. It is for this reason that Catalan art serves as a thread of the beginning and end of the museographical discourse, which focuses on two historical moments: the spread of the Renaissance manner in the first half of the sixteenth century, and eighteenth-century painting, particularly with the figure of Antoni Viladomat. Thus, Catalan works stand alongside their Spanish, Flemish and Italian counterparts from the sixteenth, seventeenth and eighteenth centuries.

The itinerary starts in the sixteenth-century Low Countries, where religious fervour combined with detailed scenes from everyday life, as we observe in the set of quality panels and triptychs conceived for private use. At the beginning of the Renaissance, Catalan art was characterised by the coexistence of Gothic forms, Flemish in origin, and more innovative concepts, as we see in Ayne Bru's *Saint Candidus* and Pedro Fernández's *Saint Blaise*, which bear the humanist stamp of the new art that was being produced in Italy. The *Altarpiece of Saint Eligius of the Silversmiths*, by Pere Nunyes, and Damià Forment's *Dormition of the Virgin* are further examples of the new language. Around the end of the century Spanish painting generated works of great beauty, such as El Greco's *The Bearing of the Cross*, in which we appreciate the painter's modern concept of colour, the fruits of what he had learnt while in Venice. The *Ecce Homo* by Luis de Morales, a contemporary of El Greco's, conveys the spirit of the Counter-Reformation.

The seventeenth century begins with the frescos in the Herrera chapel by Annibale Carracci and his collaborators, from the Roman church of San Giacomo degli Spagnuoli, and continues with paintings by Italian artists such as the Genoese Gioacchino Assereto and the Neapolitans Massimo Stanzione and Andrea Vaccaro. However, the most outstanding works from this period and one of the Museum's veritable treasures are those by the masters of the Spanish Golden Age, such as the *Martyrdom of Saint Bartholomew* by José de Ribera, Diego Velázquez's *Saint Paul* and the *Immaculate Conception* and still lifes by Francisco de Zurbarán. Returning to Catalonia, the image of *Saint Cajetan* by the sculptor Andreu Sala echoes the genius of Bernini.

Coming to the eighteenth century, Antoni Viladomat's *Saint Francis* series is the only set of scenes from monastic life preserved in its entirety at a museum. On the other hand, the bold style of Francesc Pla, known as 'El Vigatà', denotes the freedom enjoyed by artists when it came to decorating the interiors of the homes of the emerging mercantile and industrial bourgeoisie and heralds developments in art during the nineteenth century.

This collection therefore reflects the penchant on the part of certain sectors of Catalan civil society for Renaissance and Baroque art, and compared to the rest of the Museum, it brings together art produced in Catalonia, the rest of Spain, Italy and Flanders, which allows visitors to obtain an overview of the evolution of European art during the sixteenth, seventeenth and eighteenth centuries.

The central compartment features the *Baptism of Christ* by St John the Baptist in the presence of the Archangel Michael, also present on the left-hand panel at the moment of the Weighing of the Souls, while the right-hand panel depicts an episode from the life of St Francis of Assisi. On the exterior of the two doors the figures of the Archangel Gabriel and the Virgin appear at the moment of the Annunciation. The entire iconographical programme revolves around the theme of redemption and renewal of faith associated with baptism. The dimensions of the piece and the escutcheon in the top right-hand corner of one of the doors suggest that this was a private commission to preside over a family chapel in a church.

The work is a paradigmatic example of the formal criteria applied by the Master of Frankfurt, a Flemish painter whose name derives from the two triptychs preserved in that city. His art resorts to eclectic solutions and formulae: the composition of the central panel derives from an engraving by Martin Schongauer, and recalls some paintings by Gerard David, while the typology of the Archangel Gabriel recalls models conceived and executed at the Van Eyck brothers' workshop, a typology that was reinterpreted also by Rogier van der Weyden and the Master of Flémalle. J.Y.

This painting depicts the Virgin, in half length, suckling the Child against a dark background. Mary wears a dress with a round neck and a white headscarf with an abundance of folds that cascade over the Child's right shoulder. This kind of small, circular piece was hung on the wall over the bed head for private worship. The *Virgo lactans* has a long tradition in Western Christian art and was interpreted by the Church as spiritual nourishment for mankind. The most famous model of this kind is the full-length one created by Robert Campin, otherwise known as the Master of Flémalle, preserved at the Städelsches Kunstinstitut, Frankfurt, of which many subsequent versions were made.

This piece is a paradigmatic example of the dissemination of Flemish artistic sources. Specifically, around forty works of this creation are preserved in museums and private collections all over the world. The exquisite piece commented on is one of the two of highest quality, the other being the one belonging to the Johnson Collection in Philadelphia. The finesse of the artist's execution is evidenced by the folds in the headscarf, of perfect lines and unsurpassable rendering of volume, and by the astonishing realism of the ears, mouth, nose, eyes, eyebrows and hair. On the other hand, the stylisation of the face, with elongated forehead and cheeks, points to a slight break away from the original model, which denotes the personality of the artist. J.Y.

Master of Frankfurt

(active in Antwerp between the last quarter of the fifteenth century and the first third of the sixteenth)

Triptych of the Baptism of Christ

1500-20

MNAC/MAC 15914

Unidentified painter

after a model by the Master of Flémalle or Robert Campin

Madonna Suckling the Child

c. 1520

MNAC/MAC 24232

The Virgin and Child, accompanied by St Joseph and the Magi in an attitude of worship, preside over the centre of the composition. The assignation of the work has been determined by stylistic comparison with the central panel, by the Master of Antwerp and featuring the same motif, of a triptych preserved at the Musées Royaux d'Art et d'Histoire, Brussels. The Epiphany was a very usual subject of paintings acquired by the Flemish ruling classes between the fifteenth and sixteenth centuries, an episode that served as a pretext for the rendering of elegant, sumptuous decorative ambiences. The painter here displays his familiarity with formulae adopted by the Italian schools, such as the inclusion of classical architecture or the presence of Cupids, although he engages in a free interpretation of these sources. At that particular moment in history, Flemish artists were gradually assimilating the Italian Renaissance model, a change in the expressive code that led to the quest for inspiration in tradition. Hesitation in the use of a new pictorial language led to a certain lack of self-confidence on the part of the artist, which took the form of *horror vacui*, evidenced here by the abundance of figures constituting the royal retinue in the middle distance. Note also the major presence of the autochthonous tradition in the luxury of details, particularly the somewhat affected attire and the landscape in the background. J.Y.

Permanent loan from the Reial Acadèmia Catalana de Belles Arts de Sant Jordi de Barcelona; admission, 1906

This saint, depicted as a knight, stands on tiled paving before a golden backdrop that highlights the monumental quality and elegance of his bearing. His splendid attire consists of dark armour, a shield, halberd, sword and a sumptuous fur-lined green tabard. His hair is shoulder-length and he wears a red cap with a medal featuring the bust of Christ. A purple stole hangs from his left forearm as he points towards his heart. St Candidus was a soldier in the Theban legion who was martyred together with St Maurice. This particular painting might have been one of the doors of the high altar at the monastery of Sant Cugat del Vallès, where the relics of St Candidus, discovered miraculously in the thirteenth century, were worshipped. This work and the *Decapitation of Saint Cucufate* (MNAC/MAC 15840), the patron saint of the monastery, are the only two remaining paintings from the altarpiece by Ayne Bru, one of the major painters of the fifteen hundreds in Catalonia. We know nothing of the life and times of this itinerant artist 'of northern origin', whose work reflects the modernity of the Renaissance model in all its purity. However, while the highly precise facture denotes his central-European training and a strong Flemish substratum, the courtly pose of the knight and the humanist spirit he conveys relate him directly to Italian culture, specifically to the style that emerged in Venice from Giovanni Bellini's workshop that would later generate the *maniera moderna* of Giorgione. M.M.C.

Master of the Epiphany of Antwerp
(active in Antwerp during the first half of the sixteenth century)
Epiphany
c. 1520
MNAC/MAC 5718

Ayne Bru
(a painter from Lummen, in the Duchy of Brabante, documented in Catalonia between 1500 and 1507)
Saint Candidus
1502-7
MNAC/MAC 64049

The Virgin, with the Child Jesus, the infant St John and a choir of angels holding a baldachin, is seated on a throne holding a book from which she shows us a miniature depicting the Pentecost. At the side we observe a biblical quotation from the Ecclesiastes (24, 3-6) speaking about Wisdom. Mary is the intermediary between the divine will and the history of mankind, since she made the incarnation of the Son possible, who revealed the truth disseminated by the Church. For this reason, God the Father presides over the composition from the sun enveloped in clouds, while the Holy Ghost perches on his head in the form of a dove. Mary, a simple mortal, is placed in the tangible physical setting of a landscape with architectural elements in the background featuring several scenes that complete the iconographical cycle: the episodes of Christ's Childhood (the Annunciation, the Birth, the Epiphany, the Slaughter of the Innocents and the Flight into Egypt) and the Fathers of the Latin Church. The central group has affinities with the *Madonna with the Monkey*, an engraving by Albrecht Dürer, who was a source of inspiration for many painters of the period. In 1944 Diego Angulo put forward the hypothesis, basing his theory on stylistic comparison, that this panel is the work of Joan de Burgunya; bearing in mind this hypothesis as well as the painting's facture, we should date it from between 1515 and 1525. J.Y.

St Blaise, in the foreground, is seated on the parapet of a portico that looks over a landscape, holding the Bible and the wool-carding machine that was the instrument of his martyrdom. He is richly attired, in keeping with his status as a bishop, in a white dalmatic, red tunic, blue stole and a green cape with plant-motif embroidery against a gilt background. He also bears a white mitre inlaid with precious stones. The saint's enigmatic gaze might suggest that doctrine, together with the supernatural virtue of faith, constitute the road to truth, two concepts symbolised respectively by the book and the carding machine. Of almost imperceptible brushstrokes, the facture of this work denotes direct knowledge of both the style of Bramante and Lombard portraiture, while also revealing the influence of Leonardo and Raphael. The portrait betokens a notable degree of psychological analysis, a relationship of serenity between the figure and space that uses perspective to extol the intellectual calibre and enhance the majestic bearing of the saint bishop of Sebaste.

This panel might have been a compartment of the same polyptych to which another depicting *Saint Gregory* belonged, today preserved at the Harvard University Fogg Art Museum. Given their style, both paintings have been attributed to the artist conventionally known as Pseudo-Bramantino, now identified as Pedro Fernández, a native of Murcia who between 1519 and 1521 executed the *Altarpiece of Saint Helen* for Girona Cathedral and who figures among the main introducers of the Renaissance language into Catalonia. M.M.C.

Joan de Burgunya (?)
(a painter from Strasbourg documented in Valencia and Catalonia after 1503; he died in Barcelona in 1525 or 1526)

The Virgin, the Child Jesus and the Infant Saint John
1515-25

MNAC/MAC 5690

Pedro Fernández
(a painter from Murcia documented in Girona between 1519 and 1521)

Saint Blaise
c. 1517

MNAC/MAC 122690

The Portuguese Pere Nunyes was the protagonist of one of the most attractive episodes in Catalan painting of the first half of the sixteenth century. His works reflect the influence of Albrecht Dürer's engravings as well as familiarity with the work of Raphael and Michelangelo, either first-hand or through prints by Marcantonio Raimondi and Marco Dente. In 1993, Nicole Dacos suggested that Nunyes may have trained in Italy and contributed to the murals at the Vatican, a fact that might explain much of his poetics.

In 1526 the Barcelona guild of silversmiths commissioned Pere Nunyes to paint and gild the altarpiece in their chapel at the church of La Mercè. By 1529, the piece had been completed. In 1749 the work was transferred to another chapel, that of Santa Maria dels Socors, in the same church, and in 1773 the altarpiece was disassembled and eventually replaced by another. Only the door paintings were preserved, the whereabouts of the rest is unknown. The door interiors depict six episodes from the life of St Eligius, the patron saint of silversmiths: on one side the *Birth of Saint Eligius*, the *Weighing of the Saddles Before King Clotarius* and the *Episcopal Consecration of Saint Eligius*, and on the other the *Baptism of Infidels*,

the *Transferral of the Body of Saint Martial* and the *Death of Saint Eligius*. The outer side of the doors features a single theme, the *Annunciation*, the highly modern rendering of which most probably reflects the lessons Nunyes learnt in Rome, since it is highly unlikely that he would have attained such a degree of quality by simply basing his work on engravings. The piece freedom of execution might be due to the fact that it was a simple grisaille on the outer side of the doors—a work with fewer demands on the part of the patron, visible only when no ceremony was being held and in poor light conditions. J.Y.

Pere Nunyes
(a painter from the diocese of Viseu, Portugal,
documented in Catalonia and Aragon between 1513 and 1556)
Doors of the *Altarpiece of Saint Eligius of the Silversmiths*
1526-9

MNAC/MAC 15893, 24250, 24252, 24253, 24254 and 24255

This rectangular relief worked in different thicknesses depicts the bust of Emperor Augustus as a young man, seen in profile and wearing a radiate crown with infulae. In the background, a triumphal arch bears the inscription PROVIDENTIA, a classical motto that refers to the divinity. The source of inspiration for this image by an Italian Renaissance sculptor was the art of ancient Rome, most probably a coin. In 1988 Joaquim Garriga put forward the hypothesis that the piece might be the work of someone linked to Mino da Fiesole's workshop and executed after the master's death, given the graceful forms of the relief that bring Florentine sculptors to mind. Nonetheless, it must be remembered that Mino da Fiesole ran his workshop in Rome between 1454 and 1480 and that by the end of the *Quattrocento* many Tuscan artists were working in the Eternal City.

Whatever the case, the relief was purchased in Rome by a Catalan dignitary, Miquel Mai, who was Emperor Charles V's ambassador at the court of Pope Clement VII between 1528 and 1531 and vice-chancellor of the Consejo de Aragon between 1533 and 1546. We know for a fact that Mai had dealings with sculpture workshops in Rome, since he sent a marble fountain to Toledo as a gift for the Emperor. The *Bust of Augustus* formed part of the collection of twenty-one circular marble reliefs, many of which are preserved at the MNAC, that Mai kept at his Barcelona home, as we learn from his wife's post-mortem inventory. J.Y.

Permanent loan from the Reial Acadèmia de Bones Lletres to the Museu Provincial d'Antiguitats de Barcelona, 1879

Saint Sebastian was a Roman centurion born in Gaul who was denounced for exhorting two of his comrades-in-arms not to abandon the Christian faith. The outcome of this was that Emperor Diocletian attempted unsuccessfully to execute him. He was tied to a post in the middle of the Campus Martius, Rome, where he served as a target for archers. In Italian Renaissance art, which extolled the human body, the saint's torture was a very popular theme and became a pretext for the rendering of the pagan typology of the naked Apollo.

The anatomy of this figure of *Saint Sebastian* is carefully studied: a trunk treated in the classical style, a muscular neck and robust legs. His physical presence in space is highly imposing while, on the other hand, the narrow shorts suggest that the piece was executed in the centre-north of Italy (Bologna, Ferrara or Venice) during the last quarter of the fifteenth century by a sculptor familiar with the Tuscan models of the period. In this context, we might observe the similarities between this piece and the *Saint Sebastian* by Antonello da Messina, dated 1475 and preserved at the Gemäldegalerie, Dresden, a sculpture that exemplifies a confluence between the attention to detail characteristic of Lombard art and the restrained style of Piero della Francesca. J.Y.

Attributed to a follower of Mino da Fiesole
(Florence, end of the fifteenth century or beginning of the sixteenth)
Bust of Augustus
1490-1510
MNAC/MAC 9947

Unidentified sculptor
(active in the north and centre of Italy in the last quarter of the fifteenth century)
Saint Sebastian
1480-90
MNAC/MAC 4541

In his last will and testament, dated 1544, Jeroni Descoll (who must not be confused with his father, of the same name and vice-chancellor of the Consejo de Aragon between 1548 and 1553) expressed his wish to be buried in the chapel 'del sepulchra de la gloriosa Verge Maria', which he had had built in the Barcelona church of Sant Miquel. The *Dormition*, to which these *Three Apostles* belong, had been attributed to both an unknown Italian sculptor and to Martí Díez de Liatzasolo until in 1992 Joan Bosch ascertained that it was Damià Forment and his workshop who had executed the work. We also know that in 1535 Enric de Borgonya, a regular collaborator at Forment's studio, worked on the piece. Forment was in Catalonia intermittently between 1525 and 1537, during which period he would have become familiar with works by Bartolomé Ordóñez and Giovanni da Nola, which marked a change in his style as we learn from the high altarpiece at the cathedral of Santo Domingo de la Calzada. The Barcelona *Dormition* is crucial to an understanding of the evolution of the sculptor's poetics. On the other hand, however, the quality of this group is very uneven, due mainly to two factors: the intervention of Forment's assistants, among whom Gregorio Pardo and the abovementioned Enric de Borgonya have been identified, and the eventful life the work had led up until the demolition of the church in 1868, during which the Virgin was replaced by an image of Christ and the figure of at least one further apostle was added. J.Y.

Permanent loan from the Reial Acadèmia de Bones Lletres to the Museu Provincial d'Antiguitats de Barcelona, 1879

The Pontiff is seated in a gentle diagonal to the right, making a gesture of blessing with his right hand while his left rests on a voluminous tome on his lap. He wears a black-and-gold brocade chasuble over a green tunic with a wide vertical band forming a cross over his chest, in the middle of which we observe a brooch of precious stones and pearls. His tiara and pontifical gloves are adorned with brooches similar to the one on his breast and three rings. At the bottom we read the inscription SANTO GREGORIO PAPA DOCTOR in cursive Gothic script. The sitter's halo stands out against the golden, punched, goffered background featuring plant motifs. This panel is linked to a further three depicting *Saint Peter*, *Saint Jerome* and King *David*, now in private collections, which together might have belonged to the predella of an altarpiece. This work dates from the artist's last years, in which the humanist spirit stands side-by-side with the archaic language of the gilt background. Even so, this *Saint Gregory* has been linked to the series of illustrious personages who emerged from the brush of this painter from Castile, who introduced the Renaissance into the Peninsula and became one of its geniuses. M.M.C.

Damià Forment and collaborators
(Valencia, *c.* 1475 – Santo Domingo de la Calzada, 1540)
Three Apostles (Dormition of the Virgin)
1534-7
MNAC/MAC 9848

Pedro Berruguete
(Paredes de Nava, c. 1450 – prior to 1504)
Pope Saint Gregory
c. 1495
MNAC/MAC 113233

The artist responsible for this panel was the native of a town in the duchy of Modena, near Ferrara, where he would have trained alongside such masters as Cosme Tura, Francesco del Cossa and Ercoli de Roberti. San Leocadio came to Valencia in 1472 to execute the cathedral's high altar, summoned by Roderic de Borja, future Pope Alexander VI. In 1945, Leandro Saralegui noted the stylistic affinities between this panel and two altarpieces the Italian painter executed in Gandia around the year 1507. The scene depicts the moment of mourning over the body of Christ after his descent from the Cross. In the foreground and from left to right we see Mary Magdalene, Mary Cleofas, the Virgin, St John, Nicodemus with his pincers and Salome; behind, Joseph of Arimathea with the crown of thorns and one of his servants with the three nails of the Passion. The background consists of a landscape and two scenes—a group of soldiers kill off the two thieves crucified with Christ, Dymas and Gestas, and another composition with a rider and three soldiers with their backs turned to us. The landscape consists of a river, hills, sky, clouds and a walled urban nucleus, ancient Jerusalem in the guise of a medieval village. J.Y.

Depicted in half length and in left three-quarter profile, the young gentleman rests his right forearm on a piece of furniture while he stands haughtily with his left hand on his hip, sporting a ring on his little finger. He wears a black cap from which his fair hair emerges at chin level, and a dark embroidered doublet with light-coloured shiny sleeves, suggesting silk. The ruff and the white cuffs highlight the colour of his skin in contrast with the dark attire and background. Although we have no idea as to the identity of the man, to judge from his finery he may have been an occasional patron, most probably one of the European ambassadors or nobles who posed for the master in his Venetian workshop. The man seems to want to engage in dialogue with the observer, a characteristic of Tintoretto's expressionism that focuses attention on the face and hands through the application of *impasto*, while the clothing is rendered by quick, flowing brushstrokes. In this way, and with a minimum of media, the artist conveys the inner force of the gentleman.

The painting would date from around 1554, given its affinities with the *Gentleman* at the Barber Institute, Birmingham, the portrait of *Lorenzo Soranzo* (?) at the Kunsthistorisches Museum, Vienna, and the *Gentleman* in Christ Church, Oxford, all from the same period. Furthermore, its provenance is a prestigious one, having belonged to Don Gaspar Méndez de Haro y Guzmán, as we learn from his inventory and from his heraldic anagram on the reverse. M.M.C.

Paolo da San Leocadio
(San Valentino, *c.* 1445 – Valencia, 1519)

Mourning Over the Dead Body of Christ
c. 1507
MNAC/MAC 64105

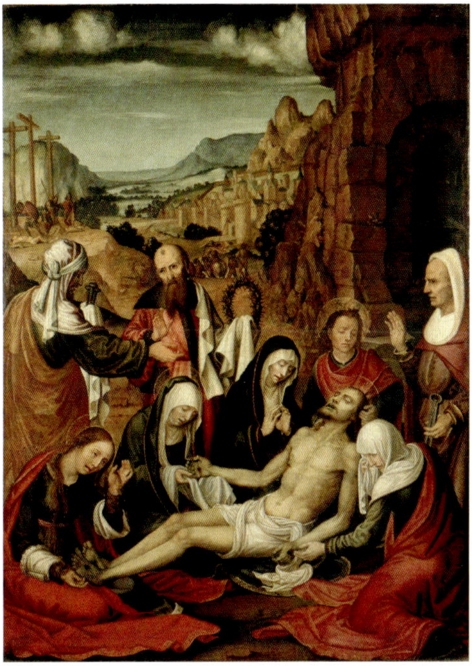

Jacopo Robusti, known as 'Il Tintoretto'
(Venice, 1519-94)

Portrait of a Gentleman
c. 1554
MNAC/MAC 24206

In this small picture of the *Calvary*, Jacopo Bassano exploits the blackness of the slate support to create a night scene. The painting would have been executed around 1575, when the artist was experimenting with the use of artificial light, and paid particular attention to the Life and Passion of Christ. These innovations secured him an extensive clientele, and his small-format *notturni* for private worship became highly prized. Although works of this kind were common on the art market of the period, very few painted on slate have been preserved. Of vertical format, the painter eliminated the figures of the two thieves, thereby highlighting the body of Christ and paying especial attention to the interplay and movement of the lances and the ladder, which fill the darkness of the deep void behind. The refined, ingeniously executed work of a virtuoso, Bassano's *Calvary* features warm tones (red and golden-yellow to represent the artificial light) and almost clotted patches of white on the figures in the foreground, which together further enhance the darkness of the night. At the same time, fine touches of gold emanate from the head of Christ and spread like a beam of light over the wooden Cross. This, in short, is an extraordinary piece whose small dimensions contain all the poetics, boldness and technical mastery of the Venetian artist. M.M.C.

Christ is alone in his suffering, wearing the crown of thorns, his face emaciated, mouth half open, his cheekbones standing out, his eyes flooded with tears and blood running over his naked skin, as Pilate had to present him to the Hebrews and proclaim 'Ecce homo' ('Here is the man'). The source of inspiration for the image is from the Gospel according to St Matthew: 'They stripped him and put a scarlet robe on him, and then twisted together a crown of thorns and set it on his head. They put a staff in his right hand…' (27, 28-29). This passage satisfied to perfection the devotional feelings of believers who supported the Counter-Reformation, since its reading and contemplation increased the intensity of their inner life. The theme, therefore, was very much in demand among the artist's clientele and became a common motif in his output, since several versions have come down to us, of which this is one of the best. Superb in execution, it presents meticulous treatment of the hair and beard and a mysterious interplay between light and shadow, pearl-grey shades, which contrasts with the dark, plain backdrop and the scarlet chlamys. A vision of Christ in pain with his fingers entwined around the staff doing for a scepter with exquisite elegance, asking himself and the observer about the reason for his suffering. This is a work rich in pathos with an intense emotional charge that leads to the mystical experience. M.M.C.

Jacopo Bassano
(Bassano del Grappa,
c. 1510/15 – *c.* 1592)
Calvary
c. 1575
MNAC/MAC 108373

**Luis de Morales,
known as 'the Divine'**
(Badajoz, *c.* 1519-86 [?])
Ecce Homo
c. 1570
MNAC/MAC 11547

The Bearing of the Cross is a creation by the Cretan artist depicting Jesus crowned with thorns and amorously caressing the Cross, which he carries with serene bearing and expression. For this Christ the Cross is not a heavy burden, quite the contrary, and both his body and his gaze rise lightly upwards, inviting us to follow. This painting, the execution of which is of exceptional quality, captivated the painter and art critic Aureliano de Beruete (1845-1912), who owned it before it was acquired by the Catalan collector Santiago Espona (1888-1958).

Dating from the same period is *Saint Peter and Saint Paul*, an astonishing work by virtue of its thematic and chromatic richness. Apparently at least, the central theme is the encounter between the two apostles who had been in disagreement, a reconciliation suggested discreetly by the hands that cross without actually touching. The gesture seems to be one of ceding or recognition on the part of Peter, depicted

The Bearing of the Cross
1590-5
MNAC/MAC 65577

here as a weary old man against a backdrop of clouds that part to reveal the blue sky above and accentuate this saint's halo. At his side appears the imposing image of Paul—without a halo—wearing a green tunic and vermilion mantle, in the plenitude of middle age, proudly gripping his attribute, the sword. M.M.C.

Doménikos Theotokópoulos, known as 'El Greco'
(Candia, 1540 or 1541 – Toledo, 1614)

Saint Peter and Saint Paul
1595-1600
MNAC/MAC 5083

On February 26 1602 the Castilian noble Juan Enríquez de Herrera dedicated a votive chapel to St Didacus of Alcalá at the church of San Giacomo degli Spagnuoli in Rome, for which Annibale Carracci was commissioned to paint the murals. Having completed the Galleria in the Palazzo Farnese, Carracci set to work on his new commission in 1604. The master from Bologna designed all the cartoons and personally supervised the work *in situ* until he fell seriously ill. Subsequently his collaborators, including Giovanni Lanfranco, Sisto Badalocchio and Francesco Albani, had to complete the murals. When the Herrera chapel was dismantled halfway through the nineteenth century, the frescos were removed from their original site and transferred to canvas thanks to the intervention of sculptor Antoni Solà. Later they were sent to Spain, where they were shared between the Museo del Prado and what is now the Reial Acadèmia Catalana de Belles Arts de Sant Jordi, from which they were transferred to the MNAC as a permanent loan.

Assumption of the Virgin
Late 1604 – early 1605
MNAC/MAC 5676

The *Assumption of the Virgin* and *The Apostles around the Empty Tomb* were originally on the entrance arch to the chapel and were painted by Francesco Albani between late 1604 and early 1605 on the basis of the cartoons by the master. The remaining fragments preserved at the MNAC correspond to the interior decoration and depict scenes from the life and miracles of the patron saint: the *Miracle of the Flowers*, the *Preaching of Saint Didacus*, the *Healing of a Blind Youth*, the *Apparition of Saint Didacus on his Tomb Before Pilgrims and the Sick*, as well as the *Eternal Father* from the cupola and the apostles *Saint Peter* and *Saint Paul* who flanked the altar. M.M.C.

Permanent loan from the Reial Acadèmia Catalana de Belles Arts de Sant Jordi, 1902; admission, 1906

Annibale Carracci and collaborators
Mural Paintings from the Herrera Chapel
1604-6

Annibale Carracci (Bologna, 1560 – Rome, 1609) and
Francesco Albani (Bologna, 1578-1660)

The Apostles Around the Empty Tomb
Late 1604 – early 1605
MNAC/MAC 24284

The monumental figure of a middle-aged man sitting on a stone plinth in three-quarter length slightly turned to the right stands out against a plain, earth-coloured background. He wears a coarse brown mantle that covers his red tunic and conceals the voluminous mass of his body. His hair is black, his curly beard is greying and his deeply wrinkled skin is tanned by the sun. A halo of light that stands out against the darkness denotes his saintliness. The fingers of his left hand peep timidly over the voluminous tome that indicates his status as an apostle. In the top left-hand corner the inscription S. PAVLVS links the personage to the apostle of the gentiles in the absence of the sword, his only known attribute. On the other hand, while the halo confirms that he is a saint, his markedly intellectual air evokes the philosophers that José de Ribera painted. Recognised unanimously by critics as a work by Velázquez, it was August Mayer who in 1921 put forward the hypothesis that the canvas belongs to the same series as the *Saint Thomas* preserved at the Musée des Beaux-Arts, Orléans. Both pictures have been associated with those that Antonio Ponz (1778) saw at the Carthusian monastery of Las Cuevas, Seville, and with a painting of the Apostles formerly at the monastery of San Hermenegildo, Madrid. This *Saint Paul* is a superb example of Velázquez's early work in Seville and, in this context, it has stylistic affinities with the portrait of *Ramon Llull* (see entry below), two 'Riberan' works that constitute fundamental points of reference regarding the assimilation and spread of the influence of Caravaggism in Spain. M.M.C.

Against a dark background the three-quarter profile of an old man appears meditating on a text he holds in his hands. He is dressed in black, with white collar and cuffs and is seated in a barely visible armchair at a writing desk. Reflected light enhances the tanned complexion and wrinkles on the face and illuminates the hands, white hair, beard, sheets of paper and books on the table. This is an imaginary portrait, removed from hagiographical exaltation, in which the subject resembles a philosopher far more closely than a saint. The inscription on the reverse side identifies the figure as Ramon Llull, the Majorcan mystic who was the first to use Catalan as a language for written philosophical thought, and relates the canvas to the one listed in the inventory of Don Gaspar Méndez de Haro y Guzmán: 'Un lienzo de cinco quartas de alto. Retrato de Raimundo Lulio, original de Francisco Ribalta.' Neither the concept nor the facture of the canvas, formerly attributed to Velázquez, would have been conceivable in Ribalta's early work; consequently, we must assume that it dates from his mature period, by which time the artist had assimilated Caravaggism and had become familiar with José de Ribera's portraits of philosophers. Whatever the case, the atmosphere here is the same one that impregnated Velázquez's early output in his native Seville (see entry above). This canvas is therefore a highly interesting point of reference in the spread and assimilation of Naturalism in Spanish painting of the Golden Age. M.M.C.

Diego Velázquez
(Seville, 1599 – Madrid, 1660)
Saint Paul
c. 1619
MNAC/MAC 24242

Francisco Ribalta
(Solsona, 1565 – Valencia, 1628)
Ramon Llull
c. 1620
MNAC/MAC 24244

The apostle Bartholomew, almost naked except for the white sheet that only barely covers him, gazes helplessly at us from the stone on which he lies. A drunken executioner skins him alive with sadistic relish, without even allowing his assistant to hold his victim steady. A classical sculpture featuring the head of Apollo, which we should nonetheless identify as that of the god Baldach, lies in smithereens on the floor. In the background, their heads covered, two priests witness the harrowing act of torture taking place in the open air and in broad daylight. The painting is loyal to the text by Iacopo da Varazze in the *Golden Legend*, a subject that is the Christian version of the fable of Marsias, the faun who suffered the same punishment as the apostle Bartholomew. In both cases the theme is one of martyrdom and physical torment that 'Lo Spagnoletto' masterfully rendered in its twofold Christian and pagan versions. This extraordinary canvas, one of Ribera's best, might have been the one that Louis Philippe d'Orléans had in his Spanish Gallery in Paris between 1838 and 1848, and it inspired the poet Théophile Gautier (1811-72) to write the following lines in his book *Ribera* (1845): 'Tu sembles enivré par le vin des suplices,... / Avec quelle furie et quelle volupté / Tu retournes la peau du martyr qu'on écorche / Pour nous en faire voir l'envers ensanglanté'. Such admiration would have been shared by the illustrator Alexandre de Riquer (1856-1920), who purchased this painting for his own collection and eventually sold it to the Museum. M.M.C.

José de Ribera o Jusepe Ribera, known as 'Lo Spagnoletto'
(Játiva, 1591 – Naples, 1652)
Martyrdom of Saint Bartholomew
1644
MNAC/MAC 24162

The very young, radiant Virgin with shoulder-length curls and her hands joined in prayer directs her intercessor's gaze heavenwards. She wears a pink silk tunic and a dark blue mantle, at the same time sporting a necklace of precious stones with the anagram A(ve) M(aria). She rests on five cherubim sitting on the horns of a moon as transparent as a crystal ball. Thirteen stars and innumerable tiny angelic heads merge with the clouds forming the halo around her head and opens towards the firmament. In the sea of cumuli bathed in golden light two cavities open with naked angels bearing lilies and roses (attributes of Mary's untarnished conception and virginal maternity) and two marble tablets feature inscriptions from the *Song of Songs*: QUAE EST ISTA and AURORA CONSURGENS ('Who is she who emerges like the dawn, beautiful as the moon, radiant as the sun?' (6, 10). On either side, the symbols of the litany: Untarnished mirror, Jacob's ladder, Gates of Heaven and Morning star. Below, outside the supernatural scenario, a backlit landscape with more Marian allusions and two collegiates who raise their eyes upwards while reciting stanzas from *Ave Maris Stella*. The theme here is the 'glorious privilege' of Mary as the only mortal who was freed from original sin, a doctrinal argument with a long tradition that was highly popular in Golden-Age Spanish painting. Zurbarán executed many versions of the theme, but this one is undoubtedly the best of those to emerge from his brushes and ranks among the finest works of world painting. M.M.C.

The static effigy of St Francis stands in frontal position in the middle of the composition just as he emerges from the dark abyss of death. From the left a strong beam of light models the volumes and folds of the rough cloth that covers his body, while his face, with half-open mouth and eyes gazing heavenwards appears, between light and penumbra, immersed in the cavity of the hood. On the right-hand side, on the surface of his habit, we observe the stigma that Christ endowed on him. The source of inspiration for this astonishing image is the discovery of the incorrupt corpse of the saint by Pope Nicholas V in 1449 in the crypt of the basilica of Assisi. The Jesuit Pedro de Ribadeneyra relates the episode in his *Flos sanctorum* of 1599: '...he was standing...with his eyes open like a living person and his eyes raised to heaven...his hands covered with the sleeves of his habit over his breast, in the style of the Friars Minor...' Early in the seventeenth century Thomas de Leu engraved the scene and gradually the light-hearted medieval poet was transformed into a post-Tridentine ascetic, as the Franciscans sought to present him: a patron saint in accordance with counter-reformist criterion that called for strict penitence. Zurbarán, without depicting the discovery of the incorrupt corpse of St Francis, restricts himself to rendering abstractly and avoiding anecdote the saint's intact body. Three versions are known of this invention of the master from Extremadura: this magnificent canvas, the one at the Musée des Beaux-Arts in Lyon and the third at the Boston Museum of Fine Arts. M.M.C.

Francisco de Zurbarán
(Fuente de Cantos, 1598 – Madrid, 1664)
Immaculate Conception
1632
MNAC/MAC 65578

Francisco de Zurbarán
(Fuente de Cantos, 1598 – Madrid, 1664)
Saint Francis of Assisi After the Vision of Pope Nicholas V
c. 1640
MNAC/MAC 11528

St John the Evangelist, kneeling in the foreground, leads us into the scene while the remaining apostles, Mary Magdalene and the Virgin watch in ecstasy as Christ, who presides over the top of the canvas, ascends into heaven to join the Eternal Father. Below, his footprints are marked on the rock as evidence of his presence on earth. This theme is fundamental to Catholic doctrine: it explains the triumph and glorification of Jesus Christ according to the prophecies in the Holy Scriptures. The theme appears in the Old Testament, the Psalms and the New Testament, and in the gospels according to the evangelists Luke and Mark, although the details are in the Acts of the Apostles (1, 9-10): 'After he said this, he was taken up before their very eyes, and a cloud hid him from their sight. They were looking intently up into the sky...' The footprints are a detail from the medieval tradition that Albrecht Dürer disseminated through his engravings. On the other hand, the clouds transfixed by beams of light and Jesus's attire moved by the rising wind are characteristics of the Baroque. The rich gamut of reds, blues, greens and pinkish glazes evokes the work of Venetian painters, while the composition echoes that of Titian's *Assumption of the Virgin* for Santa Maria Gloriosa dei Frari in Venice. A fine altar painting that faithfully reflects the devotional feelings and the innovative *maniera* of this Madrid painter, who would certainly have been wholly familiar with the Venetian canvases belonging to the Spanish royal collection. M.M.C.

Mary floats triumphantly, crowned with stars and with the dove of the Holy Spirit fluttering to her right, in a firmament crammed with cherubim raising symbols of the litany. More courtly than celestial in appearance, the Virgin is dressed in white and blue, bejewelled like a lady and enveloped by stormy nimbuses with her mantle swollen by a rising whirlwind. José Antolínez painted this spectacular *Immaculate Conception* with all the force and splendour of the decorative Baroque when, although by now somewhat appeased, the struggle still persisted to secure acknowledgement of this kind of Marian devotion. Since the Middle Ages, the Spanish Church had been the great champion of this doctrine, highly consolidated among the people, which the Catholic Church did not raise to the category of dogma until 1858. About halfway through the seventeenth century renderings of the theme became more showy and far removed from the respectful absorption characteristic of traditional iconography, Mary's 'glorious privilege' of being the only mortal free from original sin. This canvas reveals a strong Venetian influence, an exquisite altar painting whose sky, full of naked cherubim, piously evokes the *putti* of Titian's bacchanals that the Madrid artist would have observed in the royal collection at the Alcázar. M.M.C.

Francisco Camilo
(Madrid, *c.* 1615-73)
Ascension
1651
MNAC/MAC 24228

José Antolínez
(Madrid, 1635-75)
Immaculate Conception
1666
MNAC/MAC 24234

Four life-size quinces stand out monumentally against a black background, while a strong beam of light from the left models the fruit, their golden colour reflected on the edge of the metal dish. A white cloth is in the bottom-right foreground. Nothing is known about this painting from before it entered the Museum as an individual still life, as it is presented today. Nonetheless, the original canvas is relined and X-ray studies suggest that this canvas was cut from a larger one in order to make it an independent painting. It might have been a detail from a domestic religious interior scene, the bowl of fruit alluding to Redemption, as it frequently does in Zurbarán's work. Since discrepancies exist as to its dating, this is a subject that should be treated with some degree of reservation. The facture and composition suggest that it was painted in around the 1630s by virtue of its affinities with the *Still Life with Basket of Oranges* at the Norton Simon Foundation (Pasadena, California), from 1633, although it may also be related to works from his last period such as the *Madonna and Child with the Infant Saint John* (1658) at the San Diego Museum of Art and the canvas of the same title at the Museo de Bellas Artes de Bilbao, dated 1662. Regardless of when it was executed, though, this painting is remarkable for its beauty, mastery and mystery, enhanced by its current fragmented state, which allows us to admire it in all its purity, without symbols, a supreme example of visual art for its own sake. What might have prompted Rafael Alberti to write 'And the quince is pure thought / that the fruit bowl gathers in chiaroscuro'? As we contemplate it today, the canvas conveys the deep silence and 'poetry of quietude' of Zurbarán's art. M.M.C.

Arranged from left to right, in the manner of a frieze, are differently shaped receptacles in different sizes: a tin plate containing a gilt metal cup, a Sevillian pitcher of the 'eggshell' type, a vase from the Indies and another metal plate containing a pitcher full of water, all life-size. From the left, a strong light source models the volumes of the objects and causes their golds, reds and whites to stand out against the dark background. This is a mysterious creation of highly special characteristics that endow the composition with an avant-garde quality and denote all Zurbarán's compositional skill, rigour and serene quietude. Without even a hint of living nature and in the midst of absolute silence, the almost ritual arrangement of vessels in a row might evoke, in keeping with the Baroque spirit, an altar table. On the other hand, the reader must realise that these are not everyday objects, since both the gilt cup and the Indies vase were rare pieces that normally served a decorative purpose. Francesc Cambó possessed two identical copies of this work, both signed by the master from Extremadura: this one and another preserved at the Museo del Prado. Experts disagree over the exact date of execution, some placing it between 1635 and 1640, while others have recently contended that it dates from Zurbarán's last Madrid period, that is, between 1650 and 1664. M.M.C.

Francesc Cambó Bequest, 1949; admission, 1951

Francisco de Zurbarán
(Fuente de Cantos, 1598 – Madrid, 1664)
Still Life with Dish of Quinces
1633-64
MNAC/MAC 10092

Francisco de Zurbarán
(Fuente de Cantos, 1598 – Madrid, 1664)
Still Life with Four Vessels
1635-64
MNAC/MAC 64994

A wicker basket full of apples and quinces stands out against a black background in the centre of the composition. In the right foreground there are three pomegranates, one of them open revealing its bright red pulp and, on the left, two whole quinces and half another one with its interior in view. The stems and leaves of the fruit, still green, suggest that the fruit has recently been picked. Although nothing is known about this superb work, which entered the Museum as an original by Velázquez, it was William Jordan who, in 1985, convincingly identified it as by Juan de Zurbarán, basing his judgement on its similarities with the *Basket of Fruit and Cardoons* at the Gösta Serlachius Fine Arts Foundation (Mäntta, Finland), signed in 1643 and identical in execution. Indeed, the modelling of the pomegranates, the leaves and the quinces, on the basis of short, pasty brushstrokes, is identical in both canvases, as is the intense light that creates a remarkable plastic effect. These paintings constitute points of reference for the identification of the work of Juan de Zurbarán, the son of Francisco, magnificent examples of the evolution of his style, which developed away from the balance and austerity of his father's. An avant-garde, sensual manner that reached high levels of quality and led Juan to become independent from the family workshop. M.M.C.

On a wooden support and against a neutral backdrop, in the foreground a splendid crusty cut loaf appears on a wavy-edged ceramic dish, also containing a folded serviette and a knife with a hallmark on the blade. Behind, a white, plain glazed Talavera jar with a simple ochre border on the edge and a rope-shaped handle. At its side stands a bottle of wine with its stamp of origin, reflecting the window through which the light that illuminates the ensemble penetrates. Three melons tied together with the string from which they will hang in a cool, dark place mark their curved outline next to an unglazed terracotta vessel covered with a piece of cloth tied with string. In front, clusters of black and white grapes appear with leaves and shoots twisted together beside a number of apples. On the table, a number of loose shoots and grapes are about to fall. This magnificent minutely detailed canvas denotes the painter's concern for observation from life, the result of which is faithful, studied reproduction lacking in symbolic intentions, which responds to the tastes of the enlightened spirit of Carlos III's Spain. Given the absence of major commissions, Meléndez devoted himself almost exclusively to rendering objects and still lifes to meet the demands of a clientele he had to please for the sake of his own survival. And in this context we must recall that one month before his death the artist described himself as 'a poor man of solemnity'. M.M.C.

Juan de Zurbarán
(Llerena, 1620 – Seville, 1649)
Basket of Apples, Quinces and Pomegranates
c. 1643
MNAC/MAC 24259

Luis Egidio Meléndez
(Naples, 1716 – Madrid, 1780)
Still Life with Apples, Grapes, Melons, Bread, Jar and Bottle
c. 1771
MNAC/MAC 24246

St Peter of Alcántara (Alcántara, 1499 – Arenas de San Pedro, 1562), beatified in 1622 and canonised in 1669, is regarded as a reformer of the Franciscan Order, although after the split in 1517 between 'Conventuals' and 'Observants' he introduced no new reforms, preferring to consolidate and extend the branch of Observance. In the sculpture, the saint is depicted at the moment of receiving divine inspiration just before he was about to write it down. His face absorbed in concentration and his gaze fixed, he raises his right hand, holding a pen, while in his left hand he holds a book. He wears the monastic sackcloth of the Observants or *Alcantarinos*, greyish in colour with a short hood, patched and tied with an alb ribbon. The artistic model derives from the work of Alonso Cano, a sculptor who collaborated with Pedro de Mena in Granada prior to 1658. Mena personalised this iconographical type in different versions after his journey to Castile in 1663. The artist strove to exteriorise the inner religiousness of his subject, and to this end he endows the image with mystic spiritual values. The saint's innermost fervour is conveyed through his physical appearance, particularly in his marked facial features. Such emotion had to be contained within certain limits, as we observe in the austere attire. Outer severity and inner fire, the contradiction of the ascetic, which reveals the heights that religious fervour reached in seventeenth-century Spain, masterfully reflected here by Mena. J.Y.

St Cajetan of Thiene, founder of the Theatine Order, stands erect dressed in the habit of the congregation of regular clerics (a black cassock and white smock), while in his hands he holds a lily and an open book, the rule that Pope Clement VII approved in 1521. The saint crushes a malign character, an old bearded man with his head resting on an open book, who represents the Lutheran heresy. The work originally presided over the façade of the Theatine monastery of Barcelona.

In 1800 Ceán Bermúdez mentioned this piece in the biography of the sculptor Sala, although he was under the impression that the artist's Christian name was Miquel. The stylistic affinities between this work and the *Saint Francis Xavier* in the chapel of Saint Pacianus in Barcelona Cathedral, signed by the sculptor, leave no doubt as to its authorship. Andreu Sala was one of the best sculptors active in Catalonia during the second half of the seventeenth century. Although emphasis has always been laid on his training in Barcelona at the workshop of Francesc Santacruz, he might also have trained in his native city of Cardona, where sculptors such as Miquel Vidal and Josep Ribera had their own workshops. Whatever the case, Sala was familiar with Roman Baroque sculpture from the first half of the seventeenth century, since his work reflects the influence of Gian Lorenzo Bernini, Alessandro Algardi and François Duquesnoy. J.Y.

Permanent loan from the Reial Acadèmia de Bones Lletres to the Museu Provincial d'Antiguitats de Barcelona, 1879

Pedro de Mena Medrano
(Granada, 1628 – Málaga, 1688)
Saint Peter of Alcántara
1663-73
MNAC/MAC 8343

Andreu Sala
(Cardona, 1627 –
Barcelona [?], *c.* 1700)
Saint Cajetan
1685-90
MNAC/MAC 14826

This depiction in three-quarter length of Agnes of Rome shows the saint in direct communication with the Almighty, in a mystic trance, her head slightly raised, mouth half open, the fingers of one hand open over her breast (near her heart) while with her other hand she caresses the Mystic Lamb. The saint's neckline shifts sideways to reveal part of her shoulder, the highest degree of eroticism in the work of Stanzione. Agnes was the daughter of a noble Roman family who was martyred in the third century, during persecutions subsequent to the death of Decius, because she had refused to marry one of the prefect's sons. According to the *Golden Legend*, Agnes claimed she was joined to Jesus, hence the fact that she is invariably associated with the Lamb of God or *Agnus Dei*, the symbol of Christ. The resemblance in Latin and Italian between *agnello* ('lamb') and *Agnese* ('Agnes'), although the respective etymological origins differ, contributed to the lamb's becoming established as the saint's attribute. In 1954, José Milicua attributed the work to Massimo Stanzione as well as pointing out the parameters that converge in his style: a naturalism distantly reminiscent of Caravaggio and Bolognese classicism filtered through the oeuvre of Guido Reni. J.Y.

Massimo Stanzione
(Orta di Atella, 1585 [?] – Naples, 1656)
Saint Agnes
1635-40
MNAC/MAC 65579

These two paintings belong to a series of six depicting scenes from the Book of Tobit, the father of Tobias. The MNAC preserves four, the two we are commenting on here together with *Tobias and the Fish* (MNAC/MAC 11522) and *Rachel Blessing Sarah before Departing from Ecbatana with Tobias* (MNAC/MAC 11523). The remaining two are in private collections: *Old Tobit in the Presence of a King of Assyria* and *Tobit Blessing his Son Tobias before the Latter Departs for Rages*. Of the six works, all except one refer to the most significant events in Tobias's travels during the exile of the Israelites in Nineveh (Assyria, in present-day Iraq). The series constitutes a narrative sequence in which figures and colours are repeated according

Tobias Cures his Father's Blindness
c. 1640
MNAC/MAC 11541

to a single objective and programme. The Neapolitan painter Andrea Vaccaro signed three of the canvases with his monogram, A.V. In these works, Vaccaro combined his tenebrist training, tempered by the luminous Naturalism of Caravaggio's last period and the oeuvre of José de Ribera (active in Naples as from 1616), with the classicist trends of the Bolognese school that had been made fashionable by painters like Guido Reni and, above all, the Neapolitans Massimo Stanzione and Bernardo Cavallino. The use of markedly classical architecture provides the fundamental basis for dating the canvases from around 1640. J.Y.

Andrea Vaccaro
(Naples, 1604-70)

Tobias's Encounter with the Archangel Raphael
c. 1640
MNAC/MAC 24177

Between 1722 and 1724, once the War of Spanish Succession had ended, Viladomat painted the series of twenty canvases devoted to St Francis of Assisi that decorated the main cloister of the convent of Sant Francesc, Barcelona, which stood next to the sea wall. The paintings remained in their place of origin until the Napoleonic invasion. Subsequently they were placed under the custody of what is today the Reial Acadèmia Catalana de Belles Arts de Sant Jordi until they entered the Museum as a permanent loan in 1906. This is the only cycle of paintings on the life of a saint preserved in its entirety at a museum.

The iconographical programme, which as was the custom illustrated the virtues and most important episodes from the life of the founder of the Order, is based on the *Little Flowers of Saint Francis*, an anonymous account written between the thirteenth and fourteenth centuries. Francis, as the *alter Cristus* and whose effigy is faithful to the prototype described in Franciscan literature, is the protagonist of all the scenes, be they interiors or exteriors, urban or rural, the inspiration for these latter being the coastal regions of the province of Barcelona. The limited resources available to Viladomat in early eighteenth-century Catalonia explain the restricted, monotonous range of colours and the precarious quality of the pigments. Even so, the series, which portrays society of the time, contains all the elements of peninsular Baroque monastic painting, while its subject matter even recalls Francisco de Zurbarán's oeuvre. M.M.C.

Permanent loan from the Reial Acadèmia Catalana de Belles Arts de Sant Jordi de Barcelona, 1902; admission, 1906

Antoni Viladomat
(Barcelona, 1678-1755)

A Madman Lays Down his Cape for the Infant Saint Francis to Walk Upon
1722-4
MNAC/MAC 11534

Bernard of Quintavalle Divides his Goods Among the Poor
1722-4
MNAC/MAC 11551

These four canvases depicting the Four Seasons present a theme with a long tradition in Western art and highly popular in the eighteenth century. In this particular series, the annual cycle is illustrated on the basis of an optimistic plot including scenes from everyday life in the spheres of both work and leisure, set either in the city or the country, and showing tasks characteristic of each of the seasons. As compositions they resemble stage sets in which perspective, diagonals and depth play a major role.

Summer depicts bathers happily splashing each other near a portico, with classical buildings in the distance and ships unloading their cargoes in what may well be the port of Barcelona. *Autumn* addresses the theme of the grape harvest in a landscape setting reminiscent of the coastal range in the Maresme, where the golden light of sunset bathes a picnic of merry peasants. The facture is entirely characteristic of

Spring
1730-5
MNAC/MAC 24268

Autumn
1730-5
MNAC/MAC 24279

Viladomat's, which leaves absolutely no doubt about the authorship, and the canvases would have been painted at about the time when the artist was decorating the chapel of Los Dolores in the church of Santa Maria, Mataró.

This series unequalled by any other Catalan painter of the period pays especial attention to the landscape and possibly heralds interest in this genre that emerged in the following century. Also to be taken into account is the influence of the painter-set designer Ferdinando Galli, known as 'Bibbiena', with whom Viladomat collaborated at the Barcelona court of Archduke Charles of Austria. M.M.C.

Antoni Viladomat
(Barcelona, 1678-1755)

Summer
1730-5
MNAC/MAC 24277

Winter
1730-5
MNAC/MAC 24267

In 1778 Carlos III of Spain issued the decree by which the ban was lifted on Catalonia's trading with the Americas. This marked a turning point in the life of the Catalan bourgeoisie, whose power rose considerably in the last quarter of the eighteenth century. Part of the profits they made from industry and commerce was invested in the construction and decoration of their own houses. The main lounge of one of these homes, most probably built on the outskirts of Barcelona, was decorated with Pla's series of paintings devoted to the life of the Virgin. Of the complete series of seventeen canvases, twelve are preserved at the Museum. In 1987 Santiago Alcolea Gil made the paintings known, the indisputable work of Francesc Pla, otherwise known as 'El Vigatà', one of the artists most in demand when it came to painting the interiors of Catalan bourgeois mansions. His style broke away from the academic canons of the period, his flowing, quick, vigorous brushstrokes having affinities with the Rococo.

Visitation
c. 1780
MNAC 202171

The *Visitation* narrates the visit that Mary paid to her cousin Elizabeth and includes popular details that enhance the realistic nature of the scene, such as the pouch and water bottle that St Joseph carries, accompanied by his mule, and the basket of chickens borne by the maidservant. *The House at Nazareth* depicts an ordinary day in the life of the Holy Family: Joseph and the child Jesus busy in the carpentry workshop and Mary occupied in her daily chores in an atmosphere of harmony symbolised by five angels, two of whom play musical instruments. J.Y.

Francesc Pla, known as 'El Vigatà'
(Vic, 1743 – Barcelona, 1805)

The House at Nazareth
c. 1780
MNAC 202174

The Cambó Bequest

The collection of pictures making up the Cambó Bequest is a series of paintings unprecedented in Catalonia, a repertory with an identity of its own spanning the history of European painting from the fourteenth century to the beginning of the nineteenth century. These works speak to us of the perfection of the Italian *Quattrocento*, of the sensuality of the great Venetian masters of the *Cinquecento*, of the economic boom of the Low Countries in the sixteenth and seventeenth centuries, without forgetting the greatness of the Spanish Golden Age, until we come to the fullness of European Rococo. This is the most valuable disinterested donation the Museu Nacional d'Art de Catalunya has received in the course of its existence and has done more than any other to enrich the Renaissance and Baroque holdings. Francesc Cambó was born in Verges in 1876 and died in Buenos Aires in 1947. He planned his collection with an eye to the future, rather than according to personal taste and pleasure. This patron of the arts took an ambitious and generous long-term approach to collecting that was to enrich the country's public heritage. He wanted to put together a selection of paintings by the great masters which would complement the medieval series and fill the gaps in the Museo de Barcelona, a museum which in the course of time was to become the Museu Nacional d'Art de Catalunya and to which he wanted to give the same universal condition as to his native land. Indeed, to achieve this, Cambó deployed all his means and invested a large part of his fortune, guided by his refined instinct and by experts like Wilhem von Bode, Bernard Berenson, Adolfo Venturi and Joaquim Folch i Torres. In his stubborn determination to get hold of first-rate works, he did not hesitate to contact the entire international art market, from Berlin to New York, taking in Venice, Zurich, Paris and London. At times he employed a sophisticated system of acquisitions that allowed him to build up almost all of his collection in the space of less than ten years (between 1927 and 1936). Of particular interest is the strategy he thought up to acquire the group of twenty-seven early Italian works, almost half the collection, at the public auction held in Berlin in 1929, from their owner, the Frenchman Joseph Spiridon.

The last will drawn up by this eminent Catalan in Argentina on 4 November 1946 left fifty works to the Museu d'Art Antic in Barcelona. When he died, on 30 April 1947, the items destined for Barcelona were scattered between the Musée Cantonal des Beaux-Arts in Lausanne, where they had been deposited for safeguarding during the Second World War, the Museo del Prado in Madrid and the Villa Mon Repòs, Cambó's residence in Buenos Aires.

By December 1954 the pictures belonging to the Cambó Bequest in Barcelona had been gathered at the Palau Nacional on Montjuïc. The presentation to the Barcelona public took place in October 1955, coinciding with the *III Bienal Hispanoamericana de Arte* in Barcelona. The chapel of Santa Àgata provided an incomparable setting in which to exhibit the panels by the early Italians, while the Saló del Tinell housed the rest. From 1956 to 1985 the Cambó Bequest was deposited and exhibited at the Palau de la Virreina, after which it was moved to the Throne Room at the Palau de Pedralbes for an exhibition that closed the following year. In 1987, the then Museu d'Art de Catalunya began a new project for the restoration and study of the collection with a view to exhibiting all the sixty items that had once belonged to Francesc Cambó. This process culminated in the exhibitions of the whole of the former Cambó Collection held in Madrid and Barcelona between October 1990 and April 1991. In April 1997, to mark the fiftieth anniversary of the donor's death, the Museu Nacional d'Art de Catalunya honoured him by exhibiting the Cambó Bequest officially for the first time on the premises of the Palau Nacional on Montjuïc, thereby adding this valuable treasure to its holdings for ever more.

The spirit of the Florentine *Quattrocento* informs the frontal of this nuptial chest or *cassone*, since it constitutes a humanistic allegory with reference to personages from classical Antiquity: *The Seven Liberal Arts*, piece that forms a pair with *The Seven Virtues* (MNAC/MAC 64967), also from the Cambó Bequest. In 1940, Roberto Longhi attributed the works to the then anonymous Master of the Adimari *Cassone* or Master di Fucecchio, subsequently identified as Giovanni di Ser Giovanni, also known as 'Lo Scheggia', Masaccio's younger brother. However, in 1990 Luciano Bellosi and Monica Folchi put forward the hypothesis that given its more modern conception, *The Seven Virtues* might have been executed at the workshop of 'Lo Scheggia' by his son, Anton Francesco dello 'Scheggia', who made it between 1465 and 1470.

Giovanni di Ser Giovanni, known as 'Lo Scheggia'
(San Giovanni in Valdarno, 1406 – Florence, 1486)
The Seven Liberal Arts
c. 1460
MNAC/MAC 64968

The seated Virgin has a book in her left hand while with the other she holds the Child, standing on her lap. The couple is accompanied by an angel, with a flower in his hand, against a background of dog roses. In 1929, Oskar Fischel attributed the panel to an unidentified Ferrara artist, a follower of Piero della Francesca's belonging to the circle of Francesco del Cossa and Ercole di Roberti. In 1990, Giovanni Romano narrowed the attribution down to Francesco del Cossa, although he did not rule out other possibilities, as the hitherto unidentified painter of the *desco da parto* (a painted tray that in those days was presented as a gift to mothers after they had given birth) preserved at the Boston Museum of Fine Arts, the obverse side of which features an angel of characteristics very similar to those of the Child in this painting. Whatever the case, we know for certain that the panel was executed in the Ferrara area around 1460, since at that time and in that place the style of the detailed drawing of Pisanello, subsequently perfected by Rogier van der Weyden, and the luminous, realist style of Piero della Francesca converged. This is a panel of extraordinary quality, which despite its apparent coldness, presents a number of figures who reach the observer by virtue of their remarkable verisimilitude. J.Y.

The figures, framed by Renaissance architecture against a landscaped backdrop, are identified through inscriptions and attributes. *The Liberal Arts* and the *Virtues* have at their feet an accompanying figure that embodies the qualities of each discipline or virtue. Thus, in *The Seven Liberal Arts*, from left to right, Logic is accompanied by Aristotle, Arithmetic by Pythagoras, Geometry by Euclid, Astronomy by Ptolomy and the Franciscan Roger Bacon, Rhetoric by Cicero, Grammar by Priscian and Music by Tubal-cain. As regards the *Seven Virtues*, Strength is accompanied by Hercules, Justice by Trajan, Charity by Marcus Aemilius Scaurus, Faith by Marcus Aetilius Regulus, Hope by Alexander the Great, Prudence by Solon and Temperance by Scipio the African. J.Y.

Francesco del Cossa (?)
(Ferrara, *c.* 1435 – Bologna, 1478)

Madonna and Jesus Child with an Angel

c. 1460

MNAC/MAC 64971

This arrogant, enigmatic lady stands in a room in three-quarter leaning slightly to the left, her face and gaze turned towards the observer. She wears a rich purple brocade dress with wide sleeves and a low-cut neckline and sports a tied-back white headdress that falls down her back, leaving her dark hair visible at the front. A white cloth covers her left shoulder and part of her left forearm while she points with her left index finger towards the open book on the oriental tapestry that serves as a decorative cloth for the table in front of her. Her right hand rests on her breast, the index finger exquisitely introduced into her bodice to indicate the depth of her personality. Behind, in the top right-hand corner, hangs a knotted green curtain and, on the opposite side, a window opens onto a landscape bathed in the golden light of a splendid Venetian *tramonto*. Although the precise identity of the woman is unknown, according to some she may either be the poetess Vittoria Colonna or her friend and contemporary Giulia Gonzaga, who, according to Vasari, was portrayed by Sebastiano del Piombo in 1530. Although the attributes of the lady may correspond to those of either of the above-mentioned, the time when the painting was executed does not favour these hypotheses. What does seem clear, on the other hand, is that the subject is a *mulier docta*, in other words, a letters lover. Whoever she may be, the gestures of her hands denote the richness and ambiguity of her knowledge—very rich regarding the qualities characteristic of educated courtesans of the time. M.M.C.

This fine canvas is a replica from Titian's workshop of the *capolavoro* from 1515 that belonged successively to the collections of Gonzaga in Mantua, Charles I of England and Van Dyck and is now preserved at the Louvre. The replica, too, enjoyed equal prestige, for it belonged to the Imperiale and Balbi families of Genoa, to Christina of Sweden, to the Azzolino, Odescalchi and Benedetto families of Rome and the Orléans family of Paris. The subject is complex and therefore admits several different interpretations—it may be a double portrait, a genre scene or an allegory. Early in the eighteenth century it was described as follows: 'Titian's self portrait together with his loved one dressed naturally in her own clothes and half naked, with Titian behind holding a mirror.' In fact, what we see is a young woman arranging her hair and about to perfume herself while a man (her lover?) holds two mirrors, one in front of her and the other behind. The canvas might conceivably be a *vanitas*, with Beauty contemplating herself in a mirror while bewailing the ephemeral nature of her existence, in which case what at first sight appears to be an erotic theme would have a moralising purpose. Other interpretations suggest that the source of inspiration may be Petrarch's sonnet *Il mio adversario*, the theme of which is the triangle composed of the loved one, the mirror and the lover, the latter envious because it is the mirror that receives the gaze of the object of his love. Whatever the case, the theme enjoyed great success from the very outset—it was reinterpreted by the octogenarian Giovanni Bellini, among others—and denotes an extraordinary technical skill of Giorgionesque origin that evolved masterfully at the service of beauty. M.M.C.

Sebastiano del Piombo
(Venice, *c.* 1485 – Rome, 1547)
Vittoria Colonna (?)
1520-5
MNAC/MAC 64984

Tiziano Vecellio and workshop
(Pieve di Cadore, 1488/90 – Venice, 1576)
Girl Before a Mirror
After 1515
MNAC/MAC 64985

The style, subject matter, technique, execution, dimensions and provenance of these paintings suggest that they were conceived to form a pair. In both canvases the action takes place in the carnival-like atmosphere created by a crowd of simple folk, elegant ladies, children, masks, charlatans and stall-holders, who together constitute the true protagonists. They are veritable genre scenes depicting the Carnival of Venice, an annual event that inevitably attracted European travellers of the period to the lagoon city, descriptions of the world in which the painter lived, stimulated by the same elements that inspired the theatre pieces by Carlo Goldoni, in which he de-mystified society of the time. The Carnival is thereby the emblem of a people who renounce their own identity by concealing it behind an ephemeral appearance.

The Charlatan
1756

MNAC/MAC 64988

In *The Charlatan*, the crowd is captivated by the skilful manipulations of a trickster, while in *The Minuet* it is presumably Pantalon and Columbine who, accompanied by other masks, dance in the gardens of a villa on *terra ferma*. The predominantly anecdotal narrative style describes the festive customs and traditions of the Venetians. And all this enriched by the mastery of the Tiepolos, with their adroit handling of colour and ingenious use of light: clear and transparent in the sky, golden as it is reflected on the architecture and slipping between the shadows enveloping both figures and vegetation, a combination that results in two gems, exquisite spectacles of humour and irony. M.M.C.

Giandomenico Tiepolo
(Venice, 1727-1804)

The Minuet
1756
MNAC/MAC 64989

The sitter was the wife of Thomas Howard, patron of artists and intellectuals, second Count of Arundel and Earl Marshall of James I and Charles I of England; in short, a person of high standing at the British court. Furthermore, the couple belonged to the rare elite of the British Catholic nobility. Rubens portrayed the lady in her mature years, focussing on her character rather than attempting to endow her with a beauty she clearly lacked. Evidence of Lady Aletheia's strong will is the ostentatious way she displays a highly-valued family jewel on her bosom, a trigram with the name of Christ, IHS, thereby leaving no room for doubt about her religious convictions. The portrait was painted in 1620 in Antwerp, where on a stopover on her way to Italy Her Ladyship agreed to pose for Rubens for a group portrait now preserved at the Alte Pinakothek in Munich, in which she is accompanied by the British ambassador, her dog, her dwarf and her jester. The date of the visit coincided with the young Van Dyck's presence at Rubens's studio, and the master may have invited his pupil to contribute to the portrait of Lady Aletheia, since it turns out that after the encounter, Van Dyck travelled to London that same year and worked for the Arundels. Indeed, while the sitter's face and general pose reveal the mastery of Rubens, the treatment of the embroidered neckline and wrists, together with the way the hands are modelled, are identical in facture to some of the works Van Dyck executed in England. M.M.C.

The theme of the ill-matched couple enjoys a long tradition in Western culture, above all in the literary world, although it did not appear in the visual arts until the last quarter of the fifteenth century, reaching the heights of its popularity during the first half of the following one, particularly in Germany and Flanders. In this tradition, the woman is presented as a dangerous creature, a source of sin, humiliation, perdition and death. The theme, the origins of which date from the Middle Ages, was subsequently reformulated and led to a host of variations.

This particular version is signed and dated on the back of the panel, although it also features the artist's distinguishing mark beside the girl's arm, a small dragon with its wings pointing upwards. This panel of small dimensions and vertical format depicts the couple alone, in three-quarter length, against a plain background that gives no indication of where the action is taking place: an imprudent old man, thoroughly captivated by female charms, is robbed by a young girl, who has no difficulty in relieving him of his bag. And as she does so, she utters a guffaw of satisfaction. The theme of the ill-matched couple was one of Lucas Cranach's favourites, since it provided him with a vehicle by which to express his moralising slant. In this context it must be remembered that the artist was a friend of Martin Luther's and an interpreter of the new reformist iconography. J.Y.

Peter Paulus Rubens
(Siegen, 1577 – Antwerp, 1640)

Lady Aletheia Talbot, Countess of Arundel

1620

MNAC/MAC 65001

Lucas Cranach, 'the Elder'
(Kronach, 1472 – Weimar, 1553)

The Ill-Matched Couple

1517

MNAC/MAC 65012

Richard, with his head erect and arrogantly poised, is sitting on a block of stone next to a fountain from which his horse is drinking and loosely holding its bridle in his right hand. His red outfit is adorned with a white ruff collar and cuffs and he sports a gold chain on his breast. An ochre-coloured silk sash crosses his body diagonally and is knotted below his hip. His left hand rests on the hilt of a sabre. His brown leather boots, reaching to above the knee, match his gloves and he wears an ostrich-feather hat of the same colour with a red band. Behind him, the outline of the horse stands out against the blue sky. The figure is dressed '*à l'espagnole*', an expression that appears in eighteenth-century French texts to designate a picturesque style of attire that had no relationship with Spanish fashion of the time. In fact, it was a French style during the reigns of Henri IV and Louis XIII, the source of inspiration for which were the costumes that Rubens painted for the Mary of Medicis Gallery at the Palais du Louvre.

Fragonard, one of the epigones of the French Rococo, travelled to Italy at the age of twenty in the company of his friend and patron Jean-Claude Richard, the *abbé* of Saint-Non, and this splendid portrait may be one of the fruits of that experience. The style of the canvas defines the artist as a virtuoso of rapidity with touches of light, luminous matter, eloquent signs of gesture painting in the manner of the master at the height of his career. M.M.C.

Presented at the 1761 *Salon du Louvre*, this work is the portrait of one of the artist's close friends, who exercised as a notary in Paris between 1731 and 1775. Laideguive is sitting on a turned-about chair, his right arm resting on the back and his left hand holding a half-open tome, bookmarked in several places. Wearing a blue brocade dressing gown and a kerchief jauntily knotted around his head, he stares defiantly at the observer. His flabbiness denotes the passage of time, although his sharp eyes and intelligent gaze suggest that there is much more to the man than his somewhat flamboyant attire. This far from conventional portrait exudes sincerity and has nothing in common with the then prevailing Rococo style. It is an intimist psychological portrait that spurns flattery in favour of what might be described as almost insolent frankness, at the same time constituting an analysis of the links of friendship that united the painter and his sitter. This delicate pastel figures among the best works by an artist who introduced major innovations into the eighteenth-century portrait genre. M.M.C.

Jean-Honoré Fragonard
(Grasse, 1732 – Paris, 1806)
Jean-Claude Richard, Abbot of Saint-Non, Dressed 'à l'espagnole'
c. 1769
MNAC/MAC 65010

Maurice Quentin de la Tour
(Saint-Quentin, 1704-1788)
Pierre-Louis Laideguive
c. 1761
MNAC/MAC 65009

Though rarely, Goya did occasionally address mythological themes. This particular scene is associated with the fable of Cupid and Psyche as an allegory of Love. While many scholars contend that there is a parallel between the model who personifies Psyche and the one who posed for the two *Majas*, it seems more feasible to contend that a greater likeness exists to the Marchioness of Lazán, whom Goya portrayed in 1804. A possible source of inspiration for this canvas would be one that was acquired for the Madrid royal collections in 1571, namely *Tarquin and Lucretia*, a bedroom scene of similar dimensions that Titian painted for Felipe II and became one of the favourite paintings of Joseph Bonaparte, which he took away with him from Spain. Goya, who was familiar with this extraordinary painting by the Venetian, exchanged the aggressiveness of Tarquin and the fear of Lucretia for the tenderness of Cupid and the desire of Psyche. The result is a canvas with an erotic flavour and exceptional painterly fragments, such as the semi-transparent gauze through which the breasts of the young girl are visible, the handling of golds and interplay of light that vibrates on the face and the slight penumbra at the bedhead, along with other subtleties characteristic of the genius of Fuendetodos. M.M.C.

Francisco de Goya
(Fuendetodos, 1746 – Bordeaux, 1828)
Allegory of Love, Cupid and Psyche (?)
1798-1805
MNAC/MAC 64996

The Thyssen-Bornemisza Collection

The selection of pieces ceded on permanent loan to the MNAC by the Museo Thyssen-Bornemisza goes to form a series of paintings and sculptures that give a global view of European art from Gothic to Rococo. As well as reflecting the tastes of the Thyssen-Bornemisza family, the exhibit does not forget the links between medieval artistic trends in Catalonia and Italy or the northern European style of painting, which left its mark on Catalan art.

Outstanding among the medieval carvings are the *Dead Christ* in polychrome wood, from the first half of the thirteenth century, and the *Virgin and Child* from Sioneviller (France), produced in the workshops of Rheims Cathedral in the second half of the thirteenth century. Outside of France, the atmosphere of the *Quattrocento* can be breathed in the pair of *Angels* in blue and white glazed terracotta from the Della Robbias workshop that belong to Baroness Carmen Thyssen-Bornemisza.

Amongst the Italian paintings of the *Trecento* the archaic style characteristic of the *maniera greca* comes to the surface in the *Descent from the Cross* attributed to the Master of Forlì, and while the panels by Pietro da Rimini and Taddeo Gaddi are indebted to the poetics of Giotto that of Bernardo Daddi combines Siennese and Florentine formulae. From the *Quattrocento*, Lorenzo Monaco's *Enthroned Madonna and Child with Six Angels* and the panels by Bicci di Lorenzo continue in the orbit of the late Gothic tradition. Standing out above all of these is the serene beauty of Fra Angelico's *Madonna of Humility*, a *capolavoro* in which humanist feelings of the Renaissance come to the fore. And finally, while the *Saint Claire* and *Saint Catherine* by Francesco del Cossa bear the special mark of Ferrara, in Bernardino Butinone's *Nativity* one breathes the atmosphere of Leonardo.

Amongst the paintings of the *Cinquecento*, both the *Sacra Conversazione* by the Venetian Pietro degli Ingannati, a follower of Bellini's compositional ideas, the *Stoning of Saint Stephen* by Dosso and Battista Dossi and the small panels by the Pseudo-Boccaccino, with their links to Leonardo and Giorgione, brought landscapes into holy scenes as part of the main subject matter. In addition, Titian's *Madonna and Child* and *Portrait of Antonio Anselmi* exude the modernity of his innovative style.

At the century end and into the *Seicento* in Bologna, Ludovico Carracci directed the Accademia degli Incamminati, whose approach suffuses the *Presentation of the Child at the Temple*. Giovanni Francesco Romanelli, a pupil and collaborator of Pietro da Cortona in Rome, took an interest in landscape and used the freshness of his master's colour in the *Flight into Egypt* belonging to Baroness Carmen Thyssen-Bornemisza. European Baroque painting achieves its grandeur in the *Madonna and Child with Saint Elizabeth and the Infant Saint John*, a canvas that shows off the style of the master of Antwerp. In the northern Low Countries, the Dutch landscape painters captured reality as it was, as in Salomon Jakobsz. van Ruysdael's *Sailing Boats on the Shore Beside a Village*. The Spanish Golden Age painting is present with Zurbarán's *Saint Marina*, owned by Baroness Carmen Thyssen-Bornemisza, and the portrait-study of *Queen Mariana of Austria* from Velázquez's workshop.

From the *Settecento* we find nine canvases such as Piazzetta's *Sacrifice of Isaac* and Pittoni's *Rest on the Flight into Egypt*, and two works by the greatest talents of the Venetian Rococo, Giambattista Tiepolo and his son Giandomenico, protagonists and at the same time followers of the glories of the city of Venice. Yet in the course of the century there were also those who painted domestic interiors or even social themes, such as Amorosi's *Girl Sewing* or Ceruti's *Three Beggars*. And all of this without forgetting Canaletto's *vedutta*.

The collections of northern painting provide an account of developments in the Central European school during the first third of the sixteenth century in Charles V's domains, and at the same time close the discourse of the collection making up the permanent loan by the Museo Thyssen-Bornemisza to the MNAC. Mention should be also made of portraits by Huber, Wertinger, Mielich and Cranach, and religious pieces like Apt's *Pietà*, the *Crucifixion* and *Christ in Limbo* by an anonymous master, the *Adoration of the Magi* by the Master of the Thyssen Adoration, or the *Annunciation* by Bernhard Striegel, with the sculptural reliefs of St Paul the Hermit and St Anthony the Abbot on the reverse, produced by Christoph Scheller.

The Virgin, seated with the Child standing on her lap, is wearing a red tunic and blue mantle and holding a vase with roses and a lily in her right hand. She has an enormous golden halo with the inscription AVE MARIA GRATIA PLENA. The Child, with pink clothes and a sky-blue belt, is holding a lily flower in his left hand and resting his right arm on his mother's shoulder so that he is touching her cheek. His halo bears the inscription ALFA / OM(ega). They are set on a throne, surrounded by five angels, three of which are holding a sumptuous curtain in the manner of a canopy covering the background, while the other two are sitting at the feet of the Virgin with musical instruments (a portable organ and a lute). This panel has been identified with the work described by Vasari in 1568, at that time the property of the Gondi family in their house in Florence, and probably formed part of a triptych now dismembered. In 1857 it figured in the collection of King Leopold I of Belgium. In 1909 Adolfo Venturi attributed it to Fra Angelico, an opinion generally accepted by historiography. As regards the date, the work can be placed between the tabernacle of the Guild of Weavers (or *Linaioli*), of 1433, and the *Mourning Over the Dead Body of Christ* in the Museo di San Marco (Florence), of 1436, with other details from the *Coronation of the Virgin* in the Musée du Louvre, of 1434-5. J.Y.

In a tabernacle with a pointed arch, decorated with plant motifs in relief, are portrayed the Virgin and Child. Mary is sitting on a throne set on a pedestal, holding the Child Jesus, who is standing on her lap and making the sign of blessing. The Virgin is wearing a mantle and the Child a tunic, both with embroidered edges. Behind them are six angels, arranged symmetrically on either side and holding censers. All the figures have golden halos on their heads. The composition of the scene is simple and shows a fusion of the Siennese and Florentine pictorial traditions, typical of the style of Lorenzo Monaco, a Camaldolensian monk at the convent of Santa Maria degli Angeli in Florence who had a considerable influence on the work of Fra Angelico. The attribution was made by Roberto Longhi in 1956 and the work is datable to between 1415, the date of the *Madonna* in the church of San Ermete in Pisa, and 1420, the date of the *Epiphany* in the Galleria degli Uffizi in Florence. It is undoubtedly the central panel of a polyptych Miklós Boskovits tried to partly reconstruct in 1975 with a *Saint Francis* from a private collection in Florence on the left and the *Epiphany* from the Muzeum Narodowe in Poznan on the right. J.Y.

Giovanni da Fiesole, known as 'Fra Angelico'
(Vicchio de Mugello, *c.* 1395/1400 – Rome, 1455)
Madonna of Humility
c. 1433-5
MNAC 212817

Piero di Giovanni, known as 'Lorenzo Monaco'
(Sienna [?], *c.* 1370 – Florence, *c.* 1425)
Enthroned Madonna and Child with Six Angels
1415-20
MNAC 212808

A set consisting of two panels, of which the obverse is painted and the reverse carved. Although it now has the appearance of a diptych, originally these must have been the doors of a small altarpiece, with a compartment or central figure that has now disappeared. The pictorial part represents the scene of the Annunciation. On the left panel is the Virgin at the moment when she accepts the message from the archangel, and the Holy Spirit descending on her in the form of a dove: the mystery of the Incarnation. The Virgin, her hands crossed on her breast in an attitude of submission and with an enormous golden halo, is surprised in the act of reading, as we can see from the book on the seat at her side. The action takes place in a very austere room with a bed in the background behind the curtain and a window showing a view of a town and the surrounding countryside. On the right panel, the archangel Gabriel is portrayed standing, with the staff, a garment of swirling folds that accentuate the movement, and the phylactery above his head with the initial words of his message.

The painting is attributed to Strigel, an artist who followed the best tradition of Flemish art and who did the main altarpiece for the Klosterkirche in Blaubeuren and portraits of Emperor Maximilian of Hapsburg. As regards the carving, one side is the relief of St Paul the Hermit and the other St Anthony the Abbot seated and surrounded by animals. These pieces are attributed to a collaborator of Strigel called Scheller, although the sculptor Hans Thoman has also been discussed. J.Y.

A woman dressed in black, her head covered with a white headscarf with blue lines, is seated on a studded leather chair crowned with metal spheres. The only parts of her body that are visible are her face and her clasped hands, and she has a ring with an emerald on her left thumb, as a sign of her wealthy status. Her head, inclined slightly to the left, is framed by the headscarf. The background of blue and green tones shows the inside of a room with austere but very realistic decoration, something that sets off the form of the sitter. At the top of the picture is the inscription MEINES ALTERS IM 57 JAR ('at my age of 57 years'). The work is signed and dated half-way up the left side with the artist's monogram, H.M., and the date, '1539'. This item forms a pair with the portrait of a mature man, also seated, kept in a private collection on loan to the Huis Bergh Foundation in S-Heerenberg (Holland), attributed to the same painter. Mielich, whose portraits were much appreciated by the ruling classes in Bavaria, especially in the city of Munich, was Albrecht Altdorfer's most outstanding pupil. J.Y.

Bernhard Strigel
(Memmingen, 1460-1528)
Annunciation
c. 1515-20
MNAC 212818/2

Hans Mielich
(documented in Bavaria, 1516-73)
Portrait of a Woman Aged 57
1539
MNAC 212826

With his direct gaze, reserved and confident, though free of arrogance, the gentleman rests his left arm on a table that has now been lost due to earlier trimming. Dressed in black, the white of the ruff, the brown of the leather band around it and the flesh tones of the illuminated face are the only touches of colour standing out against the range of dark tones that fill the picture. An inscription on the back of the canvas identifies the sitter as Antonio Anselmi at the age of 38. This Bolognese intellectual and poet, who was born in 1512 and died in about 1558, spent ten years in the service of Cardinal Pietro Bembo, after whose death he entered the service of Archbishop Ludovico Beccadelli, former tutor of Rannunzio Farnese, the grandson of Paul III. Tiziano portrayed the former when he was a child. Anselmi was on good terms with literary figures of his time, amongst them the writer and close friend of Titian Pietro Aretino, with whom he kept up a long correspondence. Although the mutilation suffered by the canvas affected all four sides, the part preserved today is in good condition and we can appreciate in it Titian's magnificent skill as a portrait painter. M.M.C.

The scene shows a passage from the Gospel according to St Luke (2, 22-38) in which Mary and Joseph, after the birth of Jesus, went to Jerusalem to offer their first-born at the Temple, as laid down in Mosaic law. The Virgin Mary, with the Child in her arms, occupies the centre of the composition. Behind her is St Joseph, portrayed as a mature man, bald and bearded. The temple priest is Simeon, with a long white beard and wearing a mantle, holding out his arms towards the Child; the Holy Spirit had revealed to him that he would not die without seeing the Messiah. On the right the prophetess Anne also appears, at a very advanced age, holding a stone with an inscription. The scene includes other characters, one of whom is holding two turtle doves as an offering that was made on these occasions. In the distance we can see the city. The background of the picture shows the architectural setting formed by the temple, of classical inspiration, much in the style propounded by the Accademia degli Incamminati, an institution set up in about 1585-6 by the Carracci family (Ludovico and his cousins Agostino and Annibale), which emerged in their workshop on Bologna and was directed by Ludovico Carracci until his death. The work is related to the painter's stay in Piacenza (between 1605 and 1609) and the *Birth of the Virgin* he painted for the cathedral, today the Episcopal Palace of this town in the Emilia-Romagna region. J.Y.

Tiziano Vecellio
(Pieve di Cadore, 1488/90 – Venice, 1576)

Portrait of Antonio Anselmi
c. 1550
MNAC 212840

Ludovico Carracci
(Bologna, 1555-1619)

Presentation of the Child at the Temple
c. 1605
MNAC 212845

The Virgin Mary, dressed in red with the Child on her lap, is sitting on the ground and beside her is the Infant St John with a lamb, whose face Jesus is stroking. Elizabeth, behind them, bends towards the group before architectural elements of a classical order opening onto a sky with clouds. This scene, which gathers the Holy Family with St Elizabeth and the Infant St John, illustrates an apocryphal theme going back to the thirteenth century and made known through the text of the Pseudo-Bonaventure *Meditationes Vitae Christi*, which narrates a visit that brought Jesus together with his son John at the home of Elizabeth and Zachary. The subject allowed the inclusion of the child nude in sacred subject matter and was very popular with Renaissance Florentine painters. In this respect, it is worth mentioning a painting by Raphael known as *The Pearl*, kept at the Museo del Prado, which could have provided Rubens with a source of inspiration. The panel belonged to the Gonzaga family when the Antwerp master was living at the court in Mantua.

This canvas, painted in about 1618, presents a widespread invention by Rubens of which copies and replicas are known, but this version, although of unequal quality, is considered autograph and one of the best. It is a religious composition which must have had a domestic rather than a liturgical purpose and of which many prints were begun under Rubens's supervision, allowing it to circulate and become a highly popular work. M.M.C.

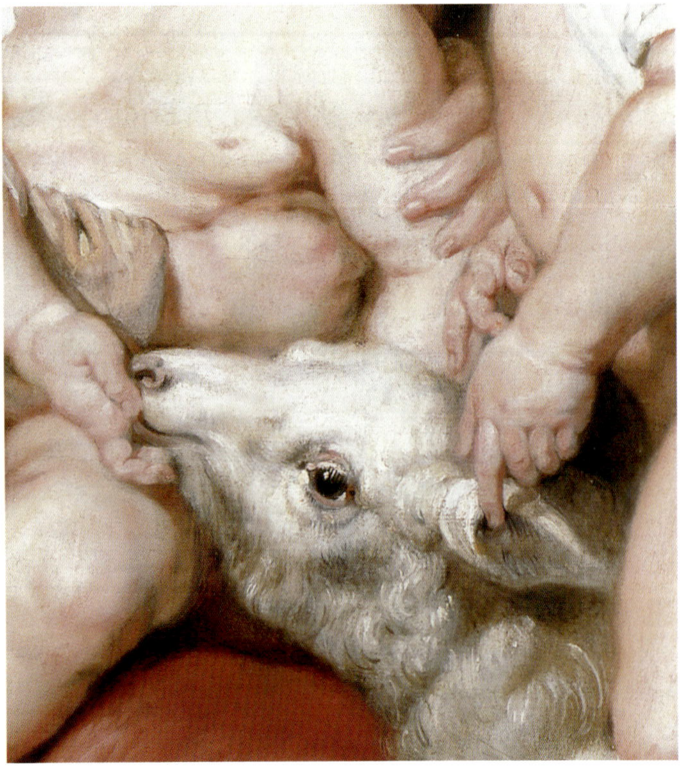

Peter Paulus Rubens
(Siegen, 1577 – Antwerp, 1640)

Madonna and Child with Saint Elizabeth and the Infant Saint John
c. 1618
MNAC 212847

The subject depicted, a favourite of this painter, immortalises the festive atmosphere that impregnated the dock of San Marco on the day of the *Sensa* (Ascension Day), an official ceremony which along with the Carnival was a great event for the citizens of Venice, as it marked the defeat of the Dalmatian pirates in 998. Since then, every year on that day the Most Serene Republic of Venice dressed in all its finery to celebrate its marriage to the Adriatic Sea. As a symbol of this union, the Doge sailed on his official boat, the *Bucintoro*, from the lagoon out to the open sea. Once there, after dropping a ring into the sea, the wedding ceremony took place.

In this scene we see the Doge's state barge with her forty oars, exquisitely decked out in red, moored at the San Marco dock outside the Palazzo Ducale after her return from the ritual outing. As the crowd welcomes her from the harbour, she is followed by an entourage of boats of all sorts, from the simple gondolas of the middle classes to the luxurious feluccas belonging to the aristocracy. The view, seen from high up, takes in the Palazzo Ducale, the *campanile* of San Marco and the Libreria Marciana, to the Punta della Dogana and the dome of Santa Maria della Salute in the distance. Boats and people inundate the pleasing, warm, luminous atmosphere characteristic of this painter, who was a historian and poet of his native country. There are various versions of this same theme from the artist's workshop, and this one, which is undoubtedly by his hand, is identified with the one that used to belong to the British collector Henry Revely (1737-98). M.M.C.

Salomon Jacobsz. van Ruysdael, uncle of Jacob van Ruysdael and one of the great masters of Dutch landscape painting, centred his interest on views of placid inland waters, either river estuaries, lakes or canals. This aquatic medium, the main source of his inspiration, provided him with the opportunity to describe atmospheric phenomena around the villages along the shores, whose silhouettes stand out against a background of cloud-filled sky with a low horizon. These are genuine freshwater seascapes in which trees are replaced by boats anchored on the shore and sailing in the distant fog. This work is a fine example of the work of this artist, whose only object is the beauty of the landscape for its own sake: an argument for the enjoyment of its contemplation, a pictorial genre which began life in Holland in the seventeenth century and which foreshadowed the genre practised elsewhere in later times. M.M.C.

Giovanni Antonio Canal, known as 'Canaletto'
(Venice, 1697-1768)

Return of the Bucintoro on Ascension Day
c. 1745-50

MNAC 212851

Salomon Jacobsz. van Ruysdael
(Naarden, 1600/3 – Haarlem, 1670)

Sailing Boats on the Shore Beside a Village
1660

MNAC 212844

Three characters, two men and a woman of very advanced age, dressed in rags, pose with a faraway look around a table, in the midst of an almost monochrome range of shades of ochre and grey formed by the light that impregnates the empty room. Ceruti was an enigmatic artist who wanted to paint those classes of his native Lombardy and the Venice region who were most in need, ordinary, unhappy but real people. Paintings of a social nature fitted in well with the ideas that flourished during the eighteenth century with the Enlightenment, and although they were in fact a protest against the conditions that existed, they are also a constructive moral lesson that raises this type of argument (poverty as a spiritual state) to the category of art. Hence the size of the canvas—almost as big as an altar painting—and the monumentality of the figures set it apart from a simple genre work and it is a creation with a new argument and reveals the talent of this artist, who is worthy of inclusion amongst the great painters of the *Settecento*. To the item's excellent quality and good state of preservation must be added a prestigious pedigree, as it was a commission made in 1736 by the collector Marshal Von Schulenberg, who took it to his mansion in Berlin. The painting was auctioned in 1775 in London along with others belonging to the German soldier and later, in 1975, it left the art market to become the property of Baron Thyssen-Bornemisza. M.M.C.

Giacomo Ceruti, known as 'Il Pitocchetto'
(Milan, 1698-1767)
Three Beggars
1736
MNAC 212852

Modern art

The collection of modern art

The MNAC's modern art collection brings together the country's most important collection of Catalan works from the beginning of the nineteenth century to the 1940s, in an itinerary that starts with the oeuvre of those artists who followed the precepts of Neoclassicism, Romanticism and Realism. Outstanding among the Neoclassicists is the painter Flaugier and the sculptor Campeny. Prominent among the Romanticists were the Nazarene painters, like Claudi Lorenzale, who specialised above all in portraiture, and the landscapists, particularly Lluís Rigalt, founder of the Catalan landscape tradition, which would continue to have its followers during the Realism period in the figures of Ramon Martí i Alsina, who introduced the ideas of Courbet into Catalonia, and Joaquim Vayreda, founder of the Olot School. Worthy of a section to himself is Fortuny, the best nineteenth-century Spanish painter after Goya, who enjoyed international success with his genre painting and whose last works heralded future developments in art. Also present are those artists who cultivated anecdote, such as Romà Ribera, Francesc Miralles and Francesc Masriera, along with the Luminists of the Sitges School, heirs to the Fortuny legacy. In sculpture, the brothers Vallmitjana are the best representatives of the Realist tradition.

One of the backbones of the modern art collections is *Modernisme*, a crucial artistic and cultural movement in Catalonia. In painting, most closely associated with this movement is the innovative strand led by Casas and Rusiñol, whose Parisian works incorporate some of the aspects of French Impressionism. Symbolism is another relevant strand within *Modernista* painting, as seen in the works by Riquer and Brull, among others. Equally important is the presence of members of the second *Modernista* generation, including Nonell, Pidelaserra, Canals, Anglada Camarasa, Raurich and Mir, who in the early twentieth century led Catalan painting to one of its high points. Also included, though their presence is merely nominal, are Spanish artists such as Romero de Torres, Regoyos, Sorolla, Zuloaga and Gutiérrez Solana, and the Frenchmen Boudin, Sisley and Rodin. Outstanding among the creations of *Modernista* sculpture are those of Blay and Llimona, which clearly reveal the influence of Rodin. The collection of *Modernista* decorative arts features exceptional examples of interior design by Puig i Cadafalch, Homar and Gaudí, from Casa Amatller, Casa Lleó Morera and Casa Batlló respectively, all three on Paseo de Gràcia, Barcelona. Also included in the collection are remarkable objets d'art in wrought iron, ceramics, stained glass and precious stones, as well as pieces of furniture by Joan Busquets and other outstanding craftsmen.

The other movement comprehensively represented at the MNAC is *Noucentisme*, which embodied the quest for the Catalan essence and Mediterraneanism. Representative of the movement are the classical compositions by Torres-García and Sunyer, vaguely reminiscent of Cézanne, and the nudes by sculptors Clarà and Casanovas. This initial phase of *Noucentisme* is completed by the sculptures of Manolo Hugué and the paintings of Nogués, markedly popular in character. Around 1917 the second generation of *Noucentistas* emerged who, although adopting a critical stance vis-à-vis the first generation, opted mostly for the figurative tradition and produced distinctive works in the context of interwar international realism. Outstanding artists here include Togores and Domingo. Furthermore, preserved in the MNAC is one of Dalí's best early paintings. The Avant-garde, sculpture in particular, is well represented with exceptional pieces by Pablo Gargallo, Julio González and Leandre Cristòfol.

Campeny's life is linked to Barcelona's Escola de Belles Arts [School of Fine Arts], where he acquired the solid training that enabled him to become a noted Neoclassical sculptor and, later, to dedicate himself to the teaching of sculpture in this same school. The eighteen years he spent in Rome on a scholarship from the Board of Commerce are crucial to his career, especially the relationship he maintained there with Antonio Canova, whose oeuvre greatly influenced his own artistic output. *Lucretia*, one of the scholarship sculptures Campeny created in Rome and possibly his most distinguished work, caused controversy due to its being considered a copy of an antique sculpture, a point refuted by various testimonies. In 1833 Campeny sculpted the example in marble that is preserved in the Llotja school building.

Campeny is inspired by the history of Rome, in particular by Lucretia, a symbol of fidelity who stabbed herself after being violated. The artist depicts her with a placid face and relaxed attitude, seated in a curule chair and dressed in a markedly transparent shift, almost nude, with the folds harmoniously disposed. As is habitual in Classicism, Campeny represents death as an abstract concept via a figure of great serenity, without drama, with the wound and dagger as the only evidence of violence, and emphasising the heroic character of the personage. M.D.

After a training period at the Llotja school, Francesc Lacoma obtained a scholarship to complete his education in Paris with Gerard van Spaendonck. In that city, where he would remain until his death, he became a recognised specialist in the genre of still life. In addition Lacoma played an important part in the recovery of many of the artistic items, paintings in the main, that had been pillaged by Napoleonic troops during the Spanish War of Independence. Thanks to this intervention he obtained the title of Chamber painter of King Ferdinand VII in 1819.

Although *Vase with Flowers* was painted in Paris in 1805, Lacoma decided to postpone its public showing until 1810, when it was exhibited in that year's Salon, in which the artist obtained a Gold Medal in recognition of his skills.

The canvas constitutes one of the paradigmatic displays of the activity undertaken by Lacoma during these years of work, and reveals the use of a figurative language that is lacking in neither conventions nor the stereotypical formulae of a genre of this type. Having said that, the final result is of an extraordinary quality and a captivating artistic beauty, to the extent that the picture may, without any misgivings whatsoever, be considered one of the finest examples that the MNAC possesses of an historic moment in which the imagery of the still life was entering a phase of gradual decline. F.Q.C.

Permanent loan from the Reial Acadèmia Catalana de Belles Arts de Sant Jordi de Barcelona, 1902; admission, 1906

Damià Campeny
(Mataró, 1771 – Barcelona, 1855)
Lucretia
Rome, 1803
MNAC/MAM 10665

Francesc Lacoma i Fontanet
(Barcelona, 1784 – Paris, 1849)
Vase with Flowers
Paris, 1805
MNAC/MAM 10440

An artist of the Bourbon monarchy, López was to occupy the position of Chamber painter of the Spanish monarchs from Carlos IV to Isabella II, although it was during the reign of Ferdinand VII that he would attain a privileged situation upon becoming the artist most coveted by the King and a part of the aristocratic clientele of Madrid. With an eclectic and heterogeneous personal language that is hard to define, yet highly convincing for its brilliant visual results, the works of Vicente López demonstrate a rich visual culture that evokes, at one and the same time, the Valencian Baroque school and Neoclassical tradition, both of which he shows himself to be indebted to in many of his creations. The all-important aspect of his style, however, is without doubt his solid academic training, which manifests itself in the perfect combination of those elements that go to form academicist praxis.

This portrait of Pedro Gómez-Havela Labrador, Marquis of Labrador, born in Valencia in 1775, a career diplomat and ambassador in different Spanish diplomatic legations, is a late expression of one of the most typical portrait typologies created by Vicente López and which, albeit involving a repeated formula, contributed so much to making him the great portraitist of his day. The mise en scène of the work follows a stereotype in which the theatrical rhetoric becomes particularly ostensible in the insignia the protagonist of the composition besports, among which the bands and crosses of the orders of Carlos III and of Isabella the Catholic can be made out, as well as the Golden Fleece. F.Q.C.

Suñol modelled this figure of the Florentine poet in Rome, where he had moved to around 1860 in order to complete his artistic education and where he resided until 1875. There, he formed part of the group of Catalan artists around the painter Mariano Fortuny. Later, he set up house in Madrid, where he would become known as the creator of various monuments. Considered Suñol's most important work, *Dante* featured in the *Exposición Nacional de Bellas Artes* in Madrid in 1864, where it was acquired by the State. The Barcelona Provincial Council commissioned this version in bronze from Suñol to decorate the Assembly Hall.

The success of this work resides in both the subject, which taps into the medievalist taste of the period, and the originality of the handling. The formal simplicity and strong expressiveness of the figure give proof of Suñol's ambition to reduce his work to the essential, and because of this he rejects the merely iconographic depiction of the personage and opts for depicting him in a moment of profound reflection. Visually speaking, with regard to the handling of the face, fine and angular, and the clothing of the time, with the folds of the tunic exceedingly well distributed, one remarks the influence of the Florentine sculpture of the Renaissance. All in all, attention may be drawn to the mildly Romantic spirit this sculpture exudes. M.D.

Vicente López
(Valencia, 1772 – Madrid, 1850)
Portrait of the Marquis of Labrador
Madrid, *c.* 1833-4
MNAC/MAM 10280

Jeroni Suñol
(Barcelona, 1839 – Madrid, 1902)
Dante
Rome, 1864
MNAC/MAM 10528

Although it never benefited from a strong personality in Catalonia, Romanticism threw up a few artists of great relevance to the genre of landscape as well as that of the portrait. Prominent among them is Rigalt, who, as one of the most important landscape painters of nineteenth-century Catalan art in its Romantic guise, interprets nature as a stage set capable of awakening evocative feelings, as is made abundantly clear in *Ruins*.

In this canvas, one of Rigalt's best-known works, his Romantic fervour for medieval architecture may be discerned, a fervour which, while it was already manifest in his drawings for some time, takes longer to come to the fore in paintings of great size. The painter concedes an equal role to all the elements of the composition, such as the notable presence of a skyscape of intense blues with thick banks of clouds that impede the shining of the sun. In any event, it seems more than clear that Rigalt focuses his interest on a church with a Romanesque east end that occupies the foreground of the composition, a structure that assumes enormous proportions in comparison with those of the figure situated nearby. Furthermore, the presence of a building in ruins surrounded by undergrowth, a manifestation of organic nature, is one of the traditional themes of the Romantic aesthetic and a symbol of the passage of time, of the fleetingness of human life and the ephemeral aspect of man's works. F.Q.C.

Fortuny's teacher at the Llotja school and a prominent representative of Romanticism in Catalonia, Claudi Lorenzale led, along with other painters of his time, an attempt at renewing mid-nineteenth-century Catalan art. Of crucial importance to this regenerative impulse was contact with the Nazarene aesthetic of the group of German painters established in Rome at the beginning of the nineteenth century and which Lorenzale knew thanks to the voyage he made on his own initiative to the city in the 1830s. Stimulated by a language founded on the rehabilitation of Italian models prior to Raphael, Lorenzale reformulated and adapted this figurative culture to a thematic content based on episodes of the history of Catalonia, which flowered from 1840 onwards.

However, it was to be the cultivating of the portrait, such as the one of his wife and children that we are commenting on, that would most contribute to consolidating the painter's reputation. This oil demonstrates the assimilation of the new Romantic sensibility along with an influence of bourgeois social and cultural values. The idea of the privacy and comfort of the nuclear family as to its living space, in which ostentatious show is made of a concept of luxury and wealth through sumptuous elements (furnishings, ornamental objects, the clothing of the sitters), forms part of the system of values defended for the new rising social class in Catalonia. F.Q.C.

Lluís Rigalt
(Barcelona, 1814-94)
Ruins
Barcelona, 1865
MNAC/MAM 10559

Claudi Lorenzale
(Barcelona, 1814-89)
Portrait of the Painter's Wife and Children
Barcelona, *c.* 1860-5
MNAC/MAM 44392

Son of the Neoclassical artist José de Madrazo, Federico was the founder of one of the most important lineages of painters of the 1800s. After a brief stay in Paris, where he came into contact with the oeuvre of Jean Auguste Dominique Ingres, Madrazo finished his training stint in Rome, where he felt drawn to the figurative culture of the Nazarenes, a group of artists of German origin who postulated the rehabilitation of the language of the Italian Primitives and in particular that of Raphael. However, on his return to Madrid and due to the demands of his clientele, Madrazo modified his creative course and cultivated the portrait. In such a context the vera *effigie* of Fortuny we are commenting on constitutes a portrait of a freer, more spontaneous facture which is a far cry from the conventions and constraints typical of official portraits. For the representation of his relatives or his friends Madrazo codified a model, already present in some of his earliest works, of reduced size in which the figure is depicted half- or three-quarter length.

In this portrait, an extraordinary example of the creative expertise of the foremost portraitist of Spanish Romanticism, the painter has managed to convincingly capture and transmit the features and faraway gaze of a great artistic personality, Fortuny, for whom he always felt great professional admiration, once the pair had established a firm friendship. In 1867, this bond became stronger as a result of Fortuny's marriage to Cecilia de Madrazo, Federico's daughter. F.Q.C.

First shown in Paris at the gallery of Adolphe Goupil, Fortuny's dealer, in April 1870, *The Spanish Wedding* met with great acclaim from critics and public alike, all of which contributed to catapulting the figure of the painter to fame and commercial success. Initially acquired by Goupil for 25,000 francs, he sold it a few days later to a French aristocrat for 70,000. The greater part of Fortuny's output falls within the category of genre painting, so much in vogue in the Parisian market during a few decades of the nineteenth century. In 1866 the artist became interested in painting interiors set in the eighteenth century yet handled in a personal way, both compositionally and technically. This version of *The Spanish Wedding*, the second that Fortuny painted, is the culmination of his artistic expertise and the finest testimony to his virtuosity with the brush, his interest in the past, and his rigour and erudition, qualities which placed him in a prominent position in the art of his time.

Furthermore, this panel is one of the most paradigmatic demonstrations of the fascination and admiration Fortuny felt for Francisco de Goya, as a number of figurative typologies and compositional resources of an unmistakably Goyaesque affiliation show. *The Spanish Wedding* became one of the icons of its time, and in it Fortuny fixed the image of one of the stereotypes most firmly rooted in the European imagination since the Romantic era, according to which Spanish society is dominated by archaic and ancestral traditions, customs and usages. Paradoxically, its picturesqueness, converted into a pictorial fashion, awoke the interest of 'modern' European society. F.Q.C.

Federico de Madrazo
(Rome, 1815 – Madrid, 1894)
Half-length Portrait of the Painter Mariano Fortuny
Madrid, 1867
MNAC/MAM 45962

Mariano Fortuny
(Reus, 1838 – Rome, 1874)
The Spanish Wedding
Rome, 1868-9. Paris, 1870
MNAC/MAM 10698

Thought to be the finest Spanish painter of the nineteenth century after Francisco de Goya, Fortuny occupied a prominent place on the art scene of the period. Educated at the Llotja school, he completed his training in Rome on a grant from the Barcelona Provincial Council, an institution which commissioned various works from him about the intervention of Catalan volunteers in the Spanish-Moroccan War that had broken out in 1859. For that reason Fortuny travelled to Tetuan at the beginning of 1860 and to Tangiers in 1862. The final result of the works in Morocco were a brace of unfinished canvases in which he depicted two of the most important clashes of the African campaign. The first, *The Battle of Tetuan*, a work of great size and in a format totally inhabitual in the artistic praxis of Fortuny, remained in his Rome studio, where it became a true emblem, until it was acquired on the painter's death in 1874 by the Barcelona Provincial Council. The second, *The Battle of Wad-ras*, is currently to be found in the Museo del Prado.

The fact that Fortuny did not finish *The Battle of Tetuan* and that the final result was very uneven and somewhat unhappy demonstrates the lack of motivation of the painter, who became increasingly aware that a history painting conceived within the genre's conventional parameters and characteristic stereotypes was at something of a remove from his painterly aspirations and his creative sensibility. On the other hand, notwithstanding the shortcomings of the staging that a *grande machine* required, the canvas is strangely compelling, given that it contains a visual poetics which paradoxically converts its compositional heterodoxy into one of the artist's chief attainments and merits. F.Q.C.

Mariano Fortuny
(Reus, 1838 – Rome, 1874)
The Battle of Tetuan
Rome, 1862-4
MNAC/MAM 10695

A prolific artist, a contemporary of Fortuny's, and one of the foremost representatives of Catalan pictorial Realism, Antoni Caba, formed in the Romantic tradition of the Llotja school in the 1850s, exemplifies the consolidation of localist inertia in the Barcelona of the second half of the nineteenth century. The author of a great number of sober and austere portraits, his compositions reflect the influence of the language codified by Federico de Madrazo during his years of apprenticeship in the Academia de Bellas Artes de San Fernando in Madrid. They also provide evidence of his training in Paris, where he managed to enrol at the Académie des Beaux-Arts in 1863.

Aesthetically and ideologically speaking, Caba's portraits are at a remove from the typologies and models of standard portraits, as well as of their scenographic obligations, with the presence of stereotyped elements that form part of the figurative repertoire of the Western portraitist. The lack of concessions to this European pictorial tradition is not to the detriment of the quality of works which stand out for their high degree of faithfulness to the person portrayed, in this case the landscape painter Joaquim Vayreda. In fact Caba settles on a standardised portrait model with identical typological features that he uses in an almost serial way when depicting people from his domestic environment or his circle of friends. Apart from the logical differences between the characters portrayed, what is evident are the formal, stylistic and compositional similarities, or even the representation of the figure, portrayed, in most instances, half-length. F.Q.C.

An extraordinarily prolific painter with an extensive output, Benet Mercadé constitutes an epigonic manifestation of the process of survival of Nazarenism in the Principality. His oeuvre has points of contact with the figurative and compositional models introduced by Claudi Lorenzale, the main representative of Catalan pictorial primitivism. Although it responds to criteria of taste and to aesthetic parameters that are distinctive, the relationship of subordination of Mercadé's output to Lorenzale's is seen in the cultivating of historical and religious imagery. It is worth remembering, in that sense, Mercadé's participation in some of the national fine arts exhibitions that took place in Madrid and which reflected the flowering of history painting in Spain. Some of Mercadé's compositions even denote the use of a very dark palette and certain earth colours, evocative of some of the more stereotyped and all-important characteristics of Lorenzale's style.

Nevertheless, the portrait we are commenting on, with a very warm chromatic register, constitutes a paradigmatic expression of the painter's adhesion to realism. A friend of the artist's, with whom she lived for several years, this mysterious woman, who according to testimonies of the day always maintained an attitude of selfless devotion and veneration towards Mercadé, was portrayed by the artist at least on one other occasion, as another painting of her preserved in the MNAC proves. As a plausible hypothesis, then, we may draw attention to the fact that Anita acted as a model for the painter from time to time. F.Q.C.

Permanent loan from the Reial Acadèmia Catalana de Belles Arts de Sant Jordi de Barcelona, 1902; admission, 1906

Antoni Caba
(Barcelona, 1838-1907)

Portrait of the Painter Joaquim Vayreda
1870
MNAC/MAM 10569

Benet Mercadé
(La Bisbal d'Empordà, 1821 – Barcelona, 1897)

Portrait of Señora Anita in a Red Dress
Barcelona, 1872
MNAC/MAM 10499

Notwithstanding his short life, the career of Simó Gómez is marked by a series of formative travels of enormous relevance, outstanding among which, given its import, is the stay he made in Paris in the 1860s, where he managed to enrol at the Académie des Beaux-Arts in 1864. During this phase he came into contact with the oeuvre of Alexandre Cabanel, whose language leaves its mark on many of the artist's pictures at this time, along with that of Édouard Manet, another of the artists who he took as a model. Having said that, Gómez's style also evinces his assimilation of the Great Masters of Western Baroque painting, basically that of the painters of the Spanish Golden Age, and by extension that of those European artists who cultivated a strong naturalism. In fact the taste for this kind of artistic expression became stronger as a result of a later stay in Madrid, in which his visits to the Museo del Prado turned into a fruitful form of apprenticeship.

A highly prolific author and a cultivator of distinct genres, Simó Gómez particularly excelled in that of the portrait, an example of which is this image of his friend Francesc Vidal i Javellí, one of the most important ensembliers and decorators of the Catalan boom era of the '*Fiebre de Oro*'. Given its extraordinary quality this portrait, a late Gómez work, constitutes a worthy contribution to the history of Catalan painting of the period. The picture forms a pair with the portrait of Mercè Puig de Vidal, wife of furniture maker Francesc Vidal, which is also preserved in the MNAC and which was painted by Gómez in 1873. F.Q.C.

The brothers Venanci and Agapit Vallmitjana occupy an important place in Catalan Realist sculpture due to their works of a religious nature, portraits and small salon sculpture, which enjoyed a certain popularity during the second half of the nineteenth century.

The visit the Spanish Queen Isabella II made in 1860 to the studio of the two brothers, at that time in the chapel of Santa Àgata in Barcelona, led to the commissioning of two sculptures, a commission the Queen herself confirmed the following year during a visit the sculptors made to Madrid. Venanci created a figure of *Saint George*, and Agapit, who had already modelled a portrait of the Queen for the Gothic patio of the Audiencia de Barcelona, sculpted, in marble, the *Portrait of Isabella II Presenting Prince Alfonso*, a consummate work of his which is today preserved in the gardens of the Palau de Pedralbes in Barcelona.

Study for the Portrait of Isabella II Presenting Prince Alfonso is one of the two sketches that, along with the plaster model, the MNAC has of the above sculpture. Of the three works which best illustrate the author's creative process, this nude is the one that enables us to appreciate the realism in which the sculptor was immersed and the plastic qualities he attained as an artist, to the extent that it may be considered one of the most interesting female nudes in nineteenth-century Spanish sculpture. M.D.

Simó Gómez
(Barcelona, 1845-80)

Portrait of the Ensemblier Francesc Vidal i Javellí
Barcelona, 1875
MNAC/MAM 114955

Agapit Vallmitjana
(Barcelona, 1833-1905)

Study for the Portrait of Isabella II Presenting Prince Alfonso
Barcelona, 1860
MNAC/MAM 67403

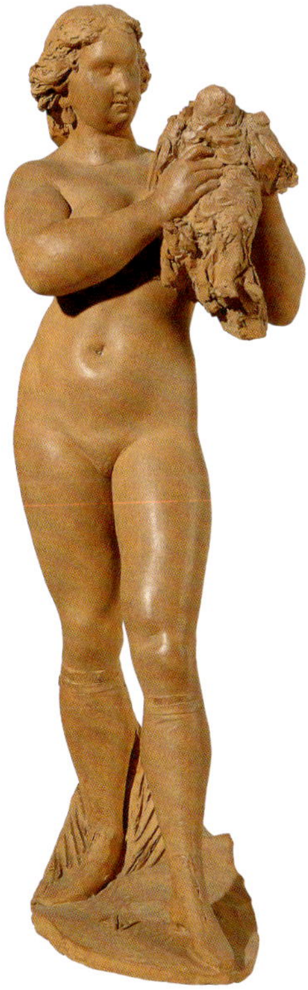

A key figure in Catalan art of the second half of the nineteenth century, Martí Alsina played a leading role in one of the most fecund and innovative episodes of the 1800s. He was a prolific artist with an abundant output that masked the existence of a studio, the most important of its day, which took on a huge number of commissions and was staffed by many assistants working under Alsina's guidance. This studio, however, also performed a pedagogical function, to the point of providing an alternative training to the official teaching imparted at the Llotja school. As such it functioned as a formative centre for many members of the next generation of painters.

As well as his portraits, the artist is notable for his depictions of urban vistas, mountain landscapes, stormy seascapes, nudes and still lifes. Thus, although landscape, following the Romantic tradition in which the painter was formed, occupies a hugely important place in his production, his way of tackling representation is the best proof of the appearance of a new poetics based on the defence of reality as the sole source of inspiration, setting aside the subjectivism and Romantic sentimentalism of the artist, who discovered in nature the reflection of his particular state of mind. An example of this militant Realism, influenced by Gustave Courbet, is *The Siesta*, Martí Alsina's finest work and one of the paradigms of Catalan Realist painting, which demonstrates the total assimilation of this new figurative culture, a culture which drinks at the source of contemporary French painting. F.Q.C.

The undeniable success that *Wounded Toreador* obtained after appearing in the *Exposición Nacional de Bellas Artes* in Madrid in 1871 marks the beginning of an interesting artistic output which situates Nobas—an artist who had worked as a goldsmith until 1870 or so—among the most prominent Catalan sculptors of his day. Although his later output was irregular, the bulk of his portraits, salon sculptures and works of a monumental kind reflect the quality he attained as a sculptor.

In its day *Wounded Toreador*, Nobas's most outstanding work, elicited varied and contrasting interpretations due to being deemed by certain critics a 'moral portrait of Spain', while others stressed what for them was an embittered jibe at a civilisation which permitted such tragic kinds of popular entertainment. Visually speaking, Nobas encapsulates in this figure his artistic ideas, based on a realism inspired in a nature whose more vulgar details he nevertheless shrinks from. To do this the artist tones down the depiction of such a dramatic subject by means of an obvious idealisation, at the same time as he seeks a balance between depth of feeling and an impeccable facture. In that respect, one might emphasise the minute detailing of the clothing, which denotes the influence of the virtuoso style Fortuny had imposed with his pictorial oeuvre. M.D.

Ramon Martí Alsina
(Barcelona, 1826-94)
The Siesta
Barcelona, *c.* 1884
MNAC/MAM 65596

Rossend Nobas
(Barcelona, 1841-91)
Wounded Toreador
Barcelona, 1871
MNAC/MAM 10493

With an output centred on landscape, mainly in the settings of Olot, Joaquim Vayreda consolidated the innovative tendency begun by his teacher, Martí Alsina, and inaugurated one of the most fertile phases in the Catalan art scene of the last third of the nineteenth century. Furthermore, his poetics, which crystallised in the founding of the Olot School, was one of the factors that most contributed to counteracting the hitherto corrupt dialectic existing between a Barcelonan artistic centre typified by a dynamism generative of new tendencies and an artistic periphery presided over by a situation of stagnation and of absolute dependence vis-à-vis this focal point, which radiated new figurative models. Indeed, grounded in a *modus vivendi* and a clearly-differentiated system of values, this world-view turns out to be one of the painter's most singular contributions. Visualised through his work is the lyrical sublimation of the rural ambit, of a set of ancestral social practices, of a way of understanding and relating oneself to the natural environment in which man lives in perpetual communion. Works like *The Harvest*, in which the landscape is converted into the indisputable protagonist with few concessions to more anecdotal details, situate Vayreda at the head of the renewal of Catalan landscape painting. In this oil, created during one of the artist's most brilliant, successful and fertile periods, the influence Vayreda underwent of the French painters of the so-called Barbizon School, who painted directly from nature, is more than evident. F.Q.C.

As his subject matter Boudin, a sailor's son, almost exclusively adopted seascapes, especially of the Normandy and Brittany coast, although towards the end of his life he also painted in the south of France and in Venice. Trouville, a fashionable resort of the period, became one of the artist's favourite locations, where between 1862 and 1871 he painted his famous beach scenes with their social gatherings, which met with great success.

Fitting within this framework, and with the artist at the height of his powers, is *Cordier Park in Trouville*, an oil painted with the spontaneity of a sketch and in which all the ingredients are subordinated to the light, delicately deployed in a play of contrasts. The location chosen by the painter on this occasion is not the beach but a little-frequented park in full sunshine. This oil, in which the trees and the lightly clouded sky are turned into the dominant elements of the composition, reflects the type of representation Boudin opted for: a landscape without figures and with a low horizon line, in which the sky occupies most of the canvas. Here, the figures, used solely as a counterpoint to suggest the magnitude of the landscape, are mere brushstrokes of bright colour that help create luminous effects and the parasols of the ladies, essential elements in these *mondaine* compositions. M.D.

Joaquim Vayreda
(Girona, 1843 – Olot, 1894)
The Harvest
Olot, *c.* 1881
MNAC/MAM 4261

Louis-Eugène Boudin
(Honfleur, 1824 – Deauville, 1898)
Cordier Park in Trouville
c. 1880-5
MNAC/MAM 50502

A follower of the nineteenth-century Catalan landscapist tradition inaugurated by Lluís Rigalt, Urgell was trained in the studio of Ramon Martí Alsina along with other artists of the period, and became one of the most outstanding disciples of the master. A friend of Joaquim Vayreda's and an admirer of his work, Urgell is one of the most interesting landscapists of his day. From an initial language indebted to the precepts and compositional formulae created by the master, the painter evolved towards a rather odd and personal style remote from the militant Realism forged during the years of apprenticeship in the studio of Martí Alsina and after receiving the fertile stimulus implied by knowledge of the work of Gustave Courbet, which he looked at as a result of a trip to Paris. Falling within this framework is *The Call to Prayer*, an excellent specimen of the Urgell manner, which he showed in the 1871 *Exposició general catalana* and which in 1876 was awarded the Runner's-Up Medal in the *Exposición Nacional de Bellas Artes*.

Painted in Gelida, it is a good example of Urgell's exclusive way of depicting crepuscular landscapes in different places in Catalonia, in which, with absolute formal economy, he transmits a strong, almost metaphysical lyricism evocative of the Romantic setting, mysterious and sad, of some of the compositions that the German Romantic painter Caspar David Friedrich had created a few years previously. F.Q.C.

Permanent loan from the Museo del Prado, 1932

A prominent painter of the Restoration era, Joan Ferrer Miró was educated in the local tradition of his hometown only to move to Barcelona a few years later, where he completed his training at the popular academy of Pere Borrell and the Llotja school. At the end of the 1870s, and as the result of a stay in Italy, Ferrer Miró transformed his style: he adopted a more luminous palette and cultivated a folkloric subject matter. Restored to Barcelona, the painter accepted the strictures of a clientele avid for mannered artistic expressions that would reflect the habits of the emergent bourgeoisie of the time, arising in a moment of tremendous economic growth. In fact his works subsume the moment of economic euphoria that Barcelona lived through during the historic period known as the '*Fiebre de Oro*'.

Presented at the 1888 Universal Exhibition, this painting, which was awarded the Gold Medal, represents a group of people contemplating a picture displayed in the window of a shop specialising in reproductions of drawings and paintings, the future art gallery or showroom. To sum up, and as is typical of anecdote, Ferrer Miró depicts an amiable and usually cosmopolitan reality in which a minutely described event leaves little room for the viewer's imagination. In fact, the success obtained by the work caused the painter to do a second version practically identical to the first. F.Q.C.

Modest Urgell
(Barcelona, 1839-1919)
The Call to Prayer
c. 1871
MNAC/MAM 11399

Joan Ferrer Miró
(Vilanova i la Geltrú, 1850 – Barcelona, 1931)
The Public Showing of a Painting
Barcelona, *c.* 1888
MNAC/MAM 10798

Romà Ribera was one of the artistic personalities most representative of Catalan pictorial anecdote, a movement which dominated the late-nineteenth-century Catalan art scene, along with other, more innovative, tendencies. Ribera is noted for employing, in this work as in others, a mannered language and a highly decorative taste. As it is, the subjects painted by Ribera are but a simple pretext to reflect the economic and social power of his clientele, which openly displays an inclination for the displaying of homes crammed with an object world of sumptuous and very expensive goods (pieces of furniture, carpets, screens, vases). In the case of the painting we are commenting on, concrete citations are not lacking to the influence that the Japanese aesthetic had among Catalan artists at the end of the nineteenth century. Ribera's work grows up around the new bourgeois values of luxury, wealth, elegance and comfort, and adds up to an authentic period portrait of a social stratum that displays a highly sophisticated and hedonist behaviour.

On the other hand *De soirée* brings us closer to the female figure as a constant of the artist's output, founded on a highly stereotyped vision in which, as aspects culturally linked to the female world, gallantry and coquetry predominate. In short, this painting is transformed into an authentic paradigm of what some writers have rightly called the phenomenon of 'high-class painting'. F.Q.C.

Rodin, the indisputable leader of modern sculpture, was the author of a group of outstanding works which presupposed both the renewal of sculpture at the end of the nineteenth century and the breaking of new ground for the twentieth. His production cannot be contained within the one tendency, since he modelled works of a naturalist Realism, splendid Symbolist representations, or others with an emphatic expressionist content, always, however, with the strength, vitality and sensuality typical of his personality. His influence was decisive on the sculptors of his time, among whom figure the Catalan *Modernistas*, who were inspired by the more Symbolist side of his output.

The Bronze Age, Rodin's first life-size sculpture, is posterior to a journey the artist made to Italy in 1875, where he discovered the great works of the Renaissance, especially those of Michelangelo, which convinced him of the importance of modelling and of direct study of the human body. From that time onwards he abandoned the decorative sculpture he had cultivated in his early days in order to devote himself to an output of an extraordinary creative force that was to break definitively with the academicism prevalent at the time. In that sense *The Bronze Age*, of which the sculptor himself ordered numerous examples to be cast, is an emblematic work of modern sculpture, given the plastic language adopted by Rodin when it comes to showing the expressive strength of the human body. M.D.

Romà Ribera
(Barcelona, 1849-1935)
De Soirée
Barcelona, *c.* 1894
MNAC/MAM 10782

Auguste Rodin
(Paris, 1840 – Meudon, 1917)
The Bronze Age
Brussels, 1876
MNAC/MAM 10001

At the beginning of his artistic career Miquel Blay, installed in Rome on a scholarship from the Girona Provincial Council, modelled a sketch in terracotta of a group consisting of an old man and a girl seated on a bench, huddling together in the cold. The following year Blay sculpted it life-size, but this time with the figures naked. This sketch was converted into the definitive piece and also into one of the most important in the artist's production; and what is more important, into one of the masterworks of Catalan sculpture.

The First Cold Spells, a sculpture falling within the naturalist Realism adopted by Blay in his formative phase, depicts an anecdotal subject treated with extreme attention to detail. One has only to observe the anatomy of the old man, especially the texture of the skin and the softness of the flesh, to discern the technical mastery of the artist. Having said that, by sculpting in marble he introduced visual elements typical of *Modernisme*, such as the *non finito* or sfumato of the girl's face, of clear Rodinian influence. In this way Blay arrived at a synthesis between conventional, sensationalist sculpture and *Modernista* sculpture, of which he himself was to be one of the finest exponents. Aside from its undoubted visual merits, though, the real strength of this work lies in the artist's ability to transform a scene of poignant tenderness into an idealised representation of human suffering. M.D.

In Catalonia the interest in Symbolism emerged on the occasion of the performing of *L'Intruse*, the play by poet and dramatist Maurice Maeterlinck, during the 'Segunda Fiesta Modernista' held in Sitges in September 1893. With regard to the pictorial realm, Symbolism took hold among such painters as Joan Brull, Josep Maria Tamburini, Adrià Gual and Alexandre de Riquer, who felt drawn to the deliquescent world of fairies and other characters related to the medieval or classical era, and such other painters as Joaquim Vancells, who dispensed with the figures and depicted misty and bleak landscapes with great lyricism.

Joan Brull, an artist who after a start linked to history painting moved towards a folkloric, anecdotal style, joined the Symbolist tendency around 1896, mainly with subject matter akin to that of European Symbolism. His heads and figures of delicate and diaphanous nymphs and fairies, often swathed in the mist of an absolutely idealised landscape, turned into images representative of decadent Symbolism. And in that respect *Reverie*, a work which depicts an ethereal woman in an unreal landscape in muted tones and which the artist first exhibited in 1906, is one of the most important landmarks of Catalan Symbolism. M.D.

Miquel Blay
(Olot, 1866 – Madrid, 1936)
The First Cold Spells
Rome, 1892
MNAC/MAM 10002

Joan Brull
(Barcelona, 1863-1921)
Reverie
c. 1905
MNAC/MAM 10882

Considered one of the finest exponents of Catalan *Modernista* sculpture, Llimona became part of Symbolism during the first few years of the twentieth century after a phase in which he had adopted an idealism deeply rooted in his solid religious convictions. Llimona, who had contributed to the founding of the Artistic Circle of Sant Lluc, the intention of which was to preserve art from the excesses of contemporary artists, did not depict the female nude, prohibited in the Circle's initial statutes, until the actual associates of the organisation considered that this prohibition was prejudicial to their artistic careers. It was then that he sculpted *Desolation*, a work he exhibited for the first time in 1907 and which demonstrates the artist's ability to communicate, via a naked female figure, feelings that reflect a deep humanity.

Desolation, a paradigm of *Modernista* sculpture, magisterially represents the formal traits of Symbolism as adopted by the more outstanding Catalan sculptors of the day, such as undulating lines and softened contours, features that derive from *The Danaide* by Auguste Rodin, their indisputable visual reference. Even so, a notable difference exists between the resigned, melancholic and chaste attitude of *Desolation* and the vitality, strength and sensuality of the French sculptor's work. With *Desolation* Llimona brought his process of sculptural renewal to a peak, while also summing up the Symbolist aesthetic of one of Catalan art's most brilliant periods. M.D.

In 1890 Casas, the most outstanding painter of the first *Modernista* generation, began his decisive second stay in Paris, which would be prolonged until 1892, in the company of Santiago Rusiñol, with whom he shared an apartment in the Moulin de la Galette. During this period, in which his hitherto far from negligible artistic career would reach its peak, he painted a great many works, works in which he followed the naturalist line he had already cultivated, while incorporating, where subject matter and composition were concerned, certain features of the painting of Édouard Manet, Edgar Degas and Henri de Toulouse-Lautrec.

Plein Air, one of Casas's most paradigmatic paintings and one of those which best illustrates the change that this artist and Rusiñol introduced into late-nineteenth-century Catalan painting, pertains to this moment. Although Casas utilised, in terms of subject matter, a number of Impressionist elements, his painting at this time is in the line of French naturalist painting. Likewise, it is worth emphasising that this is an open-air scene with the urban landscape as a backdrop. The composition is resolved in a daring manner, since the elements of the painting appear to extend beyond the edges of the canvas, and the colour is handled almost monochromatically in a harmony of greys that envelop the picture in a kind of mist which blurs its contours. It is logical, then, that this type of painting, which, moreover, posits a fleeting snapshot, the rationale of which the viewer's imagination must decide, might enter into conflict with the conventional artistic taste then reigning in Barcelona. C.M.

Josep Llimona
(Barcelona, 1864-1934)
Desolation
Barcelona, 1907
MNAC/MAM 10861

Ramon Casas
(Barcelona, 1866-1932)
Plein Air
Paris, *c.* 1890-1
MNAC/MAM 10901

Casas painted this work to decorate Els Quatre Gats, an establishment of which he was one of the main instigators and which, launched in 1897 in Barcelona's Calle de Montsió, was decisive for the consolidation of *Modernisme* through bringing together not just the artists and intellectuals who had promoted the movement, but also members of the younger generation.

The decorative purpose of this painting meant that the painter, who had begun operating as a poster artist by then, would use a technique more typical of the poster and that he would give it a humorous twist. Although the work was later trimmed back, the pedalling figures of Casas himself and of Pere Romeu, the café barman, with the silhouette of the city in the background, has become one of Casas's most popular images and, in fact, one of the most emblematic within *Modernisme*.

In period photographs of the interior of Els Quatre Gats one sees the work we are commenting on on the main wall, above the long table at which Casas and Rusiñol used to sit, along with a series of young artists like Isidre Nonell, Joaquim Mir or Pablo Picasso, people who were beginning their respective careers at the time and who in a few years would be at the forefront of Catalan art or, in the case of Picasso, of international art. For all of them this painting would be an image more known than the one that in 1900, when most of the young artists had gone off to Paris, took its place and in which the same characters are depicted, albeit now driving a motor car, a vehicle more typical of the twentieth century. Which is why when these works were reproduced in the magazine *Pèl & Ploma* they were entitled *End of the Nineteenth Century* and *Beginning of the Twentieth Century*, respectively. C.M.

This painting is a paradigmatic example of Rusiñol's Parisian output, created in the early 1890s when he lived in Montmartre together with Ramon Casas and Miquel Utrillo. As occurs in other works by the artist at this time, the depicted setting is the interior of the park of the Moulin de la Galette, used as a background for the composition, in spite of the fact that on this occasion it is practically the main feature. The foreground, in shade, has an eminently sordid air, embodied in the representation of the park's kitchen, which contrasts, in the middle distance, with the depiction of the park, a theoretically cheerful and bustling image but one which is captured in a moment of inactivity as an almost empty space, albeit full of subtle suggestions, all of which unconsciously provokes a feeling of desolation and sadness.

Rusiñol, who would become one of the main proponents of *Modernisme*, took part with this painting, plus three others, in the *Primera Exposición General de Bellas Artes*, held in Barcelona in 1891. There is nothing strange about the fact that Rusiñol presented *Laboratory of La Galette*, one of the finest pictures in quality and format terms of those he had painted in Paris around that time, in this exhibition, the first of an international character to be held in the artist's city of birth. The exhibition judges elected to give a prize to this oil, which consequently passed to the city museum, thus becoming the first work by the artist to enter our museum. C.M.

Ramon Casas
(Barcelona, 1866-1932)
Ramon Casas and Pere Romeu on a Tandem
Barcelona, 1897
MNAC/MAM 69806

Santiago Rusiñol
(Barcelona, 1861 – Aranjuez, 1931)
Laboratory of La Galette
Paris, 1890-1
MNAC/MAM 10897

This sculpture is one of the most representative of Miquel Blay's *Modernista* production and one of the most original of Catalan art from this period, both for its symbolic charge and for the fact of bringing marble and bronze together in a single work, an unusual combination in Catalan sculpture. The work dates from the period in which Blay showed himself to be most in tune with Symbolist ideas, which in formal terms meant an engagement with the production of Auguste Rodin. The fact that Blay lived in Paris between 1894 and 1906, the year in which he set up house once and for all in Madrid, brought him into direct contact with the most innovative sculpture of the era, the Symbolist version of this being the one in which he found an inspiration close to his own sensibility.

In *Pursuing the Dream* Blay depicts the sculptor's struggle with inspiration, his aim being to attain the artistic ideal. The figure of the naked man, of well-rounded physique, highlighted by the attributes of the bronze modelling, contrasts with the gentle, sinuous curves of the tunic the female figure is sporting. The artist elected to sculpt this dreamed-of woman in marble as an image of the ideal or of perfection, and utilised the *non finito* or sfumato to give her an almost unreal appearance. Thus, when combining the two figures, their formal differences along with the contrast of the texture and colour of the two materials each contribute to strengthening the symbolic content of the work. M.D.

Clarasó, like his confrères Casas and Rusiñol, felt drawn to the technical innovations underway in Paris, but his personal circumstances, distinct from those of his friends, who belonged to the well-to-do Catalan bourgeoisie, led him to cultivate two divergent artistic paths in parallel to each other. One, the one that enabled him to live, was centred on works of a naturalist sort with anecdotal subject matter, very much to the taste of the conventional public of the day. The other, the one which has situated him among the most outstanding Catalan sculptors of *Modernisme*, linked him to the Symbolism inspired by Auguste Rodin and came to fruition in sculptures that were absolutely innovative as far as the Catalan artistic scene was concerned.

Eve, the most important of Clarasó's *Modernista* works, sums up, along with Josep Llimona's *Desolation* (see p. 246), the characteristics of this movement. The naked female figure with well-rounded forms displays an attitude of passivity and abandon, doubled over atop a half-smoothed rock. Conscious of her sins, Eve hides herself from the divine gaze, concealing her face beneath a cascade of sinuously tumbling hair. The plastic language the artist used to strengthen the symbolic character of the figure contributed decisively to shaping one of the most brilliant moments of modern Catalan sculpture. M.D.

Miquel Blay
(Olot, 1866 – Madrid, 1936)
Pursuing the Dream
Paris, 1902
MNAC/MAM 153429

Enric Clarasó
(Sant Feliu de Castellar, 1857 – Barcelona, 1941)
Eve
Barcelona, 1904
MNAC/MAM 10013

The pieces of furniture the MNAC keeps from the house of Dr. Lleó Morera, situated on the chamfered corner of Barcelona's *Manzana de la Discordia* [the 'Block' or 'Apple of Discord'], are a highly successful expression of *Modernista* interior design and a good example of the close collaboration between an architect —Lluís Domènech i Montaner—and a cabinetmaker and interior decorator—Gaspar Homar—whose workshops provided all the decorative and functional accessories of the inside of this private house: furniture, lamps, carpets, and so on. Faithful to the symbolico-ornamental programme devised by the architect, Gaspar Homar combines the quality and worth of artisanal tradition with mass-production.

The furniture (sofa-settle, chairs, armchairs) is distinguished by its fine woods and complex handicrafting—marquetry and carving—created in collaboration with artists such as Josep Pey, Joan Carreras and Joan Sagarra and sons.

A key element is the marquetry, which brings together a wide range of exotic woods (sycamore, banana, mahogany, Hungarian ash, jacaranda, palisander, etc.) and confers a luxurious appearance to these objects of everyday use, a good reflection of the refinement and comfort the bourgeois class strove hard to attain. Originally, this unit decorated one of the most emblematic rooms of the bourgeois dwelling of the Ensanche: the parlour, where the Lleó Morera family received people on visiting days. The complexity of the group and the impeccable facture make it a key piece for acceding to the exquisite and sensual world of *Modernisme*. M.F.

The technique of the classic tesserae mosaic, inspired by the facings of the Roman and Byzantine period, was introduced into Catalonia by the Genoese Mario Maragliano and his follower Lluís Bru, both of whom worked on many buildings by the architects of *Modernisme*, particularly Lluís Domènech i Montaner's. The mosaic is incorporated into the facing of façades and into the interior space as a covering for floors, handrails, domes, façades, pedestals and decorative panels, creating enclaves of great chromatic effect.

The making of mosaics was not exclusive to Maragliano and Bru. And so, as was announced in various magazines of the period, one of the specialities of the workshops of the cabinetmaker and interior decorator Gaspar Homar was the mosaic panel with compositions of figures, for instance the group which decorated the dining room on the first floor of the Lleó Morera House in Barcelona and which is currently preserved *in situ*. Gaspar Homar created an identical model to this panel, which was acquired by the Museum from his descendants in the 1960s, during the historiographical rehabilitation of *Modernisme*.

In this decorative panel it is worth recording the interventions of the ceramist Antoni Serra, who reproduced in porcelain the bas-reliefs of the hands and heads of the figure moulded from plaster models provided by the sculptor Joan Carreras, as well as the design undertaken by Josep Pey, one of Gaspar Homar's most faithful collaborators and a figure who worked assiduously with him. M.F.

Gaspar Homar
(Palma de Mallorca, 1870 – Barcelona, 1955)

Sofa with side display cabinets and a decorative marquetry panel with two figures in a garden from the Lleó Morera House
Barcelona, *c.* 1905
MNAC/MAM 71703

Gaspar Homar
(Palma de Mallorca, 1870 – Barcelona, 1955) and

Josep Pey
(Barcelona, 1875-1956)

Decorative panel depicting a picnic in the country
Barcelona, *c.* 1905
MNAC/MAM 71980

The fin-de-siècle architect, influenced by the theories of John Ruskin, Eugène Emmanuel Viollet-le-Duc and William Morris, is transformed into a multidisciplinary artist capable not only of conceiving the project and the plans of a house but also of imagining the details of the furnishings and the interior decoration. Fitting into this framework is the figure of Josep Puig i Cadafalch, an architect who throughout his artistic career experimented in the field of design, as demonstrated by the set of interiors he devised for the Amatller House on the Paseo de Gràcia, set within the so-called *Manzana de la Discordia* ['Block' or 'Apple of Discord']. This is the first Puig i Cadafalch house in the Ensanche modified by the artist himself and in which he explores the rich potential of the rehabilitated decorative arts. The outcome of a commission from Antoni Amatller i Costa, a chocolate manufacturer and art lover, Puig i Cadafalch took over the designing of, among other things, the lamps and furniture, for example the bench, ceiling lamp, coat stand and quadrangular stand from the main apartment in the building, currently on permanent loan to the MNAC. In these pieces the artist interprets the formulae of Gothic art as a style which was suited to helping preserve the history of Catalonia. The pieces of furniture, made of oak, are notable for the painstaking workmanship of their carving, with trefoil motifs, and have recourse to the characteristic openwork of medieval-style ornamentation, while the lamps recreate the candelabra, coronas and sconces of the fifteenth and sixteenth centuries. M.F.

Permanent loan from the Institut Amatller d'Art Hispànic, 1970

Antoni Serra Fiter, the chief representative of a dynasty of ceramists who for three generations worked in a single speciality, widened his knowledge in Sèvres, where he was initiated into the secrets of porcelain. He created ceramic objects of enormous quality during a relatively brief period of time, between 1904 and 1908, which coincides with the moment in which the Manufactura de Porcellanes i de Gres d'Art was open in the Barcelona barrio of Poble Nou. Wound up in 1908 because its artistic wares did not sell, this workshop functioned in a very advanced way and was a meeting place for such outstanding creators of the period as Pau Roig, Josep Pey, Ismael Smith, Josep Carreras, Xavier Nogués, Gustau Violet, Enric Casanovas and Pablo Gargallo, all of whom collaborated closely on the decorative ceramics of Antoni Serra.

With regard to Serra's porcelain vases, the ones most marked by *Modernisme* were the work of the designer Josep Pey, who came up with a host of Symbolist themes, as is visible in this vase, acquired by the Museum in the *V Exposición Internacional de Arte* held in Barcelona in 1907, in which Antoni Serra's creations won a medal for the impeccable technical and artistic level of his work as a whole. The disposition of the figures of the Annunciation, redolent with the poetics of Symbolism, has its origin in a composition by Sebastià Junyent entitled *Ave Maria*.

During the 1920s Antoni Serra was connected with the Escola Superior dels Bells Oficis, and with his sons Josep and Antoni, plus Enric Serra Abella, he continued producing ceramics in his workshop in Cornellà de Llobregat, with forms that are completely at one with *Noucentista* tradition and on occasions with Art Deco. M.F.

Josep Puig i Cadafalch
(Mataró, 1867 – Barcelona, 1957)

Ceiling lamp from the Amatller House
Barcelona, *c.* 1900
MNAC/MAM 114836

Quadrangular stand from the Amatller House
Barcelona, *c.* 1900
MNAC/MAM 114833

Antoni Serra
(Barcelona, 1869 – Cornellà de Llobregat, 1932) and

Josep Pey
(Barcelona, 1875-1956)

Annunciation Vase
Barcelona, *c.* 1901-7
MNAC/MAM 1582

One might situate the modern version of the stained-glass window and its adaptation to bourgeois households to the end of the nineteenth century in the Tallers d'Indústries d'Art of the cabinetmaker Francesc Vidal i Javellí, who organised a series of important workshops devoted to the industrial production of luxury items and to the decoration of interiors with sections devoted to upholstery, cabinetmaking, carving, metalwork and glass. Rubbing shoulders in these workshops were some of the most eminent figures of the different artistic branches of *Modernisme*: from the glassmaker Antoni Rigalt to the cabinetmaker Gaspar Homar, who took over the training of Frederic Vidal, the son of Francesc Vidal, as a draughtsman.

In 1899 or thereabouts Francesc Vidal had sent his son Frederic to The Cloisonné Glass Company in London to learn the technique of *cloisonné* in glass. On his return Frederic Vidal worked on the decoration of Eusebi Bertrand i Serra's house in the Paseo de la Bonanova in Barcelona, where he incorporated this laborious process (based on little globes of coloured glass and brass, with an effect similar to *cloisonné* enamel) into the design of folding screens, lamps and other furnishings, currently preserved in the MNAC. A fine demonstration of this is this folding screen consisting of three sections decorated with tiny rounds of *cloisonné* glass and with floral motifs having a clearly *Modernista* whiplash line.

The use of *cloisonné* glass was strictly limited and the production of works created with this material extremely brief, and therefore the pieces preserved in the MNAC must be considered as something of a rarity in this technique. M.F.

Around 1900 the reign of the diamond, abundantly used in the nineteenth century owing to the discovery of the mines of Cape Town, drew to an end. The creations of René Lalique, Georges Fouquet or Henri Beber, in which the design predominated above all else, broke radically with the trend in fashion of the second half of the nineteenth century, which valued the piece of jewellery for its size and for the weight of its precious stones. The parallel in the Catalan sphere was Lluís Masriera, the most important representative of the youngest generation of a line of silversmiths and painters. With the change of century, and with *Art Nouveau* in full flight, Lluís Masriera took over the artistic direction of the family workshop, after having consolidated and perfected his technical expertise in Geneva and Paris. Once back in Barcelona and with his sights set on confronting the fierce market competition, he renewed the output of the family business in two areas of performance: in seeking the maximum technical purity and in taking over the renovation of the designs, which transcend the eclectic forms of the Restoration period.

The birds, with cranes and peacocks predominating, flowers and insects, especially butterflies and dragonflies, as well as allegorical figures such as fairies and deliquescent nymphs of a clearly Japanesque design, are the habitual motifs of these pendants, brooches, cufflinks and bracelets, which caused a sensation in the windows of the Masriera jeweller's shop in Calle de Ferran in Barcelona. Neither must we overlook the subject of Saint George slaying the dragon, with its markedly nationalist emphasis, depicted in this pendant, delicately worked on the obverse and reverse and which has become a key piece of *Modernisme*. The work is outstanding for its nuanced polychromy, arrived at from the combination of gold as the basic metal, precious stones and *plique-à-jour* and *basse-taille* enamelwork, which opens up a range of unprecedented chromatic possibilities. M.F.

Frederic Vidal
(Barcelona, 1882-1950)
Folding screen
1899-1904
MNAC/MAM 131677

Lluís Masriera
(Barcelona, 1872-1958)
Pendant with Saint George
Barcelona, *c.* 1901-2
MNAC/MAM 71983

Bibelot-style decorative sculpture was enormously popular during *Modernisme*. Presided over by a Symbolist female figure personifying Winter, this relief is a good example of the mass-produced article that Lambert Escaler manufactured in polychromed terracotta and which he included in a huge catalogue of vases, busts, medallions, jardinieres and decorative panels.

These sculptures, intended to be an artistic accessory in the interior decoration of the late-nineteenth-century home, often depict the heads of fairies and maidens of enigmatic mien with flowers, among other things. They evoke fantasy, reverie and a strong sensuality with the suggestive titles of *Fading Kiss*, *Inspiration*, *Offering* or *Maleina*. Some of these works bring to mind the American dancer Loïe Fuller, who caused a sensation at the Folies Bergère and the 1900 Universal Exhibition in Paris with her Serpentine dances of the butterfly and the flame, and who was an iconographic reference in her own right during *Modernisme*, with connotations of an erotic import.

Created using the technique of the mould and with a modest material like clay, the price of these mass-produced objects, which were sold by catalogue, was much more accessible than that of decorative sculptures of marble or bronze, due to which they enjoyed an enormous success. M.F.

Joan Busquets i Jané, son of the cabinetmaker-upholsterer Joan Busquets i Cornet, was one of the most reputed *ensemblier* during the *Modernista* phase. To be precise, the *Art Nouveau* of Franco-Belgian origin seeped into his work at the beginning of the twentieth century and assimilated the 'elephantiasic' and arborescent forms typical of Louis Majorelle and Émile Gallé of the École de Nancy. While unceasingly interpreting and recreating historical styles, Busquets similarly embarked upon the structural fantasia of curves à la Hector Guimard, with the strong presence in his furniture of bifurcated feet and osseous forms.

Joan Busquets had also assimilated models of a more rectilinear design, with decorative motifs of a Secessionist origin that connect up with the purest Art Deco, not only as a result of his participation in the *Exposition International des Arts Décoratifs* in Paris in 1925, but long before. A good example of this is this 1911 cupboard-drinks cabinet, which was acquired on behalf of the Museum for the sum of 1,200 pesetas on the occasion of the *VI Exposición Internacional de Arte* held in Barcelona.

Two plaques of Limoges enamelwork by Lluís Masriera, which represent a bacchanalia, have been incorporated into the central panel, which is collapsible. Equally outstanding are the applications of marquetry, which give shape to ornamental details of great simplicity, and the incrustations and the metals in the hinges, locks and handles. M.F.

Lambert Escaler
(Vilafranca del Penedès, 1874 – Barcelona, 1957)
Winter
c. 1903
MNAC/MAM 113300

Joan Busquets
(Barcelona, 1874-1949)
Cupboard-drinks cabinet
Barcelona, *c.* 1911
MNAC/MAM 225

The architects of the end of the nineteenth century restored to Catalan wrought ironwork, which had attained enormous splendour during the medieval era, the prestige it deserved by adapting their designs in this technique to lamps, grilles, balustrades and gates, among other things. Gaudí occupies a prominent place in the reviving of this craft, not only for the variety and inspiration of his designs, but also for his profound knowledge of this art. Gaudí, the son of a boilersmith from Riudoms, collaborated very closely with the blacksmiths, going so far as to work himself in their forges.

This grillework double gate was designed by Gaudí with the assistance of the sculptor Llorenç Matamala as an entrance to the property of the summer residence that Manuel Vicens, a tile manufacturer, owned in the Calle de las Carolines in Barcelona, and amounts to the first important demonstration of the leading role iron would come to have as an ornamental material in Gaudí's work.

As is usual in his creations, natural forms provide a wealth of novel motifs, and nature is transformed into the eternal and unsurpassable model. In this grille Gaudí has recourse to such common-or-garden local flora as, for instance, dwarf palm leaves, agaves and French marigolds executed in cast iron. M.F.

Antoni Gaudí
(Reus, 1852 – Barcelona, 1926)
Grillework gate of the Vicens House
Barcelona, *c.* 1883-5
MNAC/MAM 153204

Josep Maria Jujol, who stood out as one of Antoni Gaudí's favourite collaborators and who designed furniture, stained glass, wrought ironwork and religious objets d'art on his own account, is the creator of an oeuvre with a touch of the modern about it that, transcending its own time, has served as a stimulus and inspiration for some of the outstanding creators of today's art.

In 1911 the artist took charge of the decorative design of the shop selling locks, keys and safes that Pere Mañach ran at number 57 Calle de Ferran in the heart of Barcelona. In his decoration, which unfortunately disappeared during the Civil War, Jujol fled from the conventionalisms of a customary commercial establishment and gave visible form to his unquestionable creative ability with solutions that come close to Surrealism. The decorative programme of the shop had as its leitmotif a mystical praisesong to the Virgin Mary consisting of intertwined rosaries and Mariological emblems.

Among the objects Jujol designed for the Mañach shop and which are still preserved today we might cite a number of seats in the form of a heart with gory wounds, and this expressionist iron doorknob from the shop's street door, which represents a heart pierced by an arrow, in keeping with the mystical potential of the interior decoration. M.F.

Josep Maria Jujol
(Tarragona, 1879 – Barcelona, 1949)
Mañach shop doorknob
Barcelona, 1911
MNAC 208126

An architect like Antoni Gaudí, who set out from the idea of the total work of art when it came to devising his architecture, could hardly establish hierarchies between the arts. Furniture constitutes a brilliant and innovative chapter in his work. In the suites of furniture designed for the Batlló House, Gaudí sets himself up as a precursor of ergonomic design and discovers the freedom of planning by breaking with academic schemas and prefiguring, in a fortuitous way, industrial design, as will do other such contemporary architects as Victor Horta, Charles Rennie Mackintosh and Eero Saarinen.

The chairs from the Batlló House propose a type of seating, hitherto unknown, which seeks after the rounded forms that might adjust to the human body. Executed in the Casas i Bardés workshops in ash wood, they have anatomical shapes which seem to be modelled from the imprint the body makes when seated. Similarly, Gaudí foregoes all reference to style in order to leave the shape unadorned, emphasising the grain and the textural qualities of the wood and setting aside the upholstery and superfluous ornamentation, frequently based on floral stylisation, that contemporary decorators like Gaspar Homar and Joan Busquets often went in for.

In the furniture field Antoni Gaudí permitted himself some unusual innovations such as the act of incorporating iron as a type of fastening or of ornamentation. A good example of this is the pew from the church of the Colonia Güell in Santa Coloma de Cervelló, in which he utilises a bar of iron and steals a march on the schemes that Le Corbusier, Mies van der Rohe, Walter Gropius and Marcel Breuer will propose years later. The construction of this two-seater pew, with its trapezoidal plan, was undertaken by the carpenter Tomàs Bernat in 1914, and it is one of the last pieces of furniture designed by Gaudí. M.F.

Pew from the crypt of the Colonia Güell. Permanent loan from the Archbishopric of Barcelona, 1991
Chair and double sofa from the Batlló House. Permanent loan from the Casa-Museu Gaudí, Junta Constructora del Temple Expiatori de la Sagrada Família, 1991

Pew from the crypt of the Colonia Güell
Barcelona, *c.* 1914
MNAC/MAM 156072

Antoni Gaudí
(Reus, 1852 – Barcelona, 1926)
Chair from the Batlló House
Barcelona, *c.* 1907
MNAC/MAM 156071

Double sofa from the Batlló House
Barcelona, *c.* 1907
MNAC/MAM 156070

In 1902 Pidelaserra, one of the few Catalan painters who fully assimilated the teachings of Impressionism, held a one-man show in Barcelona that brought together an important set of pictures, most of them urban views recently painted in Paris. These followed the tenets of Impressionism in terms of subject matter and technique and showed the particular influence of Édouard Monet, Alfred Sisley, Camille Pissarro and Gustave Caillebotte. Aside from the more progressive critics, the cold reception with which this exhibition was received and in particular the rebuff meted out to the Symbolist triptych *Life*, which constituted the most innovative contribution of the show, along with the fresh rejection that his great portrait *The Deu Family* (MNAC/MAM 43862) met with months later, drove the painter to shut himself away in the Montseny, where he devoted himself to the genre of landscape. It was then that he painted a series of landscapes, among which were the work we are commenting on, which go to form the most personal and coherent group of pictures in his oeuvre. With great formal economy Pidelaserra manages to depict the majesty of the landscape, utilising a technique peculiar to him in which he combines quasi-Pointillist brushstrokes with a sinuous and diluted pictorial handling of the cloudscapes. The lack of success that this set of landscapes met with when the painter exhibited them in his native city in 1903 led the artist to break off his personal artistic career for a long period of time. C.M.

Alfred Sisley, whose early landscapes denote the influence of the Barbizon School and of Gustave Courbet, is the only truly Impressionist painter the MNAC has in its collections. This work was acquired by the Barcelona City Council from the *Exposition d'arts français*, which was organised in the city during the First World War to display solidarity with French artists who had not been able to hold their traditional Paris Salon that year. *In Saint-Mammès. June Sunshine*, also known as *The Bend of the Loing*, is a painting expressive of Sisley's final creative phase, when he had quit Paris in order to settle in the Moret region, near Fontainebleau.

Sisley's special sensibility when it came to capturing the effects of light in fluvial landscapes meant that between 1880 and 1895 the River Loing would become the most usual setting for his aesthetic researches. The structure of this painting—an extremely low horizon line and a clear, luminous cloudscape—and the tiny juxtaposed brushstrokes are typical of the canvases of this period. Outstanding are the two areas of trees, those in the foreground that let the rays of the sun through and the others forming a compact line which follows the course of the river in a diagonal that leads the viewer's gaze to the viaduct and the village of Saint-Mammès in the background of the composition. Having said that, it is worth stressing Sisley's ability to offer us, via a light-filled, poetic nature, a personal and positive vision of the world. M.D.

Marià Pidelaserra
(Barcelona, 1877-1946)
Mountains from the Montseny. Clear Morning
Barcelona, 1903
MNAC/MAM 4086

Alfred Sisley
(Paris, 1839 – Moret-sur-Loing, 1899)
In Saint-Mammès. June Sunshine
1892
MNAC/MAM 11130

Canals, a fellow student of Joaquim Mir and Isidre Nonell's, among others, at the Escola de Belles Arts de Barcelona [School of Fine Arts] left along with Nonell in 1897 for Paris, where he remained for almost ten years. Although he arrived in the city with a scant training, his entrance into the Parisian art world did not prove too difficult. At the end of 1899 Paul Durand-Ruel, the renowned dealer of the Impressionists, took an interest in his work and became his dealer. Although the professional relation with Durand-Ruel limited his artistic freedom, given that he had to devote himself to painting pictures on Spanish themes, as requested by his dealer, it also enabled him to view at first hand the works of the main Impressionists, whose influence decisively marked his artistic future.

La Toilette, probably the artist's paradigmatic painting, amply demonstrates all that Canals had assimilated during his long stay in Paris from Impressionism in general and Pierre Auguste Renoir in particular. Subsequently, the artist evolved in the direction of *Noucentisme*, going so far, even, as to found one of the more important associations of this art movement, 'Les Arts i els Artistes', of which he was the first president. Canals participated with this painting, along with six others, in the *V Exposición Internacional de Bellas Artes*, held in Barcelona in 1907, where it was acquired by the collector Lluís Plandiura. C.M.

After commencing his artistic career in 1893 with landscapes that followed the Olot School's line in rural naturalism and having formed part of the group known as the 'Colla del Safrà', Mir spent three years in Majorca, where he arrived at the end of 1899 with Santiago Rusiñol. This stay on the island, which constituted a decisive stage in the consolidation of an absolutely personal language, unfortunately came to an end with a crisis that led to Mir's admission into the Pere Mata Psychiatric Institute in Reus.

Of the many canvases Mir painted in Majorca, *The Rock in the Pond* is a brilliant display of his potent, vigorous and at the same time poetic style, in which one perceives an intuitive, impassioned temperament. One has to take into account that in the outskirts of Barcelona Mir had not encountered the grandiose quality of such enigmatic and desolate spots as those in Majorca, where nature offered him the possibility to combine an exuberant chromatism with his own fantasies. The painter utilised a wide range of ochre, blue and emerald tones to paint the rugged rocks that are reflected in the transparent water, creating a play of light in which these colours blend with the blues of the sea. The Majorca painting earned the artist the admiration of the critics, who valued his talent for converting nature into a grandiose spectacle impregnated with lyricism. M.D.

Ricard Canals
(Barcelona, 1876-1931)
La Toilette
Paris, *c.* 1903
MNAC/MAM 3807

Joaquim Mir
(Barcelona, 1873-1940)
The Rock in the Pond
Majorca, *c.* 1903
MNAC/MAM 10891

After a stay in Majorca and a brief parenthesis in the Pere Mata Psychiatric Institute in Reus, where he was a patient for almost two years, Mir resided in the Campo de Tarragona region for a time. Until 1914 the villages of L'Aleixar and Maspujols became the focus of the creations of this phase and of his output in general. An outstanding example is *Terraced Village*, one of the finest and most extraordinary of the artist's paintings, in which the chromatic explosion in a pure state is a vivid reflection of his inner experience.

The highly innovative way of interpreting the landscape in this painting is a consequence of the genius of an artist capable of concentrating, in a panoramic vision of nature, an extraordinary descriptive talent, an innate aptitude for capturing a dazzling atmosphere and an original way of applying the stains of colour, vibrant and daring, with harmonious chromatic gradations. In short, Mir's sensibility transformed a concrete place, the environs of Maspujols, into a series of fireworks that elicit profound new sensations. That is why Mir, leader of the second generation of *Modernista* painters and the most avant-garde of them all, is not only the most genial landscapist of his generation but probably the finest, too, in modern Catalan painting as a whole. M.D.

This painting reflects the strong artistic personality of Regoyos, who, after residing in Madrid, Brussels and the Basque Country, lived in Barcelona during the last few years of his life. The contact he had maintained with the Catalan milieu in 1898, on the occasion of the part publication of his book *La España negra* in the magazine *Luz*, had already made it clear that his artistic language went far beyond the Impressionist ideas of the first Catalan *Modernistas*. Regoyos's long career and particularly the fact of his having formed part in Brussels of the group of 'Les XX' and of 'La Libre Esthétique', as well as the relation he maintained with the French Impressionists Seurat and Pissarro, had shaped his highly personal style, close to the tendencies of Post-Impressionism.

Also known as *The Rainbow* and exhibited in Madrid in 1901 as *The Downpour. Santoña Bay*, this canvas, conceived on a grander scale and trimmed back by the artist himself due to an accident, is a magnificent example of Regoyos's creative labours. With his characteristic technique based on perfunctory, at times quasi-Pointillist brushstrokes and a certain ingenuity which reflects his ambition to present a new vision of the Spain of his day, Regoyos arrives at a luminous and vibrant scene which is framed between the emphatic shadow in the foreground and the rainbow that crowns the skyscape. M.D.

Joaquim Mir
(Barcelona, 1873-1940)
Terraced Village
Maspujols, *c.* 1909
MNAC/MAM 4633

Darío de Regoyos
(Ribadesella, 1857 – Barcelona, 1913)
The Downpour. Santoña Bay
1900
MNAC/MAM 65613

Following his apprenticeship in Barcelona, Anglada, the youngest painter of the second *Modernista* generation, moved to Paris, where he lived between 1894 and 1914 and where he painted, under the influence of Edgar Degas and Henri de Toulouse-Lautrec, evocative scenes of the city's nightlife with pronounced light effects. The rejection and indifference these canvases met with when he exhibited them in Barcelona in 1900 estranged him from the Catalan art scene, at precisely the same time that his brilliant international career took off. Around 1904 he incorporated Valencian folkloric subject matter, which enabled him to give priority to the handling of colour and to accent a brilliant and artificial decorativeness.

In 1914, the year he left Paris and settled for good in Majorca, he painted a series of female figures, silhouetted against an imprecise background and beneath an artificial light that helps emphasise their presence, in which the chromatism of their clothing becomes the true protagonist of the picture. In *Granada Woman* the artist places the entire range of colours on his palette, especially the louder and brasher ones, at the service of the shawl wrapped around the woman, which produces a highly impressive effect. Although this decorative excess was considered unnatural at the time, this work is one of those that best reflect the attractiveness of his exuberant artistic creation. M.D.

Permanent loan from the Diputación de Barcelona, 1991

Hermen Anglada Camarasa
(Barcelona, 1871 – Port de Pollença, 1959)

Granada Woman
c. 1914

MNAC/MAM 156066

Francesc Gimeno, one of the most singular and forceful artists of modern Catalan painting, is difficult to place for reasons having to do both with chronology and style. Born in the 1850s, a few years prior to the first *Modernistas*, he did not create his most significant, expressionistically inflected oeuvre until after the start of the twentieth century. As a result, and notwithstanding the difference in age mentioned above, it is advisable to relate him to the artists who make up the second *Modernista* generation, even though he never formed part of the artistic and gallery circles of his time.

Throughout his career Gimeno, who also excelled as a draughtsman, cultivated the genre of landscape and that of the portrait with equal fortune. As for the figure, Gimeno's marginality meant that he would often use both himself and his family as models. Outstanding in that sense are the series of self-portraits which span much of his career, and especially renowned are those he painted towards the end of his life, like this self-portrait of 1925, in which the pronounced modernity and expressionism of his language are made patent. C.M.

When settling definitively in Barcelona following a sojourn in Paris between 1897 and 1900, Nonell, in contrast to his previous activity, devoted himself more to painting than to drawing, in search of a style that might shape his own language. The ongoing attraction he felt for marginal and deracinated characters led him from 1901 onwards to paint his well-known series of gypsy women, in which the figure usually appears isolated, with an emphatically expressionist language.

Despite the violent reaction the public and the conservative critics displayed towards the artist's work on the occasion of the two quasi-one-man exhibitions held in the Sala Parés in Barcelona in 1902 and 1903, the artist did not waver, and he shut himself away in his studio to continue obsessively painting gypsy women with colour as a fundamental element of the work. In that respect *Two Gypsy Women*, which formed part of the 1903 show, is a prime example of the works of that moment in time, works in which there predominates a palette of tones darker than that employed in the paintings in the same series, but from the years immediately before, 1901 and 1902, in which blacks, olive greens, blues and earth colours predominate. Moreover, in this canvas, in which there are two profoundly dejected and mutually isolated figures, the painter's essential interest in volume and colour is made abundantly clear.

This oil formed part of the individual exhibition that Nonell held in Barcelona in 1910, a year before his premature death, an exhibition with which he finally obtained recognition. Up until then the restrained drama and overwhelming sordidness of Nonell's painting had upset and even offended the conventional tastes of the Barcelona bourgeoisie. C.M.

Francesc Gimeno
(Tortosa, 1858 –
Barcelona, 1927)
Self-portrait
Barcelona, *c.* 1925
MNAC/MAM 65626

Isidre Nonell
(Barcelona, 1872-1911)
Two Gypsy Women
Barcelona, 1903
MNAC/MAM 4650

This 1904 painting pertains to the moment in which the artist, totally rejected by conservative critics and public alike as a result of the two quasi-one-man shows he had in this city's Sala Parés in 1902 and 1903, continued painting works given over to depicting the marginal world of gypsy women, totally oblivious to the scorn his painting was subject to. Nonell must have painted the work we are commenting on in the studio he occupied around that same year, 1904—and which he retained until his premature death seven years later—where the canvases gradually piled up in the face of the impossibility of exhibiting them publicly, given that the Sala Parés, the only art gallery at that time in Barcelona, decided not hold another show of this artist due to the hostility with which he had been received. Despite the thematic continuity in relation to the works painted in previous years, from this moment onwards the figures, although retaining their sad expression, do not display the profound attitude of dejection which had been characteristic of his oeuvre. What is more, as the work under discussion demonstrates, the gypsy women of this moment, unlike those painted earlier, no longer hide their faces but rather expose them to view with the artist even depicting the facial features of the figure represented.

Forcefully demonstrated in paintings like this one, which is fairly typical of the works of that moment, is Nonell's talent and his absolute mastery of colour, which turns, in point of fact, into the authentic protagonist of the canvas. C.M.

The Degenerates, Carles Mani's best-known work, is one of the most singular in Catalan modern sculpture since it does not correspond to the aesthetic tenets adopted by his contemporaries but instead fits within an expressionism which had no influence whatsoever in the Catalan art of that period. This peculiarity is the outcome of a personal aesthetic search all but unknown in Catalan art and of the personality of an *artiste maudit* who never obtained in life the artistic triumph he craved and who after his death fell into oblivion, with, alas, the greater part of his output disappearing.

When Mani exhibited the monumental version of this group in the 1907 *V Exposición Internacional de Bellas Artes* in Barcelona under the title *Brutalisation* it caused great astonishment among the public and the critics, incapable of grasping its profound symbolism. The two colossal, almost roughed-in human figures of outlandish, simian mien, which represent the lowest instincts of human degeneration, led to a total rejection that caused the isolation of Mani from the Catalan artistic world. Only Gaudí understood its profound symbolism and converted Mani into one of his assistants on the Sagrada Familia, although Mani's creative side remained subordinate to that of the architect's genius. M.D.

Isidre Nonell
(Barcelona, 1872-1911)
Paloma
Barcelona, 1904
MNAC/MAM 65622

Carles Mani
(Tarragona, 1866 – Barcelona, 1911)
The Degenerates
Madrid/Barcelona, 1891-1904
MNAC/MAM 145141

Solana, considered one of the most notable artists of Spanish modern painting, was a man of complex personality, obsessed by death and destruction, creator of a highly personal world of enormous expressive richness, which is reflected in his painting and in his literary oeuvre. The publication of his book *La España negra* in 1921 revealed his totally Goyaesque critical vision of a country he considered sordid and grotesque. It comes as no surprise, then, that cemeteries, religious processions, bullfights, prostitutes, grotesque characters and his own collection of such diverse objects as masks, dummies, bones and skulls should become the reference material for his pictorial oeuvre.

The Chorus Girls, the definitive version of another picture Solana painted in 1915, shows the decrepitude and misery that appear in much of his visual work, handled with the sober and forceful artistic language the painter adopted for heightening a profound and grotesque expressionism. The motley scene, in which the colour black predominates along with a few elements of a garish bright red, describes the daily life of a number of decrepit women who form part of the personal universe of Solana, an extraordinary artist who painted the hidden face of reality with great lucidity. M.D.

Torres-García's leading role in *Noucentisme* was as both a theorist and a painter. As a theorist he defended the need to define a national art that would link up directly with Mediterranean Classicism whilst avoiding parochialism and North-European influences. As a painter he contributed decisively to determining the basic characteristics of *Noucentista* painting, incorporating in his pictorial work the monumental, decorative sensibility of French painter Puvis de Chavannes, who had introduced the Greco-Latin heritage into his own way of picture-making. Puvis's influence, however, gradually diminished to the profit of a more personal painting style.

Village Women, a work created prior to the mural paintings of the Hall of Sant Jordi in the Palau de la Generalitat, is a good example of the classicism Torres-García cultivated at the time and which agreed with the essential features of his thinking. Done in the manner of a mural painting, with synthetic forms, even brushstrokes, well-delineated outlines, light colours, a Mediterranean landscape as a background and an air of serenity and harmony, this canvas exemplifies the evocation of Arcadia. A few years later Torres-García abandoned the tenets of *Noucentisme* in favour of the avant-garde and became one of the leading figures of Constructivism. M.D.

José Gutiérrez Solana
(Madrid, 1866-1945)
The Chorus Girls
Madrid, *c.* 1925
MNAC/MAM 11071

Joaquín Torres-García
(Montevideo, 1875-1949)
Village Women
1911
MNAC/MAM 202509

This oil, probably the artist's most paradigmatic work, and an outstanding example of *Noucentista* painting, demonstrates that by 1917, the work's year of execution, Sunyer had reached the summit of his career and, therefore, the high point of his creative activity. Some eight years had gone by since the painter, installed in Sitges, had embarked on a new artistic path after having partaken of French Impressionist and Post-Impressionist painting. During this period he had indiscriminately cultivated the landscape and the figure, and in some of the more outstanding works of this phase he had brought together the two genres in the one canvas. All the same, it is in *Cala Forn* that he manages to distil all his accumulated pictorial wisdom in a perfect integration of the figures in the landscape. But, and herein lies the singular nature of the work, both the figures and the landscape do not merely reproduce the painter's everyday reality but turn instead into symbols of the Catalonia of the period. On top of that, and notwithstanding the indubitable realistic content of this piece, the artist symbolises infancy, the fertile years and maturity in it.

It is also worth pointing out that in this work, with its exceedingly fine layer of paint, Sunyer moves away from the Cézannean line he kept to in many canvases of that moment and adopts a more sober pictorial language which delimits contour more and also has recourse to a non-jerky brushwork. C.M.

After a long stay in Paris between 1896 and 1908, Joaquim Sunyer held an important one-man exhibition in Barcelona in 1911 that confirmed him as the leading painter of the movement known as *Noucentisme*. The year 1917, six years after said exhibition, marked a new landmark in Sunyer's artistic career, since during it he painted *Cala Forn* (see entry above) and this portrait, decisive works in his overall production and, in fact, in the history of Catalan modern art. With this oil Sunyer undoubtedly reached the high point of his artistic career and arrived at the culmination of his skill as a portraitist, a genre which, as with landscape, he would cultivate with equal success until the end of his life.

This work, and other portraits that he painted during this same era, are the culmination of the Cézanne-like language cultivated by Sunyer. With a few masterfully conjugated elements the artist invented a work of great expressive force and exquisite sensibility, in which the sitter, the daughter of the great *Modernista* sculptor Josep Llimona, is vigorously drawn, with her strong facial features. Likewise, another exceptional achievement of this portrait is the subtle handling of colour, which in the years immediately following this work would become the artist's main interest. C.M.

Joaquim Sunyer
(Sitges, 1874-1956)
Cala Forn
Sitges, 1917
MNAC/MAM 11004

Joaquim Sunyer
(Sitges, 1874-1956)
Portrait of Maria Llimona
Sitges, 1917
MNAC/MAM 3840

An influential figure in Catalan art of the 1920s and 30s due to his fecund influence as an historian, art critic and draughtsman, Feliu Elias, who signed his writings with the pseudonym of Joan Sacs and his drawings with that of Apa, was also an outstanding painter. Even though this creative facet was more uneven, a part of his oeuvre deserves the recognition it never received at the time due to its not fitting into the ruling classicism. The still lifes and the interiors, with characters depicted with the highly detailed realism of the Dutch Old Masters, link the pictorial work of this artist to the European tendencies of the time, particularly German *Neue Sachlichkeit.*

When Elias painted *The Gallery* he had already abandoned the 'Nonellian' technique of his early days, a technique consisting of applying tiny, methodical, intersecting brushstrokes, for one of a blended brushwork which enabled him to represent the pure matter of objects with great realism. The almost photographic nature of his pictures was not, however, understood by his contemporaries, who confused the modernity of his ideas with an academic perfectionism. Nevertheless *The Gallery*, one of its author's finest works, due to both its intimist feel and the magnificent iridescence of its colour, has become one of the most singular paintings of that period in Catalan art. M.D.

Considered one of the maximum representatives of *Noucentisme*, a movement which promulgated the return to Mediterranean classicism, Casanovas cultivated a sculpture of solid and serene forms that has connections with the search for beauty of the classical Greeks. Yet if in the 1910s his canon showed echoes of a certain Hellenic archaism, in the next decade it became freer, despite remaining faithful to the spirit of the classics. In that sense *Female Nude* may be considered the synthesis of the artist's period of maturity from both the formal and conceptual point of view.

Casanovas created this *Female Nude* in marble from an earlier work, *Naked Girl*, sculpted in stone in 1922, and, despite retaining very similar characteristics in both, introduced the modifications necessary to convert them into distinctive works. As regards *Female Nude*, the sculptor modelled a woman's torso with smooth, albeit tumescent, forms, a torso that beneath the semblance of ideal beauty exudes a sense of life that humanises the figure. All the same, in spite of eliminating any detail that might upset the harmony of the whole, Casanovas concentrated on the face the expression of deep humanity that transforms an inaccessible goddess into a true woman. In that sense it is worth remarking the importance of the almond-shaped eyes and the enigmatic smile, the identifying features of his artistic creation. M.D.

Feliu Elias
(Barcelona, 1878-1948)
The Gallery
Barcelona, 1928
MNAC/MAM 11022

Enric Casanovas
(Barcelona, 1882-1948)
Female Nude
Barcelona, *c.* 1924
MNAC/MAM 11007

Modelled immediately after *The Goddess* (MNAC/MAM 90087), Clarà's best-known sculpture, *Repose* is the definitive version of a figure dating from 1909 and responds to the artist's wish to reinterpret, in his period of maturity, works from his youthful phase, as he also did in the case of *The Goddess*, but with a very pronounced formal refinement and the intention of reducing the sculpture to the essential. Although Clarà lived after 1900 in Paris, a city where he had completed his training and undertaken much of his artistic career, it was in Barcelona, in the setting of the International Exhibition held in the city in 1929, that he reached the highest point of his professional trajectory.

Repose exemplifies the profoundly Mediterranean canon of ideal beauty adopted by Clarà between 1910 and 1930, when he concentrated almost exclusively on the depiction of goddess figures with potent and vigorous forms, which are treated as true architectonic structures. Constructed, refined and mature, his art had evolved in search of complex shapes by accentuating plastic values in preference to feelings. Despite this, Clarà always remained faithful to the serenity and harmony inherited from the classics, which had led to him becoming one of the indisputable leaders of *Noucentisme*. M.D.

The estrangement of Manolo Hugué from the bohemian life of Paris and the contract he signed with the dealer Daniel-Henri Kahnweiler brought about a radical change in his life and his artistic output after 1910. In Céret, where he found the stability and atmosphere conducive to creating an oeuvre marked by his extraordinary personality, he would realise a series of works carved in stone that reflect both his relation with the Cubists and a knowledge of some of the key pieces in the evolution of modern sculpture, in particular André Derain's *Stooping Woman* (1907), a work which in fact belonged to Kahnweiler at the time.

With *Toreador* Manolo adopts a subject that will become more or less habitual throughout his life, but instead of modelling the figure he fits it into a perfectly geometrical block of stone, in such a way that the volume remains delimited by the particular dimensions of the block, as if it were a capital. The unequal handling of the surface, with polished areas that contrast with others that still bear the marks of his tools, contributes to giving the work an archaic appearance. At the same time the pompons of the clothing, which enable us to identify the personage as a toreador, and the small, parallel grooves deployed over the entire piece, produce a decorative effect of great charm. M.D.

Josep Clarà
(Olot, 1878 – Barcelona, 1958)
Repose
Paris, 1929
MNAC/MAM 10534

Manolo Hugué
(Barcelona, 1872 –
Caldes de Montbui, 1945)
Toreador
Céret, 1913
MNAC/MAM 10219

In 1915 Santiago Segura, founder of the Galeries Laietanes, commissioned Xavier Nogués to do the mural decoration of the wine cellar, which was to become a meeting place for *Noucentista* artists and writers. These paintings, all of them on themes alluding to wine, were removed and broken up in the 1940s. The group the MNAC has, consisting of 38 fragments, includes the greater part of this mural decoration.

The popular and ironical aspect of the artistic trajectory of Nogués, which had abundantly shown itself in the drawings published between 1909 and 1911 in the weekly magazine *Papitu*, encountered on the walls of the Galeries Laietanes wine cellar the ideal setting for carrying out one of the most singular and attractive works in Catalan art. While the extant photographs enable us to appreciate the decorative nature of the series, built around fictitious architectural features that divide the space in an orderly manner, each of the fragments gives clear proof of the humorous tone of the charming figures of the inebriates. Nogués summed up human weaknesses, conferring an extraordinary expressive force on them with the colour blue, which, applied with coarse, loaded brushstrokes, produces a surprising effect. The men, amusing, grotesque, down-at-the-heel, with a glass or a musical instrument in the hand are, in short, the reflection of a cordial, amiable world in which there is no room for either criticism or meanness. M.D.

Without turning his back on the depiction of the human figure and utilising a theme typical of classical sculpture, Manolo Hugué moves in the direction of the more innovative languages of modern sculpture in this work, to the point where *Bacchante*, which belongs to his mature phase, can be considered not only one of the most relevant works in the production of this artist but also one of his finest contributions to the sculpture of his time.

Sculpted after his definitive return to Catalonia, the genesis of this work, a commissioned piece, is linked to a number of highly specific factors. In point of fact Manolo received an assignment from a publisher's to model a relief which was to be placed in the upper part of a display case. The artist adapted the figure to the actual architectural space and, in contrast to the way a bacchante is usually depicted, turned her with her back to the spectator. Likewise, he cut away the figure by getting rid of the background in order to give the impression that it was a free-standing sculpture. The original position of the figure, a female body with robust, rounded forms, its accentuated dynamism, and the rough handling of the surface all contribute to emphasising the extraordinary plastic values of this work. M.D.

Xavier Nogués

(Barcelona, 1873-1941)

Fragment of the set of wall paintings from the Galeries Laietanes wine cellar

Barcelona, 1915

MNAC/MAM 42411

Manolo Hugué

(Barcelona, 1872 – Caldes de Montbui, 1945)

Bacchante

Caldes de Montbui, 1934

MNAC/MAM 113762

Francesc Domingo, an artist linked to the second generation of *Noucentista* artists, formed part of the 'Courbet' group along with a number of companions who, like him, shared an admiration for Cézanne. Thought to be one of the most interesting artists of the time, his physical distance from the Catalan art world, firstly in Brittany, and after the Civil War in Argentina and Brazil, gave rise to a forgetting of sorts of his excellent artistic output. One of the most outstanding works of his early days was *The Players*, dated to his return from a sojourn in Paris and inspired by a number of card players who gathered in a café in Caldes de Montbui. Based on a few sketches and preparatory drawings, Domingo worked intermittently on the painting for a couple of years, making various changes and modifications. Presented in the 1920 *Exposición de Arte* in Barcelona, the work garnered highly favourable reviews.

In this oil Domingo introduced a new way of painting that was at that moment innovative vis-à-vis the *Noucentistas*, with intense colours and without tonal gradations, with perfunctory, incisive brushstrokes, a bright atmosphere that confers a feeling of placidity on the whole, and a unity of rhythm among all the features of the canvas. The painter offered a subjective, personal vision of a seemingly insignificant scene, full, for all that, of surprising touches, the fruit of his sensibility and his artistic gifts. M.D.

Around 1917 a generation of artists some ten or fifteen years younger than the first *Noucentistas*, among whom were Francesc Domingo, Joan Miró, Enric C. Ricart and Josep de Togores himself, presented themselves in public in Barcelona. These artists, who, although not sharing a common aesthetic, formed a number of groups or associations, concurred in rejecting Mediterraneanist *Noucentisme* and proclaimed their admiration for Paul Cézanne, a painter who had also influenced Joaquim Sunyer, leader of the *Noucentista* style of painting against which these young artists of the so-called 1917 Generation were theoretically rebelling. The majority cultivated a figurative art which, in some cases, temporarily approximated to certain avant-garde ideas.

Togores, one of this generation's most outstanding figures, began a long stay in Paris in 1919, a moment in which he combined his artistic praxis with art criticism for a time. Following a number of difficult years, in 1921 he signed an exclusive contract with the famous dealer Daniel-Henri Kahnweiler, a contract which would be prolonged, in fact, until 1931. The following year he held an important exhibition in the galleries of his dealer, in which he included paintings created since his arrival in Paris that even hinted at a move in the direction of German *Neue Sachlichkeit*, and others done in 1921 and 1922 such as *Catalan Girls*, which at the same time reflected a return to Mediterranean classicism, a fruit of his relationship with the sculptor Aristide Maillol. C.M.

Francesc Domingo
(Barcelona, 1893 – Sao Paulo, 1974)
The Players
Barcelona, 1920
MNAC/MAM 4319

Josep de Togores
(Cerdanyola del Vallès, 1893 – Barcelona, 1970)
Catalan Girls
Banyuls-sur-Mer, 1921
MNAC/MAM 4666

In 1925 Dalí, then a young painter of 21, held his first one-man exhibition in the Galeries Dalmau in Barcelona, a springboard for the most advanced experiments of the day. This was the first chance Dalí had had to present an important group of his works. In actual fact he assembled 22 oils and drawings dating from before his first trip to Paris; before, then, he would show a preference for Surrealism. The works exhibited corresponded to the different languages the artist was experimenting with at the time, languages influenced by the Cubists, the Italian Metaphysical painters and the return-to-order tendency promoted by certain French artists, which in Catalonia, under the name of *Noucentisme*, would have a set of features of its own. One of the show's most outstanding paintings was this portrait of Dalí's father, considered one of the finest of his juvenile phase.

Dalí concentrated on the severe expression of the face and especially on the incisive and penetrating gaze, the strong personality of his father, a notary in Figueres with whom he maintained a somewhat difficult relationship that would end, a few years later, in a total break. The technical mastery the young painter had attained by this time can be seen in the sharply drawn outlines, the expressive power of the sober tones and the handling of light and shade, all of which give volume to the figure. The picture's modern spirit, at one with certain *Noucentista* theories, make it a major work of Catalan art, one in which we divine the talent of an artist who would become, with time, a consummate twentieth-century figure. M.D.

Within the sculptural output of Rebull, an artist who belongs to the second generation of *Noucentistas* and, more specifically, to the evolutionist group, *Gypsy Girl* is one of the works most representative of his youthful phase, an era in which he arrived at a highly personal language characterised by a realism of pure, synthetic forms with reminiscences of Antiquity, especially Egyptian and Mesopotamian sculpture. The Spanish Civil War and his subsequent exile gave way to the stage of artistic maturity in which Rebull would dispense with the archaism which had marked his former output.

Considered one of the most interesting Catalan sculptors of his day, Rebull was extremely prolific during the 1930s, when he modelled a series of heads and busts of great visual beauty, among which this bust of a young gypsy girl stands out. From the formal point of view, it is worth underlining the hieratic attitude of the figure, which is not devoid of human warmth, the well-rounded anatomy, the sharpness of the carving with some surfaces completely smooth, and the polychromy of the eyes, the latter being habitual in many Rebull works of this period. These special features are the outcome, however, of a process of synthesis that foregrounds the artist's ambition to successfully express an immutable ideal of beauty. M.D.

Salvador Dalí
(Figueres, 1904-89)
Portrait of Salvador Dalí i Cusí, the Artist's Father
1925
MNAC/MAM 68839

Joan Rebull
(Reus, 1899 – Barcelona, 1981)
Gypsy Girl
Barcelona, 1933
MNAC/MAM 45780

Like other artists of his generation (Jaume Mercadé and Emili Armengol, for instance), Manuel Capdevila's production is centred on two disciplines: silversmithing and painting. In the first of these he may be considered one of the jewellery makers who managed to bring an avant-garde spirit to his profession.

This series of brooches, which from a formal point of view are at one with the line defended by the group of artists known as ADLAN ('Amics de l'Art Nou'), was created in Paris in 1937 while the young artist was working in the Atelier Lacambra. In his Rue Raspail workshop Capdevila designed his own pieces of jewellery, pieces committed to a new aesthetic and an innovative set of ideas.

As far as technique and materials go, Capdevila mainly used silver, eggshell and Japanese lacquer, and he sought the assistance of the lacquerer Ramon Sarsanedas, who had learnt this artistic skill in the Polythecnicum school with Lluís Bracons, the introducer of Japanese *urushi* in Barcelona. These pieces, which are based on the juxtaposition of abstract, geometric shapes and contrasting colours, were exhibited in the 1937 *Salon d'Automne* in Paris and constitute one of the most advanced manifestations of Catalan jewellery in the international context. From an iconographical standpoint the series echoes the tragic experience of the Spanish Civil War. A good example of this is the brooch entitled *La España replegada*. M.F.

The irruption of avant-garde tendencies in Catalonia had repercussions in the world of design and of interior decoration, as can be seen in the sets of furniture designed by Josep Lluís Sert for the Roca jewellery shop, of which the Museum preserves a display case (MNAC 208630) and this armchair.

Sert, one of the most radical and loyal exponents of the group of rationalist architects known as the GATCPAC ('Grup d'Arquitectes i Tècnics Catalans per al Progrés de l'Arquitectura Contemporània'), took charge in 1933 of the planning of the shop that the jeweller Rogeli Roca had recently rented in the Paseo de Gràcia in Barcelona. Sert himself fitted out the establishment, calling on a wide range of components designed for the occasion.

This armchair consists of a framework of varnished wood coloured black and, notwithstanding its purist simplicity, in consonance with the tenets of rationalism, it evinces an image of modern refinement, comfort and luxury, with certain art deco touches, characteristic of an establishment whose goal was to sell pieces of high-class *joaillerie*. In this instance Sert leaves behind the typically late-1920s coldness of chromium plating and steel tubing as the furniture's constructional basis and gives the maximum emphasis to wood. Josep Lluís Sert entrusted the building of the furniture for the Roca jewellery shop to the cabinetmaking workshops of Josep Ribas's widow, which realised many of the designs of the GATCPAC architects' group during the 1930s. M.F.

Permanent loan from Joieria Roca, 2003

Manuel Capdevila
(Barcelona, 1910-2006) and

Ramon Sarsanedas
(Barcelona, 1896-1987)

Set of brooches
Paris, 1937
MNAC 200453-200459

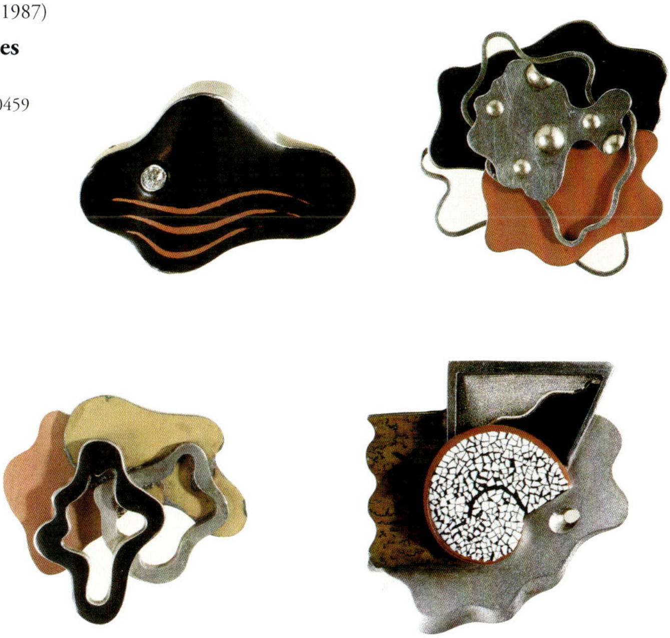

Josep Lluís Sert
(Barcelona, 1902-83)

Armchair from the Roca jewellery shop
Barcelona, 1934
MNAC 208125

Gargallo's evolution in terms of experimenting with new materials and new techniques appropriate to these materials led him to use first copper and then iron sheeting. If in the first works elaborated with these metals he employed extremely fine sheets which limited the size of the sculptures, later on he regularly used metal of greater thickness in order to arrive at plastic effects more suited to his expressive needs.

Around 1930 Gargallo, who had gradually acquired a greater mastery of technique, began to work with iron sheeting of considerable thickness, which enabled him to simplify both the more complex technical aspects of his works and to eliminate those elements which were not strictly necessary. In that respect *Grand Bacchante*, undoubtedly one of the artist's finest sculptures, represents a radical change in his production since it displays the formal purification that enabled him to simplify the creative process by utilising a smaller number of pieces, some of which are limited to insinuating a part of the female body. In this way the mature works of Gargallo, the fruits of constant research, contributed to defining the language of sculpture in iron, increased in intensity and, in short, arrived at the synthesis of his art. M.D.

Considered one of the most eminent proponents of Catalan sculpture, notwithstanding his Aragonese origin, Gargallo began as a sculptor at the height of *Modernisme* and later showed a preference for a classic language that alternated with his avant-garde ideas. In that sense his contribution to the renovation of European sculpture was fundamental as a pioneer in experimenting with new materials—lead, copper and iron—and in the utilisation of empty space as an element of volume. Installed in Paris in 1924, Gargallo experimented with a highly personal language that would in fact culminate in *Grand Ballerina*, of which he would make three versions.

Technically speaking, *Grand Ballerina*, a consummate piece from the MNAC's modern sculpture collections, is from the technical viewpoint an illuminating display of the work Gargallo accomplished with pieces of iron sheeting, cut out according to cardboard templates and subsequently welded to form a sculpture. At the same time, however, this work enables us to evaluate the consolidation of a language that, although it is still party to premises typical of traditional sculpture, has totally original features and incorporates a number of solutions proceeding from Cubism. Gargallo first exhibited *Grand Ballerina* in the Invited Artists' Pavilion of the 1929 International Exhibition in Barcelona, where it stood out for its absolute modernity, in contrast to the official art prevailing at the time in Catalonia. M.D.

Pablo Gargallo
(Maella, 1881 – Reus, 1934)
Grand Bacchante
Paris, 1931
MNAC/MAM 11653

Pablo Gargallo
(Maella, 1881 – Reus, 1934)
Grand Ballerina
Paris, 1929
MNAC/MAM 108413

A consummate figure of the European avant-garde, Julio González created a new sculptural language of his own, the fruit of his formal experimentation with iron. While influenced by Cubism and Surrealism and having the support of his friends Pablo Picasso and Pablo Gargallo, it was mainly through his own constant and single-minded labours that he created a solid oeuvre, essaying a variety of paths. Thus, in the 1930s he adopted a filiform language based on using iron wire, which enabled him to draw in space, while at the same time shaping sheets of iron to represent fragments of the human body that can be related to *Montserrat* (*c.* 1936-7), a magisterial work with which he culminated his personal research embracing tradition and innovation.

Female Bust depicts the front part of a headless, armless woman's body, in which volume is magisterially suggested despite the bust being empty behind. With an evident formal economy, yet with great creative richness, González not only managed to extract unsuspected expressive possibilities from a simple sheet of iron, but was capable of attaining a synthesis between matter and space. Starting out from a concrete formal element, on this occasion a human silhouette—a female bust—the artist transformed observed reality, yet was uninterested in creating a mere description of this reality, giving priority, instead, to the representation of the idea. M.D.

The participation of Julio González in the Spanish Pavilion of the Paris Universal Exhibition of 1937 with a work of such an emblematic character as *Montserrat* (Stedelijk Museum, Amsterdam), symbol of Catalonia's resistance to the Spanish Civil War, led the artist, in the middle of the Second World War, to a new conception of this female figure, who appears shouting in order to manifest her horror at the barbarism of war and her denunciation of repression. González died before finishing this opus, but the expression of this head displays his ability to reflect feelings that transcend the work's formal treatment.

In order to create this sculpture González did not use iron sheeting but elected instead to model it in plaster, possibly because he considered that a figurative work was more suitable to the expressionist character he wished to give to the figure of the Catalan woman. The small-sized model of *Montserrat Shouting* permits him to take the plastic, expressive values of the sculpture as a whole into account, but the fragments he made before his death, the two hands and particularly the *Head of Montserrat Shouting*, bespeak González's talent for representing his own cry against the injustice of war in a symbolic image. M.D.

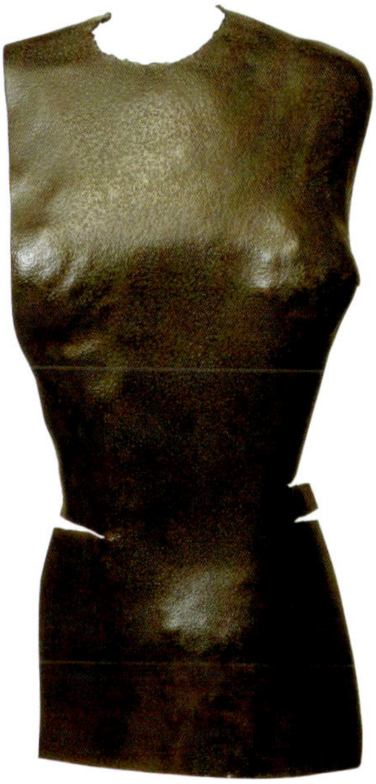

Julio González
(Barcelona, 1876 – Arcueil, 1942)
Female Bust
Paris, 1935-6
MNAC/MAM 200315

Julio González
(Barcelona, 1876 – Arcueil, 1942)
Head of Montserrat Shouting
Arcueil, *c.* 1942
MNAC/MAM 113413

Julio González was the youngest member of a family that had long since run a workshop—La Metalistería Artística, in Barcelona's Rambla de Catalunya—devoted to silversmithing and metalworking, above all in iron. In his case labouring in the workshop of his father, Concordi González, took the place of a formal education in an art school, and there he had been trained as a silversmith, an activity he complemented with the practice of painting and above all of sculpture, all of which makes it difficult to distinguish the artist from the artisan.

Instead of fitting in with the curvilinear, floral style of *Modernisme*, his jewellery, as this necklace shows, is made from sheet iron. The artist plays with the contrasts of light and shade, while seeking new chromatic effects and textures.

In 1913 Julio González opened a shop specialising in jewellery and objets d'art in Paris that sold objects and pieces of jewellery created by him, and during the same period he exhibited with a certain regularity in the *Salons d'Automne* and the *Salons des Indépendants* held in the French capital. M.F.

An artist belonging to the Catalan avant-garde of the 1930s, Cristòfol created abstract images based on organic forms or the transformation of common everyday objects into poetic objects via a spontaneous, intuitive process which has been related to the playful and oneiric objects of the Surrealists. At the start of his artistic career he participated in the exhibition of the 'Logicofobistas', one of the most resounding in Barcelona in the years prior to the Spanish Civil War. Indeed, the rupture the war presupposed in the continuity of the avant-garde movements in our country did not stop Cristòfol from following the path he had embarked upon, albeit in isolation from the more important artistic centres of the day.

In *Moonlit Night* Cristòfol came up with a genuine aesthetic creation when confronting two functional objects linked to his everyday surroundings, objects which he emptied of their original meaning in order to insert them into an abstract structure in which an allegorical or symbolic meaning is hinted at. Cristòfol's strong sculptural personality becomes evident in this work, the outcome of his ability to successfully express his inner reality in an intuitive manner and with great formal simplicity, and with a lyricism and profundity that make this opus the one that best expresses the poetic intensity of the artist. M.D.

Julio González
(Barcelona, 1876 – Arcueil, 1942)
Necklace
c. 1916-25
MNAC/MAM 113587

Leandre Cristòfol
(Os de Balaguer, 1908 – Lleida, 1998)
Moonlit Night
Lleida, 1935
MNAC/MAM 200034

The Carmen Thyssen-Bornemisza Collection

This gallery contains about twenty paintings from the collection of Catalan art belonging to Carmen Thyssen-Bornemisza and consisting of more than 350 works. In view of the wealth and heterogeneity of this collection, the works ceded to the MNAC give priority to diversity rather than to unity of discourse, with the object of giving an idea, even though it may have the conciseness of a telegram, of the plurality of this collection.

The chronological period covered by this section responds to the chapters in the history of Catalan painting from the mid-nineteenth century to the mid-twentieth century, one of the most brilliant moments in Catalan art. The nineteenth century is amply represented in the Carmen Thyssen-Bornemisza Collection and particularly stands out for the presence of Fortuny, the most important artist in Spanish nineteenth-century painting after Goya, whose influence can be clearly seen in *Bullfight. Wounded Picador*, painted in about 1867 on the occasion of Fortuny's stay in Madrid. As regards the *Modernista* movement, of which there are also leading works in the Carmen Thyssen-Bornemisza Collection, there is a particularly outstanding selection of important artists from this period such as Casas, with his *Open-Air Interior*—dated Barcelona 1892, just after his fertile stay in Paris—Anglada Camarasa, with *Le Paon blanc*—a paradigmatic painting from his Paris period—and Mir, with two paintings from two significant moments in his career, *The Cathedral of the Poor*—with the Sagrada Familia under construction in the background—which the artist painted in 1898, and *The Abyss. Majorca*, which Mir did during his prolific stay in Majorca. Equally noteworthy is the presence of *Noucentisme*, a movement deeply rooted in Catalonia, with paintings by its leading artists, amongst them Torres-García and Sunyer. Sunyer stands out for his *Mediterranean*, a programmatic work of *Noucentista* painting, and there is also a representation of younger artists than the early *Noucentistas*, who extended the *Noucentista* spirit. A brilliant colophon to this suggestive tour of the history of modern Catalan painting lies in the presence of the indisputable Antoni Tàpies.

Fortuny painted this picture during a stay in Madrid in which he produced magnificent, mostly small-format oils and watercolours on the subject of bullfights. *Bullfight. Wounded Picador*, however, is of quite considerable dimensions, although the format was subsequently altered when the left side of the canvas was cropped. The original dimensions of the picture are the ones that figure in the catalogue for the sale of Fortuny's studio in Paris in 1875, after which it became part of a series of collections until 1995, when it was purchased by Baroness Thyssen-Bornemisza.

Bullfight. Wounded Picador is based on two watercolours representing, respectively, the *picador* on horseback at the moment he sticks the lance into the bull, and the assistants removing a wounded *picador* from the ring. Fortuny merged these two scenes from the *tercio de varas* into one, creating a new composition that preserved the same sketchy nature as the watercolours. As regards the palette used by the artist, it shows a surprising contrast in the reds and yellows on the clothing of some of the figures, and very especially the yellow, pink and blue of the capes, with multiple black brushstrokes applied on a background which is also black, but more dilute, with which he represents the spectators. This way of conceiving the public, with its obvious reminiscences of Goya, and the colourful approach to the spectacle make this canvas one of Fortuny's most interesting on this subject matter. M.D.

This painting, done immediately after the artist ended his first stay in Paris, which was to be crucial to his career, is one of the most important examples of Casas's production in particular and of *Modernista* painting in general. The painter set the scene, which was to become a paradigmatic image of the newly emerging Catalan bourgeoisie to which he himself belonged, at the back of the family home in Carrer Nou de Sant Francesc, in Barcelona's old quarter, with his sister and brother-in-law as the chief characters.

After taking part in the *Exposición Nacional de Bellas Artes* in Madrid in 1892, the work was included in the third and last exhibition that Casas, along with Santiago Rusiñol and the sculptor Clarasó, held at the Sala Parés in Barcelona. These exhibitions, with the works painted in Paris by the two artists at the beginning of the 1890s, shook the city's art scene. *Open-Air Interior* stands out for its successful composition and for the exceptional way the light is handled. The chromatic ranges, which at the time were compared with Whistler's, were skilfully harmonised under the reflection of the light shining at the back of the patio subtly contrasting with the figures depicted in the gentle shade of the foreground. C.M.

Mariano Fortuny
(Reus, 1838 – Rome, 1874)
Bullfight. Wounded Picador
Madrid, 1867-8
MNAC 212856

Ramon Casas
(Barcelona, 1866-1932)
Open-Air Interior
Barcelona, 1892
MNAC 212857

This work dates from the painter's youth, when he was a member of the group known as 'La Colla del Safrà' [The Saffron Group] on account of the yellow tones with which they painted the Barcelona suburbs. First exhibited at the International Exhibition held in Barcelona in 1898 and later at the famous Els Quatre Gats, *The Cathedral of the Poor* shows a group of beggars outside the church of the Sagrada Familia under construction. In this way, to the interest of the painting on account of its unquestionable artistic value is added the iconographic value of representing one of the most emblematic works of modern Catalan architecture a few years after the start of construction.

Mir painted this canvas on the site of the actual church, which makes this a *plein-air* work, and structured the scene in two clearly differentiated parts—the building in the background and the human figure in the foregroun—thereby achieving a perfect fusion of the two. The effect of the sunlight on the walls of the church helps to pick out the presence of the beggars, sitting in the shade, and shows up a certain symbolic significance in the placing of characters who survive on charity next to a church built solely on charitable contributions by the faithful. Although at the time the critics stressed these merits in this oil, they were nevertheless unable to appreciate it as one of the masterpieces of Catalan art. M.D.

Estranged from the Catalan artistic panorama since 1900 following the limited success of his exhibition in Barcelona of the latest works he had painted in Paris, Anglada began a brilliant career in the most cosmopolitan European circles and became the Catalan painter most highly valued in Europe in the years leading up to the First World War. His suggestive paintings of elegant women from Paris night-life were purchased by some of the leading European collectors after being exhibited in Paris, Venice, London, Brussels, Vienna or Berlin. Berlin, in fact, was where he first exhibited *Le Paon blanc*, one of the most outstanding works in his production.

The central character in *Le Paon blanc* became the prototype of sophisticated womanhood, with extremely white skin, portrayed by Anglada in so many of his canvases. The urban landscape in which elegant women stroll, with their large hats, is a habitual backdrop in the paintings on Paris themes. But above all this canvas stands out for its chromatic richness and for the magnificent effect of the light on the figure, which it wraps in a golden tone. Finally, it needs to be mentioned that this is not a Symbolist work, as the title might mistakenly suggest, so much as an exceptional example of Anglada Camarasa's brilliantly decorative language. M.D.

Joaquim Mir
(Barcelona, 1873-1940)
The Cathedral of the Poor
Barcelona, 1898
MNAC 212858

Hermen Anglada Camarasa
(Barcelona, 1871 – Port de Pollença, 1959)
Le Paon blanc
1904
MNAC 212859

After a long stay in Paris from 1896 to 1908, Sunyer returned to his country, where he started out on a new path that marked the end of the previous period and at the same time formed the solid basis for his most genuine artistic language. The new paintings, along with some done in Paris, made up the important individual exhibition held in Barcelona in 1911, which made this artist the leader of *Noucentista* painting. In this respect, the fact that *Mediterranean* includes a series of prototypical elements from *Noucentista* painting, such as the sea, the lateen-rigged sailing boat, the swallows, the hills and the vegetation characteristic of the area, have turned this work into an essential iconographic reference in the definition of *Noucentista* painting and the artist, as a result, into the maximum exponent of this movement. In this work, which portrays an idealised reality with reminiscences of Arcadia, Sunyer managed to capture a synthesis of values closely tied to nature. Unlike the Paris paintings, in which the artistic elements were the work's main purpose, in *Mediterranean* he conveys a message that goes beyond the work's formal and aesthetic value. The naked figures, with their obvious ritual charge, perfectly integrated into the landscape, are the protagonists around which Sunyer renders the *Noucentista* programmatic repertory. C.M.

In 1934, Torres-García, who had become an important painter and a leading art theoretician of Catalan *Noucentisme*, settled in his native Montevideo with the intention of spreading the principles of modern art in Uruguay. One year later he founded the 'Asociación de Arte Constructivo' and published the association's magazine *Círculo y Cuadrado*. A few years earlier, Torres-García, while living and working in Paris, had taken part in the formation of an international group of artists, 'Cercle et Carrée', and formed part of the group 'Abstraction-Création', where he developed a constructivist language that was to characterise him from then on, based on the combination of geometric forms with allusions to visual reality.

In this work, Torres-García draws an orthogonal grid of horizontal and vertical rectangles based on the rule of the golden mean. He inscribed each rectangle with a graphic symbol based on the schematic form of objects like pictograms: a heart, a key, a clock, a fish, etc. The inscription at the top right, written in the personal alphabet Torres-García invented in 1935, refers to the 'Asociación de Arte Constructivo'. M.F.

Joaquim Sunyer
(Sitges, 1874-1956)
Mediterranean
Sitges, 1910-11
MNAC 212860

Joaquín Torres-García
(Montevideo, 1874-1949)
Constructive Composition
1936
MNAC 212861

This work represents Antoni Tàpies's own personal choice of Informalism. Here the artist has abandoned the figuration inscribed in the magic realism with Surrealist roots of the earlier years, linked to the 'Dau al Set' group, of which he was a founder member, and settled for matter painting. It was this type of painting at the end of the 1950s and the beginning of the 1960s that catapulted him to the top ranks of the international avant-garde. In this painting, built up from conglomerates of sands, resins and oils, the material is piled on unevenly to produce a surface in relief, a crust on which the artist draws with indecipherable incisions and which becomes a wall-object.

Tàpies uses an austere colour range, more in tune with the inner world and closely related to the Franciscan world and to the colour of excrement.

Over and above the physical attributes associated with Tàpies's art at that time (matter, texture and mural qualities) and the return to the purest and most primitive aspects of painting, there is also a rediscovery of the tradition of mysticism and of medieval alchemy, of the transmutation of materials and, at the same time, the reflection of concerns of a spiritual sort parallel to the philosophies of the Far East.
M.F.

Antoni Tàpies
(Barcelona, 1923)
Blackish Brown
1958
MNAC 212862

Drawings, prints & posters

The collection of the Cabinet of Drawings and Prints

Despite the fact that some artists are either entirely absent or scarcely represented, the Cabinet of Drawings and Prints (GDG) collections include a rich, wide-ranging selection of the most important trends and movements in Catalan art. Nonetheless, the Catalan presence does not come to the forefront until the latter part of the eighteenth century, coinciding with the foundation in Barcelona (1775) of the Escola Gratuïta de Disseny i Nobles Arts, which would become a point of reference as the consolidation of Academicism took place in Catalonia during the nineteenth century. From this period, the collections contain a substantial number of works by artists linked to the Llotja school, notably Flaugier, Rodés, Lorenzale, Martí Alsina, and by members of some of the artistic dynasties that, as the Planellas and the Rigalts, played a leading role in this artistic period from Neoclassicism to Realism. From the previous era we cannot overlook the contribution of the most remarkable Catalan Baroque painter, Antoni Viladomat, whose work is amply represented in the GDG. Recently, the collection of Catalan Baroque art was augmented by the acquisition in 2003 of a set of altar designs from the César Martinell Collection. This is a unique collection that, given its documentary importance, provides a more informed approach to the study of Catalan altarpieces of the seventeenth and eighteenth centuries.

One of the chief identifying signs of the GDG collection is undoubtedly its major collection of the work of Fortuny, of whom the MNAC keeps over 1,000 drawings and 50 prints, an inevitable point of reference for anyone wishing to retrace the creative itinerary of this brilliant nineteenth-century artist. From this same period we have a set of more than 30 drawings by the history painter Eduardo Rosales, acquired from his sister Carlota in 1912, which are linked to the *Testament of Isabella the Catholic* and the *Death of Lucretia*, two of the artist's most paradigmatic historical compositions.

The Cabinet's collections are also nourished by a substantial number of works belonging to *Modernisme* and *Noucentisme*, particularly those by Ramon Casas, one of the former movement's most illustrious representatives. Outstanding among Casas's works is the famous series of 'Charcoal Portraits', a genuine iconographical gallery donated by the artist himself in 1909. Equally important is the collection of posters from this same period, many of which were acquired from Lluís Plandiura in 1903. The six hundred posters, including a substantial number by artists from abroad, constitute both a legacy of incalculable heritage value and an incomparable record of poster production in Catalonia.

Finally, we must refer to the avant-garde movements. Sculptor Julio González is one of the artists best represented, thanks to the generous donation made in 1974 by his daughter Roberta of some two hundred drawings. On the other hand, the presence of other great creators of contemporary art like Dalí or Miró is nothing more than a small but historically important sample.

The formation process of the GDG collections was marked by two crucial acquisitions by the Board of Museums: in 1911 this institution purchased the collection of literary and art critic Raimon Casellas, and ten years later the collection that the *Modernista* artist Alexandre de Riquer had gradually accrued over the years. Despite the unquestionable value of the latter, the purchase of the Casellas Collection marked a quantitative and qualitative change in the history of a collection that had hitherto been built up on the basis of sporadic partial contributions from private collectors.

Given the specific characteristics of works on paper, the pieces are exhibited in galleries that meet the necessary environmental conditions. Nevertheless, due to their fragility these works cannot be placed permanently on show. Consequently each medium follows a stringent order of rotation to ensure that they are preserved in the best possible conditions. Therefore some of the works in this guidebook differ from those on display. Even so, the museological discourse is not altered at all.

An architect and sculptor active fundamentally in Burgos and Granada, Diego de Siloé was one of the major representatives of Spanish Renaissance architecture during the first half of the sixteenth century and responsible for some of the most important artistic interventions of the period, notably his work on Burgos Cathedral and the Capilla Real in Granada, around 1526.

Although this is a purely imaginary architectural design that draws on a set of fanciful typologies, the work nonetheless reveals the artist's knowledge of the classical language, from which he obtained much of the inspiration for his figurative elements. On the other hand, Siloé here displays his mastery of monofocal perspective, which takes the form of a convincing spatial construction that creates the optical illusion of three-dimensionality. Some of the above aspects reflect Siloé's familiarity with Italian innovations, with which he would probably have come into contact during his brief working sojourn in Naples in around 1517.

Some authors have put forward the plausible hypothesis that this composition is a clear example of Siloé's activity as a set designer, although it might also be an ephemeral, decorative work for some kind of festive celebration. Whatever the case, we have only to congratulate ourselves on the fact that the MNAC's Cabinet of Drawings and Prints preserves a work of such importance and historical significance, the only example of its kind that has come down to us. F.Q.C.

The figure of Alonso Cano occupies a prominent position in the seventeenth-century Spanish art world. He was one of the most conspicuous representatives of the Spanish Baroque and, thanks to his versatility, cultivated the different artistic disciplines—mainly painting and sculptureæ with equal success.

The nature of this drawing, featuring the image of a saint with highly specific iconographical attributes standing on a prismatic base, suggests that it may be a sculptural design, perhaps a study for an element destined for a no-longer surviving altarpiece, or a simple *divertimento* entirely independent from any particular commission.

On the other hand, and far from rejecting the opinion of other authorities in the field, the fact that this drawing has been attributed to Alonso Cano, given its undeniable quality, would seem to be plausible if we compare its stylistic traits to other works definitely known to be by the artist. From the formal point of view, there are clear affinities between this drawing and other works from Cano's sojourn in Madrid, before he moved to Granada, appreciable specifically in the way he models the bodies of the figures and in the use of a particular typology in the treatment of the hands. Furthermore, the architectural construction in the middle distance bears a close resemblance to the one in a drawing of St Joachim preserved in the Museo de la Real Academia de San Fernando, Madrid. F.Q.C.

Diego de Siloé
(Burgos, *c.* 1490 – Granada, 1563)
Scenographic Perspective
Second third of the sixteenth century
MNAC/GDG 107786 D

Alonso Cano
(Granada, 1601-67)
Saint Anthony the Abbot
c. 1645
MNAC/GDG 27205 D

The publication in Barcelona of the first edition (1764) of the *Máscara Real* [Royal Masquerade], a work produced at the workshops of Royal printer Tomàs Piferrer, marked one of the most important episodes in the history of eighteenth-century Catalan engraving and constituted a unique contribution to the world of the illustrated book of the time, since no work of these characteristics had hitherto emerged. The work commemorates the festive masquerade consisting of floats and cavalcades, mythological in theme, with which the city authorities, mainly the professional associations and guilds, sought to celebrate on two consecutive nights the proclamation of Carlos III as the new sovereign and his entry into the city of Barcelona in 1759, accompanied by his wife, María Amalia of Saxony, and the entire royal family.

The twelve prints depicting the different *tableaux* that took part in the allegorical feast were engraved by the Frenchman A.J. Defehrt after the preparatory sketches by Francesc Tramulles, now preserved at the Museu d'Història de la Ciutat de Barcelona. The remaining images, also drawn by Tramulles and constituting the initial letters of the captions, as well as the chapter headings and the tailpieces, were engraved by the Valencian Pasqual Pere Moles, the first director of the Llotja school and one of the most highly reputed Catalan engravers of the seventeen hundreds. F.Q.C.

Although Ametller worked for most of his career in Madrid, he was member of the major group of engravers who trained at the Llotja school at the end of the eighteenth century. And despite the fact that he is known above all for his teaching activities at the Real Academia de Bellas Artes de San Fernando, an institution at which in 1821 he occupied the prestigious post of head of engraving, we cannot overlook his major contribution, exemplified by prints such as this one, to the qualitative enrichment of Catalan engraving of the period.

The theme of ostrich hunting was one of the most popular motifs among engravers from foregoing periods. Indeed, it became a commonplace in the figurative repertoire of the engravers of the sixteenth and seventeenth centuries, notably Antonio Tempesta and Philippe Galle. In the eighteenth century hunting themes were popularised by Carle Vanloo, who was responsible in 1738 for a canvas that formed part of the decor Louis XV commissioned for the palace of Versailles, a decor based on the theme of exotic hunting. Indeed, Ametller's engraving, after a drawing executed by Pasqual Pere Moles during the latter's formative years in Paris between 1768 and 1774, reproduces Vanloo's painting. Consequently, the inscription that the engraver placed at the foot of the print, which attributed it to François Boucher, is mistaken. In 1803 the Real Calcografía in Madrid commissioned Ametller to complete the engraving. F.Q.C.

Pasqual Pere Moles

(Valencia, 1741 – Barcelona, 1797)

Drawing by Francesc Tramulles

Chapter heading and initial letter A. Allegory of History and of Representation, accompanied by the personifications of Love and Zeal

Barcelona, 1764

MNAC/GDG 3763 G

Blai Ametller

(Barcelona, 1771 – Madrid, 1841)

Hunting the Ostrich

Madrid, 1803

MNAC/GDG 2803 G

Vicente López occupies a prominent position in Spanish painting of the first half of the nineteenth century, of which he is one of the foremost representatives.

This work forms part of the set of studies and preparatory drawings for López's history painting *Cyrus the Great Before the Bodies of Abradatus and Panthea*, commissioned by Ferdinand VII, whose Chamber painter never managed to finish. For this scene, known through the modellino preserved in the Museo del Prado and a canvas at the Museo de Bellas Artes de Bilbao, López drew on the iconographical source of historian Xenophon's *Cyropaedia*, a literary text conceived to extol the figure of Cyrus the Great.

The female figure at the MNAC forms part of the group of women mourners who give vent to their grief beside the dead bodies of the two protagonists. The artist's intention here was clearly to emphasise pathos and rhetorical gesture as two traditional components of history painting. The same female model was exploited for the execution of further studies, of which a pencil drawing at the Biblioteca Nacional de Madrid presents the greatest number of stylistic and compositional affinities with this pastel. Furthermore, in this case we cannot overlook the moral and propagandistic implications of a theme destined to occupy one of the halls of what was then the Museo Real. F.Q.C.

Permanent loan from the Reial Acadèmia Catalana de Belles Arts de Sant Jordi de Barcelona, 1902; admission, 1906

Although Fortuny executed this work while still a scholarship holder, the watercolour *Il Contino*, painted after his first trip to Morocco, is one of the most virtuosic and emblematic creations of the artist's first period in Rome, the city to which he had moved in 1858 having secured a scholarship to further his studies from Barcelona Provincial Council. The work reflects one of the artist's first inroads into genre painting and includes, with the motif of the fountain standing in the middle distance of the composition and located in the Villa Borghese gardens, a reference to classical culture that nurtured Fortuny during this formative period.

The sitter poses with an air of distant, affected elegance, his haughty posture emphasising pride in his lineage, highlighted by his eighteenth-century attire—the traditional three-piece suit consisting of frock coat, waistcoat and blouse—complemented by the regulation ceremonial sword and powdered wig.

Fortuny's unchallenged technical skills may be appreciated in the subtlety with which he creates the effect of crystalline transparency of the water that spouts from one of the fountain masks to fall into the little pond below.

After the painter's death, some authors assigned the watercolour the new title of *A Stroll in the Garden*. F.Q.C.

Vicente López
(Valencia, 1772 – Madrid, 1850)
Head of a Woman
Madrid, *c.* 1826
MNAC/GDG 10281 D

Mariano Fortuny
(Reus, 1838 – Rome, 1874)
Il Contino
Rome, 1861
MNAC/GDG 10692 D

After his beginnings as a book illustrator during his formative period in Barcelona, Fortuny continued to work as an engraver and became one of the great nineteenth-century specialists in the technique of etching. Many of his prints reflect the artist's admiration, which often takes the form of figurative and compositional influence, for the great European masters of the art of engraving, Francisco de Goya in particular. Even so, Fortuny invariably managed to transform the presence of this tradition into in a highly fruitful stimulus to his own creative genius, never falling into the trap of imitation, which would have greatly limited his highly fertile and original talent.

In this context, this particular print, for which he made many proofs of state in his quest for chiaroscuro effects of extraordinary beauty and incomparable lyricism, denotes a thematic dependence on the models of the painter and engraver José de Ribera. The relationship becomes particularly perceptible when we compare the composition engraved by Fortuny with the Valencian artist's engraving of St Jerome. Both works share aspects evidenced in particular by the protagonist, the emaciated figure of a penitent, which in the case of Fortuny's engraving emphasises a feeling of solitude and helplessness in the midst of a desert-like crepuscular landscape, which plays a leading role in the composition. F.Q.C.

This sanguine done by Sir Edward Burne-Jones, the British painter and engraver who played a central role in the rebirth of the art of engraving in his country, shortly before his death shows the artist's loyalty to a medievalist aesthetic concept, the return to nature and a certain mysticism and ideal beauty, characteristics which, especially through his pupil Aubrey Beardsley, were to decisively influence French Symbolism and contribute to the transformation of this movement towards *Modernisme*. In Catalonia, his influence made itself felt to differing degrees in Joan Llimona, Santiago Rusiñol and Ramon Pichot and, very especially, in Alexandre de Riquer, the populariser and maximum exponent in Catalonia of the Pre-Raphaelite movement.

The presence of this drawing by Burne-Jones in the Museum's collections is due to its inclusion, nine years after the artist's death, in the *V Exposición Internacional de Arte*, inaugurated in the Palau de Belles Arts in Barcelona on 27 April 1907. Riquer, member of honour of the exhibition and official curator for Great Britain, selected the works by the English artists who were to take part and organised, prepared, installed and decorated the two galleries assigned to them, where he gathered 231 works, including paintings, drawings, engravings, sculptures and decorative arts. The exhibition was a great success as a very large number of Catalan artists took part, as well as numerous foreign artists, something that was not repeated in Catalonia until 1917 with the *Exposition d'arts français*. C.V.M.

Mariano Fortuny
(Reus, 1838 – Rome, 1874)
The Anchorite
c. 1869
MNAC/GDG 22034 G

Edward Burne-Jones
(Birmingham, 1833 – London, 1898)
Study of a Female Head
1894
MNAC/GDG 27061 D

A figure emblematic of early Catalan *Modernisme*, Casas together with other major artists headed the movement whose aim was to revive the Catalan figurative arts at the turn of the nineteenth and twentieth centuries. The artist's extraordinary talents are revealed in this remarkable drawing belonging to the famous gallery of portraits Casas donated to the Board of Museums in 1909, in which he recorded the likeness of the major artistic, musical and political figures of his day. Most probably with the intention of breaking the optical effect of repetition in series, Casas chose to vary both the posture of his sitters—standing, seated, half-length or full-length—and the incorporation of landscape or architectural features, whose purpose was to generate greater dynamism and figurative richness. An example of the latter would be this portrait, with its reference in the middle distance to the city of Paris, which we readily identify thanks to the inclusion of some of its most famous monuments, such as the unmistakable outline of the Sacré-Coeur and the sails of the popular Moulin de la Galette.

This magnificent portrait shows Picasso aged nineteen, when both painters visited the 1900 Paris Universal Exhibition. They would most probably have met in 1899 at Els Quatre Gats, one of the most dynamic and representative centres of *Modernista* Barcelona. F.Q.C.

Within the context of the highly fecund activity of the first generation of *Modernista* artists, this work documents one of the foremost cultural initiatives of late nineteenth-century Barcelona. In June 1899 Ramon Casas and Miquel Utrillo founded the journal *Pèl & Ploma*, whose title refers to the attributes—brush and pen—with which their respective professions were identified. The journal, which was published weekly until December 1903, when it was succeeded by *Forma*, became a landmark in the Catalan graphic arts of *Modernisme* and served to expose a great number of compositions by Casas alongside Utrillo's art reviews.

The rather lethargic female figure, emblematic of Melancholy, became a stereotype in Casas's rendering of women and, as time went by, a characteristic feature of his visual poetics.

The preparatory drawing for the masthead of this publication became one of its most popular publicity motifs. Indeed, this 'logotype' was put to several uses: as the heading for letter paper, as an advertisement for the weekly and even as the written invitation to Casas's second one-man show held in May 1900. The artist produced another version of the drawing, in a different format and excluding the title, for the front cover of issue no. 11 of *Pèl & Ploma*. F.Q.C.

Ramon Casas
(Barcelona, 1866-1932)
Portrait of Pablo Picasso
Paris, *c.* 1900
MNAC/GDG 27264 D

Ramon Casas
(Barcelona, 1866-1932)
***Masthead for the journal* Pèl & Ploma**
Barcelona, 1899
MNAC/GDG 41257 D

In 1893, young painters like Ramon Pichot, Sebastià Junyent and even Pablo Picasso, a tireless investigator, felt drawn towards Symbolist standpoints. Symbolism, a movement originating in England that gradually invaded the beginning of the twentieth century, exalted idealism and evoked medieval times.

Pichot, trained at the Barcelona Llotja school and later in Paris, was a member at the start of his painting career of the so-called 'Colla de Sant Martí' or 'Colla del Safrà' and from 1894 one of the youngest members of Santiago Rusiñol's circle. He had met Rusiñol in Paris and had collaborated with him in the great inaugural party at the Cau Ferrat and in all the *Modernista* parties held in Sitges between 1894 and 1898. He also travelled with Rusiñol in the south of France (1898) and later to Granada, where he painted and drew a series of works which he exhibited in 1899 at Els Quatre Gats and then in Madrid. In 1894, Pichot illustrated the intimate prose writings *Fulls de la vida*, Rusiñol's most mystic production, for which he drew 55 pictures with an obvious Symbolist connotation, very similar to this one as regards both subject matter and medium.

Pichot, whose earliest work was devoted to landscapes and who later joined Symbolist *Modernisme*, then took an interest in figure painting and in popular types, before drifting gradually towards primitivism. In the course of time, his work, currently very scattered, became irregular in its style, perhaps the result of his short artistic career and of his way of life, constantly on the move. C.V.M.

Hassall, a painter, etcher, illustrator and poster artist, completed his artistic training at the Academy of Fine Arts in Antwerp and at the Académie Julien in Paris. His first drawings appeared in 1890 in *The Daily Telegraph*. A contributor to various magazines, especially as a caricaturist, he also illustrated postcards and children's books. During the seven years he worked for David Allen and Sons, he drew almost 600 advertising posters, most of them for the same stories he illustrated. Later, he founded a school exclusively for poster artists.

The friendship between Lluís Plandiura, the first collector of posters in Catalonia, and Hassall began through the correspondence the former maintained with various foreign, especially English, poster artists. A large part of the considerable collection of Catalan and foreign posters Plandiura gathered was exhibited for the first time in October 1901 at the Artistic Circle of Sant Lluc. The poster by Hassall we are commenting on advertised the second large exhibition of posters from the Plandiura Collection held at the Reial Cercle Artístic in Barcelona on 1 January 1903. This exhibition, representing the best poster artists of the time, both Catalan and foreign, made an impact internationally. These exhibitions were the most important to be held in Barcelona at the beginning of the twentieth century. Hassall, who also took part in said exhibition, did the invitation card expressly for his friend. C.V.M.

Ramon Pichot
(Barcelona, 1871 – Paris, 1925)

Twilight

c. 1894-1900

MNAC/GDG 26903 D

John Hassall
(Walmer, Dover, 1868 – London, 1948)

Círcol Artistich. Exposició de Cartells

c. 1903

MNAC/GDG 69807 D

Apart from his interesting career in painting and drawing (as an illustrator he contributed to the best magazines of the time, such as *Le Rire, Paris Illustré* and *La Revue Blanche*), Toulouse-Lautrec was an excellent lithographer and poster artist.

This poster created to announce the presentation of the Irish singer May Belfort at the Petit Casino in Paris in 1895, like all this artist's posters, was very successful in his lifetime and was awarded a prize at an international exhibition of posters held in Rheims in 1896.

The work of Toulouse-Lautrec, which is almost exclusively devoted to subjects reflecting the atmosphere of the *cafés-concert*, the brothels and the night-life in Paris, and in particular the poster in question, shows the influence Japanese art, very much in vogue at that time, exerted on the composition, stylisation, form and arabesque of the artist's advertising posters, an influence which managed to revolutionise the graphic arts thanks to his personal approach. The extraordinary quality of all of Toulouse-Lautrec's poster work had an enormous impact which made itself felt in many of the best artists of the time working in this field, as well as among the French *Fauves* and the German Expressionists. Of the Catalan artists who received this influence, one should mention, amongst others, Ramon Casas, Santiago Rusiñol, Isidre Nonell himself and even the young Pablo Picasso. C.V.M.

This portrait is one of the last works from the artist's Parisian period, which occupied the space of nine years between 1896 and 1905. During this sojourn, and before he became one of the most illustrious representatives of the *Noucentista* pictorial movement, Sunyer's oeuvre evolved from an initial interest in rendering the city's dropouts, the popular *clochards*, towards an ever-growing fascination for the elegant, sophisticated ambience of the cosmopolitan universe. The artist immediately found his niche in the French art world, as evidenced by his contributions to *Le cri de Paris* as from 1897 and his lithographs for Jehan Rictus's *Les soliloques du pauvres.*

This particular drawing reveals the influence, or at least reminiscences, of the language of the great French painters of bohemian life. Indeed, during this second period Sunyer's palette became more luminous and characterised by a far richer colour range. *Portrait of a Woman* reveals a penchant for refined, elegant details evidenced particularly by both the model's fashionable attire and the accessories, such as the blue scarf and the hat, which constitute a hedonistic declaration of principles. In general terms, this entire period from Sunyer's career was characterised by the predominance of work on paper, both etchings and pastel drawings. F.Q.C.

Henri de Toulouse-Lautrec
(Albi, 1864 –
Malromé, 1901)
May Belfort
Paris, 1895
MNAC/GDG 748 C

Joaquim Sunyer
(Sitges, 1874-1956)
Portrait of a Woman
Paris, 1904
MNAC/GDG 39140 D

From its figurative beginnings that coincide with the artist's early period, rooted in the Catalan tradition of the last third of the nineteenth century, Mir's oeuvre evolved towards a new, innovative kind of painting with few points of thematic and stylistic contact with the work of his contemporaries. A decisive factor in the emergence of this uniquely suggestive language was the painter's sojourn in Majorca between early 1900 and 1903. The discovery of the island's landscape exerted a highly positive influence on the artist's personal maturation process, evidenced by the fact that on the basis of this fertile contact Mir's output veered towards highly original aesthetic concepts. His devotion to painting *au plein air*, with its corresponding visual consequences, opened the gates to an almost overwhelming, explosive combination of light and colour, in which the natural forms of this organicist landscape became the true protagonists of his oeuvre. Furthermore, and more remarkably still, Mir made no concessions to anecdote, guiding his work towards abstraction. By virtue of all these aspects, coupled with almost intuitive research into this new artistic language, Mir became an unavoidable point of reference in modern Catalan art. Given its stylistic characteristics, this pastel composition most probably belongs to the painter's Majorcan period. F.Q.C.

Riera Collection on permanent loan from the Generalitat de Catalunya, 1995; admission, 2002

Having trained at the Llotja school, Canals began his artistic career in Barcelona alongside Isidre Nonell, with whom he formed part of the group known as 'Colla del Safrà'. In emulation of their *Modernista* predecessors, in 1897 Nonell and Canals decided to move to Paris, where they exhibited on several occasions. In terms of subject matter, his work from this initial Parisian period, and specifically *Music Hall Interior*, denotes the cultivation of new, light-hearted hedonist motifs that focus on capturing the ambience of Paris bohemian life, of the popular types that frequented the city's cafés, without falling prey to pure description or anecdote.

Indeed, the rendering of these scenes, the projection of a stereotyped image of a frivolous city, was by no means original, since it formed part of the collective imaginary of all the artists who lived and worked in the late nineteenth-century Parisian context. Even so, we cannot ignore the brilliant artistic qualities of a composition that convincingly conveys Canals's innermost feelings and sensations. Equally admirable are the effects of vivaciousness and visual rhythm transmitted by the two main protagonists: a musician in the foreground and a ballerina who occupies the centre of the composition, whose forms are imprecise, dissipated and sketchy. F.Q.C.

Joaquim Mir
(Barcelona, 1873-1940)
Landscape
Majorca, *c.* 1900-3
MNAC 207738

Ricard Canals
(Barcelona, 1876-1931)
Music Hall Interior
Paris, *c.* 1897-9
MNAC/GDG 16097 D

The realist, powerful work of Francesc Gimeno is difficult to classify on account of his individuality and his particular approach. His art is direct, sincere and passionate, and has no bearing on the artistic trends of his day.

Although the subjects he most commonly dealt with were conditioned by his personal circumstances (his work as a painter-decorator until 1916 or 1917 kept him busy all day), he never failed to paint or draw for a couple of hours before going to work. He began a magnificent and numerous series of self-portraits and studies from nature in which his models were his wife and children, very often still sleeping. Except for a few notes, he painted his landscapes on his days off.

Without giving up his calling, for years he took part in the various exhibitions of fine arts and artistic industries that were held in Barcelona. At some he was even awarded prizes. His first individual exhibition, though, did not take place until 1915 at the Galeries Dalmau in Barcelona. Thanks to its success he was reunited with an old friend of his from Sabadell, Francesc P. Bedós i Artal, who from that moment covered his maintenance expenses in exchange for his pictorial production. This allowed him to give up his job as a painter and to once and for all devote himself to his art.

In this self-portrait, one of the series of drawings he did in his final period of daily servitude and obligation, Gimeno looks about 50 years old. C.V.M.

Isidre Nonell, one of the best Catalan painters of post-*Modernisme*, trained at the academies of Josep Mirabent and Gabriel Martínez Altés. He alternated this training with his classes at the Llotja school, where he was a pupil of Lluís Graner, with whom he shared an interest in subjects from the world of workers and common people, at the same time as he belonged to the 'Colla del Safrà'.

His sojourn in Boí in 1896 provided him with one of the subjects that were to contribute noticeably to his renown, shocking public opinion and especially the Catalan bourgeoisie. However, though at first Nonell's interests centred on the outcasts of society, cretins, beggars and repatriates, from 1905 his favourite subject was gypsy women, a subject to which he devoted himself almost full-time, both in painting and in drawing, until 1908.

If we compare his early studies and sketches from nature, many of which appeared in the *Esquella de la Torratxa* in 1894 and *La Vanguardia* in 1896, with the series on cretins begun at the end of 1896, and the watercolours with the subject of gypsy women and the extraordinary illustrations he did for the magazine *Papitu* from 1908, it becomes obvious that Nonell's sense of colour and matter as a painter never prevented or detracted from his charm and vivacity as a draughtsman. Despite the initial rejection and the fact that his work was already established by 1901, a few months before he died Nonell was still able to savour success in his last exhibition at the Faianç Català in 1910. C.V.M.

Francesc Gimeno
(Tortosa, 1858 – Barcelona, 1927)
Self-portrait
c. 1915
MNAC/GDG 41256 D

Isidre Nonell
(Barcelona, 1872-1911)
Una Buscona
1906
MNAC/GDG 26875 D

Xavier Nogués, one of the most representative figures of *Noucentisme*, who excelled as a draughtsman, illustrator, mural and easel painter and decorator of glass and ceramics, was also one of the best Catalan engravers of the first half of the twentieth century.

His earliest etchings date from 1910. Though only intermittently, Nogués worked at this engraving technique throughout his artistic career, as can be seen from the fact that all of the eight individual exhibitions he held in his lifetime, from 1917 to 1940, were of engravings, as well as the fact that in many group exhibitions he also figured only as an engraver. In his first individual exhibition, for example, held at the Ateneo de Madrid on 1 April 1917, he presented 25 engravings, nine of them done between January and March of that same year, amongst them this one, to which Nogués gave the title *The Agave*. This engraving's excellent composition, along with the figures, all in the purest and most genuine classicist *Noucentisme*, were to emerge in each of his engravings from this moment on, just as they are reflected in the mural paintings in the Plandiura Salon, one of his most extraordinary works, begun in 1917.

From this date and until 1920 Nogués's production underwent extraordinary progress. Acknowledged as an excellent draughtsman thanks to the pages of *Papitu*, he was a member of the association 'Les Arts i els Artistes', contributed to various magazines of the time, painted the murals in the wine cellar of the Galeries Laietanes and the Plandiura Salon, decorated ceramics, published *La Catalunya pintoresca* and made a name for himself as an engraver. C.V.M.

A draughtsman, caricaturist, painter, poster artist, designer, critic and art historian, Feliu Elias signed his pictorial work with his real name and used the pseudonyms Joan Sacs as an art critic and Apa for his caricatures and posters. At the *V Exposición Internacional de Arte* in Barcelona (1907) he received a first class medal for his caricature *The Hanged Man*, but it was not until 1908, when he founded the satirical magazine *Papitu*, of which he was editor until 1908, that his drawings made him known to the general public. Of his poster production, which goes from 1904 to 1934, only about twenty works have been located so far. Amongst them the poster discussed here stands out, with its distinct abstract treatment of the composition and figuration, in contrast with the hyperrealism of his pictorial work.

This poster for the Faianç Català, an establishment selling ceramics and art objects founded in Sabadell by the ceramist Marià Burguès i Serra and continued in Barcelona from 1898 by his nephew Marià Segura i Burguès, seems to have been done in about 1904 to announce the change in the numbering in the street where the shop was, the Gran Via de les Corts Catalanes.

The Faianç Català, like Els Quatre Gats, became an art gallery and a meeting-place for a group of *Noucentista* painters who in 1910 founded the association 'Les Arts i els Artistes', which made a considerable impact on the art scene of the time. C.V.M.

Xavier Nogués
(Barcelona, 1873-1941)
Agave with Figures
Barcelona, 1917
MNAC/GDG 7386 G

Feliu Elias
(Barcelona, 1878-1948)
Fayans Català
Barcelona, *c.* 1904
MNAC/GDG 420 C

Manolo, who from a very young age went to the Llotja school and frequented the *Modernista* atmosphere of Els Quatre Gats, went to Paris for the first time in February 1901. There, as well as struggling to survive and making himself popular in the most interesting literary and artistic circles of the time, he began to define his work.

A meeting with the art dealer Daniel-Henri Kahnweiler made it possible for him to move to Céret in 1909, where he produced his best early work, which was to become internationally acknowledged. Manolo's great personality drew a series of artists to him, first from 1910 to 1914 and then from 1916 to 1927, amongst them Aristide Maillol, Henri Matisse, André Derain, Georges Braque, Juan Gris, Max Jacob, Pablo Picasso, Pierre Brune and Chaïm Soutine. This was the start of what has since been called the Céret School, an essential point of reference in the history of twentieth-century art.

It was after his second stay at Céret, coinciding with his maturity as an artist, that Manolo introduced the subject of bullfighting into his repertory (in 1922 the new bullring was inaugurated in Céret), a subject that was inevitably of interest to him, along with the colour of the images that preside the whole ritual of the event. It was in Céret that same year that he carved his first relief of a *picador* and the magnificent bas-relief of the two bullfighters, a subject he continued to work at after 1929, when he had definitively settled in Caldes de Montbui, and which he repeated in paintings and drawings until 1942. C.V.M.

Riera Collection on permanent loan from the Generalitat de Catalunya, 1995; admission, 2002

In this work, one of the most representative from Salvador Dalí's youth, the artist sets aside his concern for composition and colour and begins a period we can consider one of the most balanced of his artistic production, although, as he himself says in his *Secret Life*, it was a period he experienced as exalted and frantic, otherwise in keeping with his hypersensitive and passionate temperament.

In this drawing, of which there is another almost identical version in a private collection in Barcelona, the father, portrayed three-quarter length sitting side-on looking to the right, brings to mind the same figure in the oil portrait Dalí painted a few months later (see p. 288). But it is in this drawing, one of the many he did that summer, especially of his sister, that he reaches a purity of line which shows itself in the precise detail of the faces, which are very delicately worked, a particular approach that was later to characterise his Surrealist works for ever more. C.V.M.

Manolo Hugué
(Barcelona, 1872 – Caldes de Montbui, 1945)
Bullfight
1927
MNAC 212712

Salvador Dalí
(Figueres, 1904-89)
Portrait of the Artist's Father and Sister
Figueres, 1925
MNAC/GDG 66171 D

Though we cannot be sure of the exact date this pastel drawing was done, we can guess at it as we know that González worked on this theme and this technique in depth from 1914. Despite having used it from time to time before, between 1905 and 1910, it was not until 1915 that he exhibited six works using this procedure at the *Salon des Indépendants* in Paris. After that, he made frequent use of it until 1919.

This female face, one of his favourite subjects at that time, belongs to a series of portraits done in this technique, in which the magnificent *Self-portrait* (MNAC/GDG 113452 D) kept in the Cabinet stands out. González, who before being a sculptor had been a painter, used these two disciplines in his work throughout his life. His mastery of pastels, one of the most difficult techniques there is, was perfect and he adapted it, through the use of colour, to give his drawings volume and depth, playing with the procedure's pasty material and with the space, and creating a solid, admirably constructed work that makes it doubly interesting. C.V.M.

In González's drawings we find everything from figurative character studies to Cubist sketches, but without entirely abandoning sensitive form, which the artist kept coming back to throughout his life. This diversity and this contrast in style, a result of his laborious research, can also be found in his subject matter, which come and go throughout his artistic career, at the same time as the techniques he used helped him to perfect and improve his work.

After 1905 he showed his first portraits drawn with conte pencil, with light touches of pastel, a technique he went on developing and which he used almost exclusively on dark coloured paper during the period from 1910 to 1919.

This is one of the best periods Julio González went through in his entire life, both on a personal level and artistically. From 1914 and almost without a break until 1918, González produced maternities and girls or young women combing their hair, washing or dressing, like this one. In all the works from this time, he reflects a love of life and shows a certain sensuality in the line and colour, a rare concession he never again allowed himself in his work. C.V.M.

Julio González
(Barcelona, 1876 – Arcueil, 1942)
Sweet Expression
c. 1914-18
MNAC/GDG 113535 D

Julio González
(Barcelona, 1876 – Arcueil, 1942)
Woman Washing
c. 1914-17
MNAC/GDG 113538 D

From 1936, González, concerned at the events of the Spanish Civil War, made a number of drawings which he used to carry out his sculpture *Montserrat*, one of his most emblematic works and one of the best-known as a symbol of resistance. It was exhibited for the first time at the exhibition *Origines et développement de l'art international indépendant*, held at the Jeu de Paume in Paris between July and October 1937. At the end of that same year, González once again presented *Montserrat* at the Spanish Pavilion at the Universal Exhibition in Paris, where it was an extraordinary success.

Later, González resumed this subject in studies of which there are several variants, like the series of figures of peasant women standing with their arms raised in an attitude of despair, or that of *Heads Shouting*, dated between 1938 and 1941, a subject he kept working on and developing until his death. This drawing, dated May 1940, belongs to this last series and was done when González had settled with all the family in Lasbonygues (Lot), a period when the Second World War, which had broken out the year before, forced the artist to limit his production to drawing and clay modelling. C.V.M.

Julio González
(Barcelona, 1876 – Arcueil, 1942)
Montserrat Shouting
1940
MNAC/GDG 113554 D

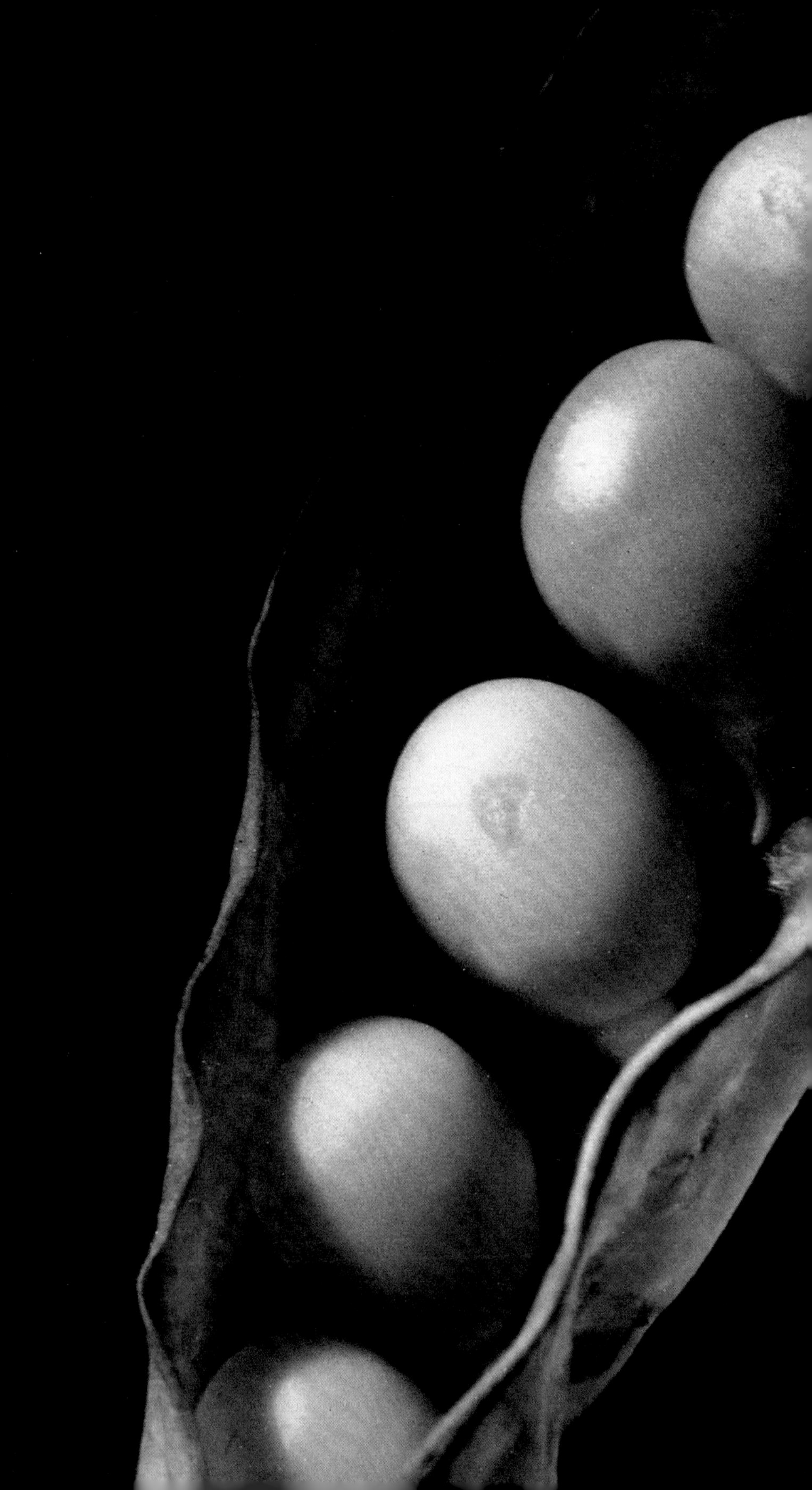

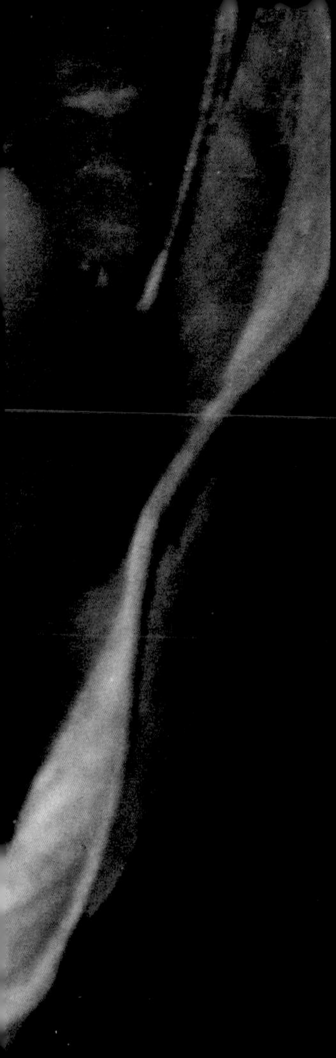

Photography

The collection of photography

The MNAC decided to include photography in its collections in 1996 as a response to the demand from several cultural and patrimonial entities who made urgent calls for commitment on the part of the Museum to the photographic heritage. This response took the form of the creation of the Department of Photography, whose mission is both to provide exhibition space for photographers and their works and to meet the moral obligation to rescue major legacies in the genre from oblivion and material destruction.

The Museum's aim is to bring together works ranging from the origins of photography in 1839 until the present day in a collection representative of the history of photography that lays especial emphasis on the work of Catalan photographers.

The collection constitutes an itinerary through the different artistic movements, starting at the very beginning with works by Disdéri, Jean Laurent, Francis Frith, Charles Clifford and Gaston Braun, among others. Next comes the Pictorialist period, which began around 1888 and continued in Catalonia until the mid-twentieth century with figures of the stature of Antoni Campañà, Claudi Carbonell, Pere Casas Abarca, Josep M. Casals i Ariet, José Ortiz Echagüe, Joaquim Pla Janini and Joan Porqueras. This is followed by the historical avant-garde movements, with outstanding photographers such as Antoni Arissa, Josep Batlles, Pere Català Pic, Emili Godes, Josep Lladó and Josep Masana. The most prominent graphic document from the next period, corresponding to the Spanish Civil War, is the work of Agustí Centelles. The postwar period saw the emergence of the new avant-garde with Otho Lloyd and Joaquim Gomis, followed by the neo-realism of Francesc Català-Roca, Colita, Joan Colom, Oriol Maspons, Xavier Miserachs, Leopoldo Pomés, Ton Sirera, Ricard Terré and Julio Ubiña. This leads finally to the contemporary period, dating from the transition back to democracy in Spain, with such representative names as Manel Armengol, Toni Catany, Manuel Esclusa, Joan Fontcuberta, Pere Formiguera, Jordi Guillumet, Kim Manresa, Jorge Ribalta and Humberto Rivas.

The Department sets out to safeguard all this material by recovering, restoring and drawing up an inventory of it to foster its study and dissemination, in accordance with criteria that take in both historical photography and its more experimental and avant-garde aspects.

In short, it is the MNAC's wish that its Department of Photography, by virtue of its rich collections, will become an indispensable point of reference for photographic research and creation in our country.

Given the specific characteristics of photography as material sensitive to light, all the works comprising the collection are exhibited in galleries that meet the necessary environmental conditions. Nevertheless, due to the fragility of some of the processes some pictures cannot be placed permanently on show. Consequently each process follows a stringent order of rotation to ensure that they are preserved in the best possible conditions.

The works in this guidebook therefore constitute a reference to the periods featured in each of the galleries, as a result of which the visitor may find that some of the works on show differ from those published. Even so, the museological discourse will not be altered as the pictures on display will still belong to the same periods, their quality will be comparable and they will be accompanied by their corresponding technical entry.

Photo on pp. 338-9: **Emili Godes**. ***Peas,*** detail, *c.* 1930. Permanent loan from the Godes family, 1997

From the origins to Pictorialism, 1839-88

This section retraces the advent of the medium in Catalonia during the nineteenth century, and the social, technological, and cultural conditions of the first decades during which photography evolved. This was the pre-industrial era, that is, a time when photography was yet to attain the technological simplicity that would place it within reach of practically everyone. Similarly, it was a time when the media had yet to enjoy the advantages of photomechanical printing, which would not be invented until the end of the century and not become widespread until the interwar period. The advent of the printed page marked a major turning point in the history of photography.

During this initial period, photography served mainly to graphically record travels and picturesque sights, historical monuments and great works of architecture and engineering. This was a photographic activity characteristic of the initial period of photography in the global sense, the best examples of which were fruit of public commissions and colonial geographical expeditions. These enterprises were associated on the one hand with the will to conquer and exploit natural terrain and, on the other, with the beginnings of travel, the forerunner of tourism, a social and cultural trend the modern roots of which are to be sought in the enlightened mentality, which regarded travel as a formative experience. In this context, photography came to form part of the eighteenth-century tradition of views and engravings.

The other sphere in which photography played a crucial role was that of the portrait. The second half of the nineteenth century witnessed the emergence of the first photographic studios and the popularity of the portrait among the bourgeoisie grew and grew, first in the format of the daguerreotype, an unrepeatable image that preserves the exquisite quality of the cameo and the miniature, and later in the form of visiting cards, which thanks to the reproduction process led to greater democratisation in access to the portrait. D.B.

Francis Frith
(Chesterfield, 1822 – Cannes, 1898)
Barcelona
Undated
MNAC 212762

Permanent loan from the Fondo Fotográfico de la Universidad de Navarra. Fundación Universitaria de Navarra, 2003

José Martínez Sánchez
(Bicorp, 1808-74)
Barcelona. Pont del Diable
Martorell, *c.* 1865
MNAC 212764

Permanent loan from the Fondo Fotográfico de la Universidad de Navarra. Fundación Universitaria de Navarra, 2003

André-Adolphe-Eugène Disdéri
(Paris, 1819 – Nice, 1889)
Infante Princesse Victoria de Bourbon, Comtesse de Mascali
c. 1860
MNAC 212757

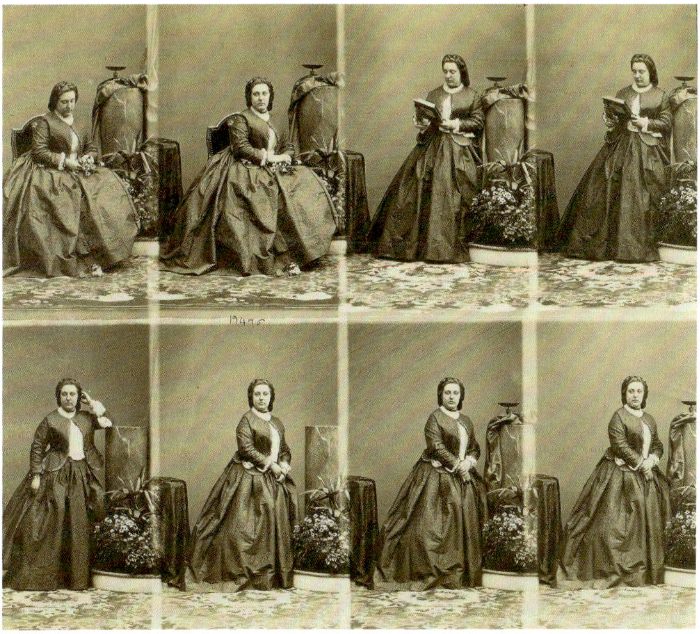

Permanent loan from the Fondo Fotográfico de la Universidad de Navarra. Fundación Universitaria de Navarra, 2003

From Pictorialism to the avant-garde movements, 1888-1917

The mass industrialisation of photography with the invention in 1888 of the new Kodak cameras marked the widespread emergence of a phenomenon crucial to the technological evolution of the genre: 'amateurism'. This also led to what might be regarded as its elitist counterpart, Pictorialism, which sought to secure photography's recognition as an art form. In the face of technological standardisation and documentary utilitarianism, Pictorialism applied pigment processes that evoked painting and its symbolic themes, both picturesque and sublime, in accordance with the aesthetic paradigms of nineteenth-century modern art based on the Romantic principle of the genius. In the Catalan context, major figures belonging to this strand were Pere Casas Abarca, José Ortiz Echagüe and Carlos Yñigo.

Although from today's point of view—shaped largely by the fact that the different modern photographic movements of the twentieth century condemned it—Pictorialism may be regarded as a prolongation of the old academy, in other words as reactionary, we must not forget that it was initially a progressive movement, a breakaway, photography's first artistic strand and the prelude to the great discourses that legitimised modern photography. D.B.

Pere Casas Abarca
(Barcelona, 1875-1958)
La danse
c. 1900
MNAC 207769

José Ortiz Echagüe
(Guadalajara, 1886 – Madrid, 1980)
Sermón en la aldea
1903
MNAC 212777

Permanent loan from the Fondo Fotográfico de la Universidad de Navarra. Fundación Universitaria de Navarra, 2003

Late Pictorialism, 1917-36

The modernity of the precepts and practice of Pere Català Pic, Josep Masana, Emili Godes, Antoni Arissa, Josep Sala, Joaquim Gomis and Josep Lladó, among others, did not put an end to Pictorialism, against which they rebelled. On the contrary, they were forced to live with it for a number of years more. Their innovations were counteracted by those photographers who remained loyal to the principles and spirit of Pictorialism in a gesture of defence of the values of the fine arts against the revolutionary modernity of photography understood as an applied art. Josep Maria Casals i Ariet, Claudi Carbonell, José Ortiz Echagüe, Joan Porqueras and Joaquim Pla Janini were among the most prominent second-generation Pictorialists. These photographers engaged in symbolist 'picturesquism' and used pigment processes. Although at first sight it may seem that this second wave of Pictorialism and modern photography were worlds apart, on closer examination we discover points of contact and overlap between both strands. Thus we find photographers who combined Pictorialist techniques, modern aesthetics and the quest for abstraction—such as Antoni Campañà, Joan Porqueras and Antoni Arissa—alongside modern photographers who could not disguise a certain nostalgia in terms of subject matter and retouching and manipulation techniques, like Josep Masana. The eclectic nature of the work of Joaquim Pla Janini illustrates the complex way in which modernity and tradition coexisted. In Catalonia, Pictorialism dominated as a trend in photography until well into the 1950s, a phenomenon most probably influenced by the history of this country in comparison to that of its European neighbours. Modernity here was somehow counteracted and held back by the historical forces it strove to supersede. D.B.

Joaquim Pla Janini

(Tarragona, 1879 – Barcelona, 1970)

La hora del fantasma

Undated

MNAC 201174

Josep Maria Casals i Ariet
(Viladrau, 1901 – Barcelona, 1986)
Untitled
Undated
MNAC 205164

Permanent loan from the Fons d'Art de la Generalitat de Catalunya, 1999

Claudi Carbonell
(Barcelona, 1891-1970)
Forest of the Virgin
Undated
MNAC 209381

Permanent loan from the Agrupació Fotogràfica de Catalunya, 2003

Joan Porqueras
(Barcelona, 1889-1969)
Les goudronneurs
1931
MNAC 208649

Permanent loan from the Agrupació Fotogràfica de Catalunya, 2003

Antoni Campañà
(Arbúcies, 1906 – Barcelona, 1989)
Drawn by Blood
1933
MNAC 205163

Permanent loan from the Fons d'Art de la Generalitat de Catalunya, 1999

Modern photography, 1917-36

This section presents an itinerary through the period when the artistic discourses of modernism emerged and evolved during the first third of the twentieth century. More specifically, modern photography was born in Europe between the two world wars and coincided with the advent of the avant-garde movements. In the Catalan context, this period came to an end with the outbreak of the Spanish Civil War. It was a time when a discourse of radical photographic renovation was put forward and took root internationally: Talk was heard of new vision, new objectivity, new photography and so on in reference to the prevailing idea at the time that a genuine renaissance was taking place in photography, which for the first time in its history had attained the age of majority as an art form on an equal footing with painting. Furthermore, this was the period that witnessed the emergence of the first illustrated publications devoted to avant-garde art and the first journals

Pere Català Pic
(Valls, 1889 – Barcelona, 1971)
Crystal Glass
1935
MNAC 205167

Permanent loan from the Fons d'Art de la Generalitat de Catalunya, 1999

specialising in photography. *D'Ací i D'Allà* and others journals were key elements in the development and dissemination of photographic modernism in Catalonia. In the early nineteenth thirties the photographer, professor and critic Pere Català Pic, one of the local pioneers of modern photography, published a number of key articles that had a fundamental influence on the construction of photographic modernism in Catalonia, in which he contended that modern photography is the equivalent of advertising. This concept of photography as an applied art, as opposed to the notion of an independent art characteristic of the fine arts and of the tenets of traditional aesthetics, is linked to the avant-garde movements, which in the same interwar period burst onto the scene in the major European capitals, each one with its own contextual peculiarities. The most influential photographers from this period include Antoni Arissa, Ramon Batlles, Pere Català Pic, Emili Godes, Josep Maria Lladó and Josep Masana. D.B.

Josep Masana
(Granollers, 1892 – Barcelona, 1979)
Untitled
1934
MNAC 205401

Permanent loan from the Fons d'Art de la Generalitat de Catalunya, 1999

Emili Godes
(Barcelona, 1895-1970)
Cactus
c. 1930
MNAC 202136

Permanent loan from the Godes family, 1997

Antoni Arissa
(Barcelona, 1900-80)
Untitled
Undated
MNAC 203161

Permanent loan from Margarida, Maria dels Àngels, Concepció and Maria Antònia Arissa i Serra, 1998

Josep Maria Lladó
(Igualada, 1903-56)
Untitled
Undated
MNAC 202653

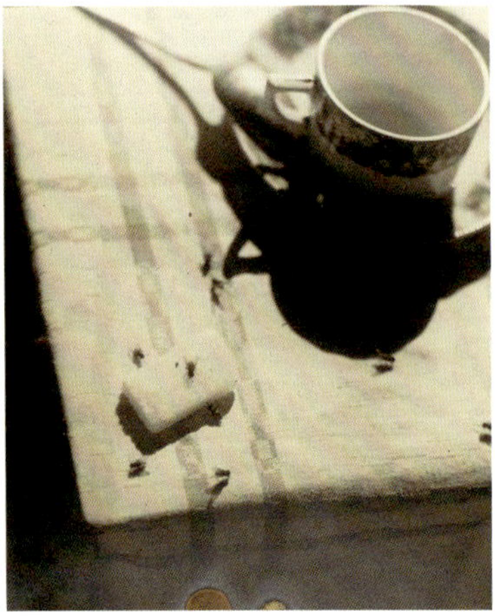

The Civil War, 1936-40

The advent of the printed page was a key factor in the definition of modern photography. This was also the moment that saw the birth of photographic reportage, which corresponded to the historical period of the emergence and consolidation of illustrated journals and of small-format cameras and new materials that made high-speed shots possible. In this context, the Spanish Civil War became the first testing ground for new techniques and for mass reproduction in anticipation of the imminent outbreak of World War II. Indeed, a historical relationship exists between photographic reportage and wars. More specifically, we might contend that modern reportage was born with the Spanish Civil War thanks to figures such as Robert Capa and Agustí Centelles, since it was the first armed conflict to enjoy wide coverage in the press. D.B.

Permanent loan from the Fondo Fotográfico de la Universidad de Navarra. Fundación Universitaria de Navarra, 2003

Agustí Centelles
(Grao de Valencia, 1909 – Barcelona, 1985)
Riot Police
Barcelona, 19 July 1936
MNAC 212780

The new avant-garde, from 1939 to the late 1960s

This period reflects the persistence or reconstruction of modernist discourses in the post-war years and during the Franco regime. Unlike the preceding one, this period was marked by realism and reportage, while on the international scene illustrated reviews reached their zenith of popularity and influence. The traumatic aftermath of war transformed visual experimentation and the quest on the part of the first avant-garde movements for abstract forms into a new documentary imperative—marked almost certainly by the photographers employed by the great

Francesc Català-Roca
(Valls, 1922 – Barcelona, 1998)
The Columbus Monument
1950
MNAC 205176

Permanent loan from the Fons d'Art de la Generalitat de Catalunya, 1999

Joaquim Gomis
(Barcelona, 1902-91)
The Eiffel Tower
Paris, *c.* 1950
MNAC 205323

Permanent loan from the Fons d'Art de la Generalitat de Catalunya, 1999

American journals—that in the case of Europe found responses adapted to post-war circumstances: Humanism in France and Neo-Realism in Italy and Spain.

The discourse of photographic modernism linked to the aesthetics of reportage was closely associated with the idea that modern photography was not an independent but rather an applied art at the service of illustration and magazines. In this context, it is a significant fact that the Catalan photographers of the period coined the term 'useful photography' as synonymous with modern photography.

Xavier Miserachs
(Barcelona, 1937-98)
El Born
Barcelona, 1962
MNAC 205417

Permanent loan from the Fons d'Art de la Generalitat de Catalunya, 1999

Oriol Maspons
(Barcelona, 1928)
Eivissa
1954
MNAC 205736

Permanent loan from Oriol Maspons, 1999

In Catalonia, the critic and historian Josep Maria Casademont coined the term 'new avant-garde' to describe the photographic aesthetics that prevailed between the mid-1950s and the early 1960s, characterised by respect for the principles of photographic reportage and documentary style.

The great pioneer of this movement was Francesc Català Roca, while its most influential and renowned representatives include Xavier Miserachs, Oriol Maspons, Julio Ubiña, Colita, Ricard Terré and Ramon Masats, some of whom were mere amateurs. In terms of aesthetics, the movement reached its culmination point in the early years of the sixties, specifically in the work of an amateur, Joan Colom, author of an unforgettable document on Barcelona's red-light district, the '*Barrio Chino*'. This report stretched the formal and poetic possibilities of new avant-garde photographic realism to their ultimate consequences in that it comprises a set of snapshots, a kind of pseudo film sequence, which made a permanent breakaway from the idea of the single image.

This period marked the swan song of the hegemony of the reportage as an avant-garde photographic form. Historical circumstances governing the role of photography in the media changed during the sixties, which determined the future destiny of reportage.

Parallel to the photographic movement linked to realism, another strand emerged of informalist and abstract experimentation in the best modern photography tradition. The most prominent figures here were Otho Lloyd, Joaquim Gomis, Leopoldo Pomés and Ton Sirera. D.B.

Colita
(Barcelona, 1940)
Carmen Amaya and Los Tarantos
Barcelona, 1963
MNAC 205217

Permanent loan from the Fons d'Art de la Generalitat de Catalunya, 1999

Joan Colom
(Barcelona, 1921)
From the 5th District Series
Barcelona, *c.* 1960
MNAC 211142

Permanent loan from the Agrupació Fotogràfica de Catalunya, 2003

Ricard Terré
(Sant Boi de Llobregat, 1928)
Sant Boi de Llobregat
1958
MNAC 205509

Permanent loan from the Fons d'Art de la Generalitat de Catalunya, 1999

Leopoldo Pomés
(Barcelona, 1931)
Paral·lel
Barcelona, 1957
MNAC 205437

Permanent loan from the Fons d'Art de la Generalitat de Catalunya, 1999

Otho St. Clair Lloyd
(London, 1885 – Barcelona, 1979)
Untitled
Undated
MNAC 202105

Permanent loan from Salvador Martínez, 1997

Ton Sirera
(Barcelona, 1911 – Lleida, 1975)
Lichen on Rock
c. 1959
MNAC 205493

Permanent loan from the Fons d'Art de la Generalitat de Catalunya, 1999

Francesc Esteve
(Sabadell, 1932)
The Sixth Fleet and the Angel Tobias
1958
MNAC 206995

The contemporary period, from the mid-1970s to the mid-1990s

This period stretches from the reinstatement of democracy in Spain in the mid-1970s to the mid-1990s. This was a time when major transformations took place not only in the political sphere but also in the cultural industries in general. Broadly speaking, as from 1975 photography went through an ever-widening schism between photojournalism on the one hand and, on the other, photography as an art form in its own right.

Thanks to newfound freedom of expression, photojournalism found not only new terrain but also a new social and political role during the initial years of the Transition, and parallel to the apparition of new publications, a new generation of photographers emerged onto the scene.

The language of new graphic journalism was based on the same principles as those of the new avant-garde from the previous decade, from which it inherited the spirit of denunciation that has characterised illustrated reportage throughout its history. Even so, such principles were no longer emblem of artistic avant-garde but rather, and to the contrary, they were often defended as the traditional quintessence of a hypothetical photographic authenticity linked to the notion of photographic realism. As from this moment, photojournalism became a prestigious genre in its own right that enjoyed ever-increasing attention and support.

Manel Armengol
(Badalona, 1949)
Demonstrations on 1 February 1976. Demonstration Call: 'Freedom, amnesty, statute of autonomy'
Barcelona, 1976
MNAC 212790

Kim Manresa
(Barcelona, 1961)
The Little Girl Kadi Undergoing Female Circumcision in a Sub-Saharan Country
1997
MNAC 205741

Enric Folgosa Martí
(Barcelona, 1959)
Funeral at Kosovo
Dragobil, 5 October 1998
MNAC 212751

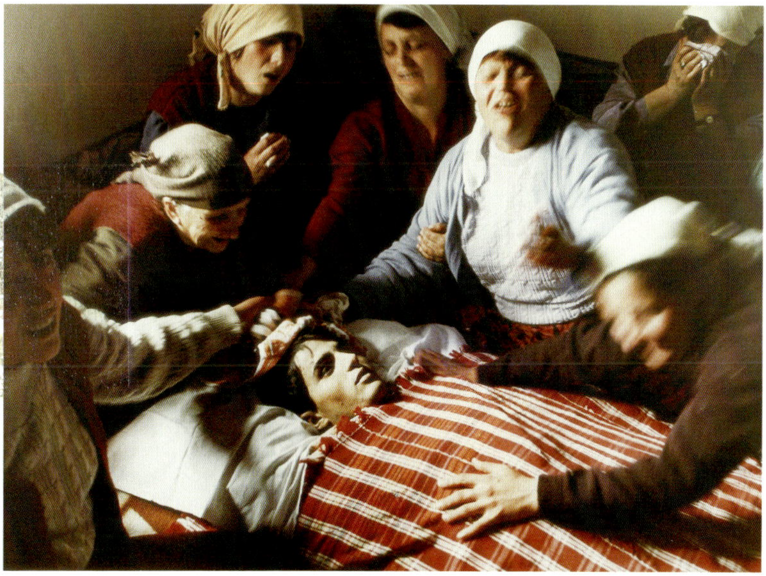

As opposed to photojournalism, the branch of photography that continued to advocate artistic autonomy remained loyal to modernising principles that linked back to previous photographic avant-garde trends, although the prevailing model was no longer identification of the avant-garde as a form of social instrumentalisation.

The quest for artistic independence gave rise to approaches opposed to reportage, which was now identified exclusively with photojournalism, and led to critical and

Manel Úbeda
(Mollet del Vallès, 1951)
Tibi
1978
MNAC 205515

Permanent loan from the Fons d'Art de la Generalitat de Catalunya, 1999

Manuel Esclusa
(Vic, 1952)
Shipwreck
1984
MNAC 205248

Permanent loan from the Fons d'Art de la Generalitat de Catalunya, 1999

aesthetic rejection of photographic realism in favour of experimentation with photographic fictions.

During the first years of the 'Transition' period, the decline of realist approaches in the face of photographic fictions involved a change in attitude on the part of photographers towards the country's political and social circumstances—from critical denunciation to a ludic celebration devoid of political connotations.

Manuel Laguillo
(Madrid, 1953)
Barcelona
1983
MNAC 205387

Permanent loan from the Fons d'Art de la Generalitat de Catalunya, 1999

Ferran Freixa
(Barcelona, 1950)
Palazzo Pitti
Florence, 1981
MNAC 205304

Permanent loan from the Fons d'Art de la Generalitat de Catalunya, 1999

Martí Llorens
(Barcelona, 1962)
Industrial Premises and Folch Chimney
Barcelona, 1987
MNAC 205393

Permanent loan from the Fons d'Art de la Generalitat de Catalunya, 1999

Humberto Rivas
(Buenos Aires, 1937)
Maria
1979
MNAC 205469

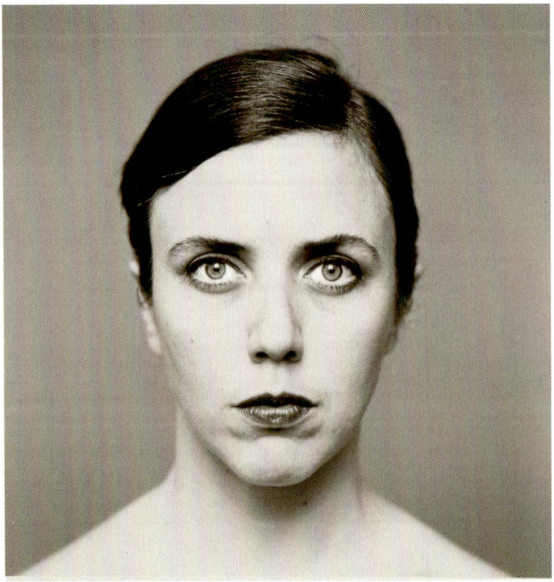

Permanent loan from the Fons d'Art de la Generalitat de Catalunya, 1999

Pere Formiguera
(Barcelona, 1952)
Father
1991
MNAC 205285

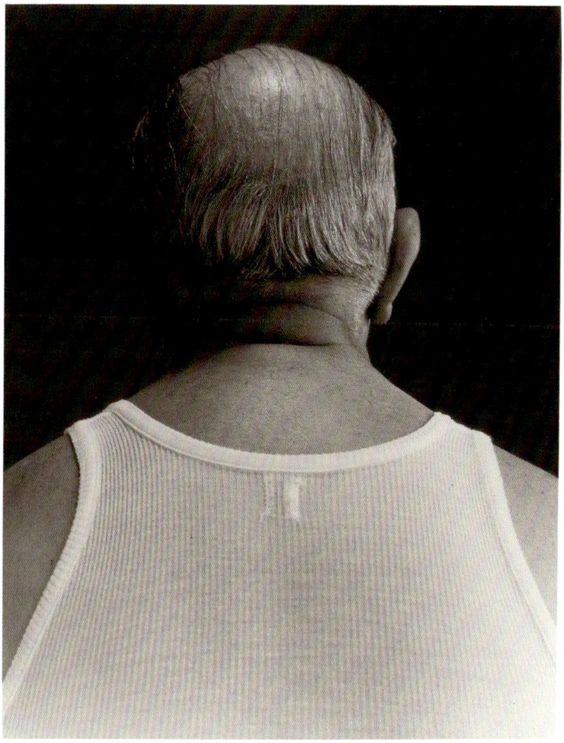

Permanent loan from the Fons d'Art de la Generalitat de Catalunya, 1999

Toni Catany
(Llucmajor, 1942)
Still Life, # 136
1987
MNAC 206220

From the early 1980s to the mid-1990s the artistic debate was dominated by the different discourses of Postmodernism, which led to wide-scale questioning of the models of modern art and generated reflection on the universe of the image. Photography came to be seen as the emblematic medium in this critique of representation. And in the long run, the postmodernist debate and the critique of representation would lead to photography's becoming a dominant presence on the art scene as from 1980. Hegemony of the critique of representation in the practice of photography would persist among the younger generation of artists, who revealed implicit understanding of the fictitious and conventional character of photographic realism and whose works tended mainly towards visual fictions. D.B.

Joan Fontcuberta
(Barcelona, 1955)
Braohypoda frustata
1984
MNAC 205274

Permanent loan from the Fons d'Art de la Generalitat de Catalunya, 1999

Jordi Guillumet
(Barcelona, 1953)
Untitled
1988
MNAC 205382

Permanent loan from the Fons d'Art de la Generalitat de Catalunya, 1999

Jorge Ribalta
(Barcelona, 1963)
Journeys of Invention
1987
MNAC 205452

Permanent loan from the Fons d'Art de la Generalitat de Catalunya, 1999

Numismatics

The collection of the Numismatic Cabinet of Catalonia

The Numismatic Cabinet of Catalonia (GNC) was created in 1932 as an institution devoted to research into and dissemination of the history of coins and medals in Catalonia. Today, the Cabinet's collection consists of over 130,000 pieces in a wide variety of materials. The coin holding comprises over 100,000 pieces featuring the main numismatic series, the most emblematic of which are those issued in Catalonia and include both extremely rare and unique coins. The collection begins with the series of ancient coins, prominent among which are those minted in Hispania, with pieces as significant as the first silver coins issued on the Peninsula by the Greeks of *Emporion*.

The transition from Antiquity to the Middle Ages is documented in particular by an interesting collection of Visigothic currency. Outstanding among the medieval, modern and contemporary issues are the series of Catalan comital coins, those of the War of Separation (Reapers War) and those of the Napoleonic invasion. Furthermore, the Cabinet preserves a number of major monetary findings, such as the coins unearthed during excavations that took place in Empúries and hoards that document key periods in the use of currency in Catalonia.

The collection of medals comprises over 7,500 pieces, ranging from the first ones struck in Italy during the second half of the fifteenth century to those of the present day. Although a considerable number of European and American countries are represented, Spanish medals constitute the core of the collection, particularly those made on the occasion of the proclamation and pledging of monarchs, as well as a very interesting set of medals and plaquettes from the *Modernista* era.

Another major section of the Cabinet is given over to valuable paper, ranging from banknotes, bonds and credit vouchers to different kinds of credit documents such as bills of exchange, shares, debentures and cheques. In this context, worthy of especial attention are the bonds and credit vouchers issued by Catalan municipal councils during the Spanish Civil War (1936-9).

Just like all numismatic cabinets, the GNC also includes items directly linked to coins and medals, such as Roman tesseras, *pellofes* (a kind of token), weights, weighing scales and dies. Furthermore, it also includes a small collection of objects less directly related to coins and medals, such as medieval and modern seals, decorations and insignias.

An outstanding document of the early period of the use of coinage in the Greek colony of *Emporion* is a hoard that was recovered in 1926 in the eastern area of the archaeological site of Empúries, designated a neapolis by modern historians. The coins were inside a small pitcher of pseudo-Ionic ceramic ware hidden in the subsoil of a *taberna* near the entrance to the agora, the city's main square. The deposit, concealed around 385-75 BC, contained 897 small silver coins, the total weight of which was no more than 840 g.

Almost all the coins in the hoard were from the *Emporion* mint and the vast majority of the pieces, 879, corresponded to the issue which shows the head of the goddess Athena and an owl between the initials of the city, EM. This series, dated to around 395-75 BC, copies the Athens trioboles of the fifth century BC. The only differences between the mintings of the two workshops are the substitution of the initials of Athens by those of *Emporion* and the adoption of a metrology typical of the peninsular colony based on a unit of 0.94 g.

The copying of these designs must be related to the great prestige the coin issues of Athens enjoyed and to their wide diffusion throughout the Mediterranean. There is nothing odd, then, about the *Emporion* workshop deciding, in a period in which it had to continually choose new iconographies for its issues, to adopt the designs of the prestigious mint of Athens, whose mintings must have been well known in the small colony of *Emporion*, whither they arrived brought by the merchants who tied up in its port. M.C.

There were three Iberian workshops that minted silver coinage: *Iltirta* (Lleida), *Kese* (Tarragona) and *Ausesken* (the *Ausetanos*). Since the weight of the units of these issues was identical to that of the Roman denarius they are known by that name. On the obverse of its denarii *Iltirta* engraved the head of a male divinity surrounded by three dolphins, and on the reverse a horseman with a chlamys and bearing a palm. Inscribed in Iberian signs below the horseman is the legend *Iltirtasalirban*, consisting of three elements: the name of the issuing authority, *Iltirta*, the lexical element, *salir*, to which a value is attributed relating to money or coinage, and the suffix *-ban*, of uncertain function.

Generally speaking, the origin of the Iberian denarius has been related to the warlike conflicts between indigenous peoples and Romans in the second century BC, and with the payment of tributes to Rome. Having said that, neither the scant production and short lifespan of the *Iltirta* mint, nor those of *Kese* and *Ausesken*, indicate the regular handing over of taxes or the financing of great war ventures. The issuing of these denarii seems to correspond instead to payments of a precise order, the nature of which is unknown to us, but which present a wide range of possibilities: the specific financing of troops, the paying of enterprises relating to the reorganisation of the area, or to urban development at the end of the second century and beginning of the first century BC. M.C.

Hoard from the neapolis of *Emporion*

Beginning of the fourth century BC

MNAC/GNC 76000-76897

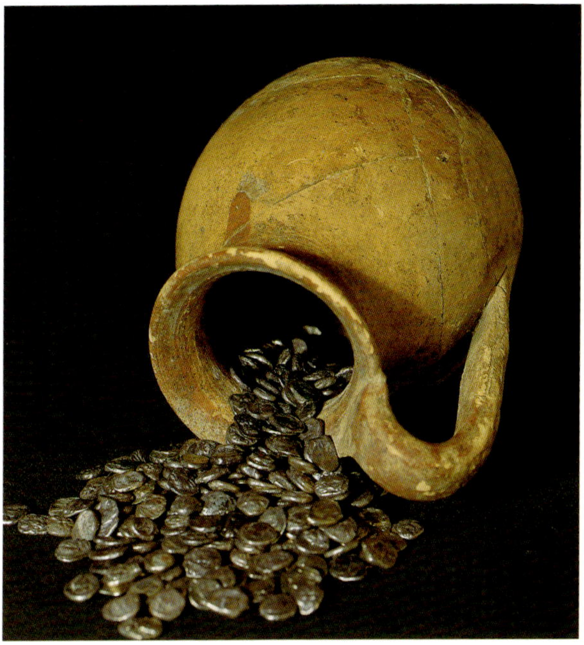

Denarius from *Iltirta*

Second half of the second century BC

MNAC/GNC 109407

∅ 18 mm

Recovered in 1913 in the excavations in Empúries was a small hoard of 45 denarii of the Roman Republic. The bulk of the denarii are mintings of the period of the Civil War, firstly between Caesar and Pompey the Great and afterwards between Caesar and the sons of Pompey. Of note in the composition of the hoard are the mintings of a military character, made under the responsibility of the generals, to whom the Roman Senate had conceded a military *imperium*, that is, the command of the fighting troops.

One must ask oneself what are the reasons for this strong presence of issues of the period of the Civil War in a place relatively remote from the theatres of war, as was Empúries. The answer is found in a text by the historian Titus Livius (XXXIV, 9, 3): 'A third type of people were the Roman colonists settled by the divine Caesar after the defeat of the sons of Pompey.' After the Battle of Munda, then, in which Caesar had defeated the Pompeyans, Caesar's followers, Roman colonists, settled in Empúries. Some of them must have arrived there with large quantities of denarii from the period of the Civil War, received in all likelihood in payment for services rendered during the fighting.

One deduces from all this that this small hoard could have been the property of a veteran of the Civil Wars who, the fighting done, may have arrived in Empúries immediately after 45 BC, as one reads in Livius and as the date of issue of the newest denarius indicates, an example from the mint in Rome manufactured in 44 BC. M.C.

Tarraco was the most important mint of north-eastern Hispania, in accordance with its importance as a capital of the great province of *Tarraconensis*. Augustus resided in the city during the years 26 and 25 BC, following the Cantabrian wars, and governed the Empire from it. Later, in 15 BC, the emperor travelled once more to Hispania and repeated his stay in *Tarraco*.

The *Tarraco* mint issued an enormous amount of bronze and orichalcum coinage, probably from 2 BC onwards. During the reigns of Augustus and Tiberius, sesterces, dupondii, asses, semises and quadrans were manufactured, on which there was engraved, in a more or less abbreviated manner according to the occasion, the juridical status, epithets and name of the city, C (olonia) V(rbs) T(riumphalis) T(arraco). Missing, however, is the reference to the qualifier *Iulia* that the colony also had, and may have been conferred on it sometime later.

At his death Augustus was deified, and *Tarraco*, as capital of the province, played a fundamental role in the organisation of the imperial cult, a role which is reflected in its monetary issues. During the reign of Tiberius (14-37) the iconographies of the *Tarraco* mint made constant allusions to the memory of Augustus and to his deification. Thus, on the obverse of this example Augustus appears seated on a curule chair, a patera and sceptre in his hands and accompanied by the inscription DEO AVGVSTO. The iconography on the reverse alludes to the temple that the city of *Tarraco* built in honour of Augustus. M.C.

Hoard of Roman denarii from Empúries

Shortly after 44 BC

MNAC/GNC 105023-105090

Tiberius, dupondius from *Tarraco*

After 21-2 AD

MNAC/GNC 15096

∅ 32 mm

The Visigoths, who invaded the lands of the Roman Empire at the end of the fourth century, were one of the most deeply Romanised barbarian peoples. Thus, for instance, they adopted the Roman monetary system based on the solidus as a unit of gold and on the tremissis, or third part of the former. This fraction became the basic value of the issues that the Visigoths minted. The first issues were undertaken when the Visigoths were established in southern Gaul and faithfully imitated Romano-Byzantine imperial issues.

Later, expelled from Gaul by the Franks, the Visigoths settled in Hispania. There, they founded a kingdom that lasted until the Muslim invasion of 711. During the reign of Leovigild, and with the object of creating a distance from the imperial power, they first minted a coinage in the name of their sovereign, who, furthermore, adopted the royal insignia. Minted in Barcelona, this coin testifies to these innovations. On the obverse there is a royal bust engraved in a highly schematic style and the name of the monarch. On the reverse, on the other hand, a cross appears on top of several steps, in imitation of a contemporary Byzantine type, and the name of the mint next to the king's title. A.E.-R.

The authority of the Carolingian kings over part of the area of what is now Catalonia led, among other things, to the establishment of counties and the introduction of a new monetary system based on the currency of silver. The unit of highest value was the pound, which was divided into 20 solidus, 1 solidus into 12 deniers and each denier into 2 oboles. Of this system of theoretical equivalences, which lasted throughout the Middle Ages, only deniers and oboles were minted during this period.

The growing autonomy of the Catalan counts meant that not only would they end up controlling the issuing of coinage, but also, at a given moment, cease minting coinage in the name of the Carolingian monarchs and do so in their own names. This step was taken in Barcelona at the time of Count Ramon Borrell, who manufactured deniers and oboles with his name and a cross on the obverse, and the abbreviation of Barcelona and three rings on the reverse. It is supposed that the rings derive from an issue by King Odon (888-97) in Toulouse, on the reverse side of which there figured, in monogram form, the monarch's name, ODDO. In any event the extremely rare deniers and oboles of Ramon Borrell are exceptional coins manufactured in good silver. A.E.-R.

Like other medieval prelates, the Bishops of Vic obtained the right to mint coinage in the tenth century, retaining it until the beginning of the fourteenth. The types chosen for deniers and oboles varied throughout that period, but they always had a religious character—keys, crosses or a hand giving the blessing—that alluded to the Church as an issuing authority.

The most representative coin of the episcopal issues of Vic is, without a shadow of a doubt, what was then called 'ox coinage or money'. These are examples minted in good silver and of great artistic and technical quality. On the obverse are the face-to-face profile busts of St Peter and St Paul—identified by inscriptions—who hold up what seems to be a processional cross. On the reverse there appears a man with a staff leading a pair of oxen and the inscription AVSO-NA. Although the name of the bishop under whose pontificate they were minted does not appear, these issues are attributed to Sunifred Berenguer de Lluçà (1078-99) because in the documents mention is made of this. A.E.-R.

Leovigild (573-86), tremissis from Barcelona

MNAC/GNC 9869

∅ 18 mm

Ramon Borrell (992-1017), denier from Barcelona

MNAC/GNC 11367

∅ 19 mm

Episcopal denier from Vic

Second half of the eleventh century

MNAC/GNC 15262

∅ 15 mm

The volume of coinage in circulation in the counties occupying the territory in the north of what is now Catalonia was enriched between the end of the tenth century and the first third of the eleventh by the introduction of Muslim gold. This was very common in transactions in the form of dinars or Muslim units of gold, which in the Christian documentation went by the name of *mancusos*. This term derives from the Arab word *manqus*, which means 'engraved' or 'minted'. When genuine dinars were lacking because, despite arriving in lesser quantities, demand for them remained constant, it was necessary to manufacture imitation *mancusos*. Initially, these *mancusos* faithfully copied the iconographic types of the models, although with time the formal aspects were disregarded.

The Òdena hoard, discovered in 1943 in a pit near this locality in the Anoia area, provides clear-cut evidence of the circulation of *mancusos*. The fortuitous circumstances of the find explain its rapid dispersion and our lack of knowledge of such important aspects as the total number of coins or the type of container they were kept in. As it is, in the GNC eleven examples are preserved, of which ten are gold *mancusos* from Barcelona and the remaining one a dinar of Muslim gold minted in Ceuta by Yahyá al-Mu'tali. This composition is especially relevant inasmuch as it subsumes, in a circumscribed, contemporary context, a Muslim coin and the Barcelonan Christian examples that imitated it. In short, it provides conclusive proof of the joint circulation of Muslim dinars and their Christian imitations. A.E.-R.

One of the clearest signs of the economic growth of the thirteenth century was the introduction in the monetary systems of denominations minted in good silver and with a higher value than preexisting deniers and oboles. Thus, the Italian republics began minting the solidus, something hitherto only employed as a unit of counting with a value of 12 deniers. In Catalonia this value was introduced by Peter the Great in 1285, when he ordered the Barcelona *croat* to be manufactured as a thick silver coin. This monarch also created a divisor with a value of a half *croat* and later, in the fifteenth century, other, smaller fractions were established.

The *croat* type copies that of the ternal deniers and oboles of the reign of James I the Conqueror. Thus, on the obverse the crowned bust of the sovereign is shown in profile and on the reverse the cross with rings and points in alternate quadrants. The inscriptions mention, on the obverse, the name of the king and his title and the dedication 'by the grace of God', with the city of Barcelona on the reverse. Peter the Great died shortly after ordering the first minting of *croats*; hence, *croats* bearing his name are rare. His successors went on manufacturing this denomination, while changing the name of the sovereign, until the beginning of the eighteenth century. A.E.-R.

Hoard from Òdena

Mid-eleventh century

MNAC/GNC 80047-80057

Peter II (1276-85), *croat* from Barcelona

MNAC/GNC 34137

∅ 24 mm

The Kings of Majorca implemented a politics of prestige aimed at reinforcing their autonomy vis-à-vis the monarchs of Aragon and France. In particular, James II of Majorca adopted in 1300 an exclusive monetary system initially made up of denominations in silver and billon. In 1310 he added as a new value the gold real, which was a coin of great modulus manufactured in almost pure gold, of which the exclusive monarchs of Majorca only minted a limited number of units, which turns them into rare pieces. It was not until the incorporation of the kingdom into the Crown of Aragon, once Peter III the Ceremonious had conquered it, that various divisors were introduced, for example the half, quarter and eighth real.

The final goal of the manufacture of the real was eminently political, with the object of making the authority and prestige of its monarchs obvious. Its design is extremely elegant, its facture careful, and it draws its inspiration from contemporary French issues. Depicted within a lobed border on the obverse is the sovereign seated on the throne in a majestic pose, displaying the attributes of royal power: the crown, sceptre and the orb topped by a cross. On the reverse there appears a cross with a double crosspiece within a lobed border, which came to be one of the royal symbols. The inscription is continuous—it begins on the obverse and continues on the reverse—and reproduces the name of the monarch alongside his titles as King of Majorca, Count of Roussillon and Cerdaña and Lord of Montpellier. A.E.-R.

At the end of the fifteenth century the most valuable foreign exchange in gold on the international market was the Venice ducat. Many areas of Europe, notable among which were those of the Crown of Aragon, imitated or adapted their currency to the model of the ducat. Ferdinand II the Catholic was the monarch who in 1493 established a set of rules by which the gold coinage of Catalonia was reformed in order to adapt it to said model. In particular, he created the gold *principat*, a new denomination which took the place of earlier gold issues and which was manufactured in the mints of Barcelona and Perpignan. As well as this unit divisors like the half *principat* and multiples like the double and ten *principats* were minted.

The iconography of these coins shows the bust of the sovereign on the obverse and different heraldic variants on the reverse. This double *principat*, produced in the Barcelona mint, features a crowned shield with the combined arms of Sicily, Aragon and the heraldic group specific to Naples with the symbols of Hungary, Anjou and Jerusalem. The inscription is continuous—it begins on the obverse and ends on the reverse—and proclaims Ferdinand as the King, by the grace of God, of Aragon and Count of Barcelona. The execution of the die-stamps used for manufacturing the coin show great mastery in the technique of engraving, which is evident in the elaboration of both the coat of arms and the royal bust. On top of that, the effigy of the sovereign is testimony to the adoption of the Italian taste for the portrait of the monarch. A.E.-R.

Sancho (1311-24), gold real from Majorca

MNAC/GNC 104445

∅ 23 mm

Ferdinand II (1479-1516), double *principat* from Barcelona

MNAC/GNC 308658

∅ 28 mm

In 1989 a hoard of coins was located in the subsoil of the house of the abbot of the monastery of Sant Pere de Rodes (Alt Empordà). The find, made during an archaeological dig, is one of the great numismatic discoveries of recent years in Catalonia, both for being an intact whole, circumscribed and well documented in archaeological terms, and for its particular monetary content, which is exceptional. To be precise, it consists of 658 pieces; 348 are of gold and the rest, 310, of silver. The coins had been placed, forming rolls, in an apothecary jar. The silver coins were separated in the bottom part and the gold ones in the top.

The more modern coins in the hoard indicate that the concealment must have occurred around 1520-30, although there are various examples from the second half of the fourteenth century. For some reason the person who hid the hoard never recovered it, and this fortuitous circumstance has enabled us to have access to an extraordinarily rich and varied collection of the high-value currency which was manufactured in much of Europe. The bulk of the issues in gold follow the model of the Venetian ducat, the strong foreign exchange of the time. The origin of the coins is very varied: Catalonia, Valencia, Majorca, Castile, Portugal, France, Bohemia, Hungary, the Archbishopric of Salzburg, the Knights of the Order of St John of Jerusalem in Rhodes, Milan, Savoy, Modena, Ferrara, Urbino, Saluzzo and Mantua, among others. With regard to the silver issues, the great many *croats* from Barcelona, which had yet to circulate, is noteworthy. A.E.-R.

During his long reign the Emperor Carlos had to face serious territorial problems, mainly relating to the constant threats of France and of the Turks. The conflicts with the two powers had one of their most intense moments in the Tunisian campaign, which the Emperor led in person.

In order to defray a part of the costs of the campaign Carlos I ordered a new issuing of gold, silver and billon coins. Much written documentation exists about this issue, but the source which provides the most precise description of it is the Royal Decree of 30 May 1535. In it the monarch gave all sorts of indications of how the metal, weight, fineness and type of coinage had to be. In terms of the gold coins, it was established that they would be called imperial escudos and would have a degree of fineness of 22 carats, like the best Italian escudos. On the iconography, the document indicates that the obverse should be engraved with the royal arms with an imperial eagle rampant and the inscription CAROLUS QUINTUS IMPERATOR, while the reverse was to show a cross surmounted by imperial crowns and the legend HISPANIARUM ET UTRUSQUE SICILIE REX.

The manufacture of these gold escudos marked the transition between the old medieval mintings of gold—like the ducat or the *principat*, with a higher degree of fineness—and the modern ones, which were now made in other territories. Based on this model, escudos were minted in the different Castilian mints, with a variant on the reverse: the cross surmounted by crowns was replaced by a Jerusalem cross. M.C.M.

Hoard from Sant Pere de Rodes

c. 1520-30

MNAC/GNC 308647-309304

Carlos I, gold escudo from Barcelona

1535

MNAC/GNC 301805

Ø 25 mm

During the reign of Felipe III the mint in Barcelona began to manufacture new issues of gold—trentins and half trentins—in accordance with the Concession of 16 September 1599. The word *trentin* is related to its equivalence with silver coinage. The trentin was worth 2 ducats and initially equalled 35 silver reales. Later, from 1618 onwards, the ratio was reduced to 33 reales.

Trentins and half trentins, which were also minted under the government of Felipe IV, were copies of the double excelentes and its divisors manufactured in the name of the Catholic Monarchs in the different Castilian mints after the 1497 Pragmatic of Medina del Campo. On their obverse these coins feature the face-to-face busts of the Catholic Monarchs, and a mark which identified the mint. On the reverse a crowned shield was engraved with the arms of Castile, Leon, Catalonia-Aragon, Sicily and Granada, protected or otherwise according to the denomination by the eagle of St John. In fact without detailed examination it was difficult to tell the trentins from the original excelentes, since the sole variation was the mint mark situated between the busts of the monarchs. M.C.M.

In Catalonia discontent with the political centralism of Felipe IV led to a long rebellion, the War of Separation (known as *dels Segadors*, the Reapers' War) (1640-52). During the conflict new denominations were minted, firstly in the name of Felipe IV and then of the Principality of Catalonia, at the same time as thirty or so municipalities began to manufacture currency to pay the troops and other costs typical of a state at war.

On 12 February 1641 the Council of Vic decided to start minting silver coins following the model of the Barcelona ones. As for the examples of 5 real pieces, the first issues showed on the obverse the shield of crowned bars and retained the name of King Felipe IV on the legend. The inscription on the reverse alluded to the city of Vic, CIVITAS VICEN 1641, and was divided in four by a cross similar to the one on the *croats*. Shortly afterwards, still in 1641, the workshop in Vic started to manufacture currency in the name of the Principality of Catalonia. M.C.M.

In February 1808 the French armies occupied Barcelona and did not leave until May 1814. During these years the city remained isolated from the rest of the Principality, something which brought about a severe lack of currency. In order to solve the problem the Count of Ezpeleta, Captain General of Catalonia, after meeting with the Real Acuerdo, Knight Intendent, City Council and Coinage Board, decided to reopen the Barcelona mint.

According to the accords of this meeting, revealed in an edict of 21 August 1808, the Barcelona mint was to manufacture provincial coinage of gold and silver with the same fineness and weight as the issues from Madrid, along with coins of copper. The typology chosen was of great simplicity, at the same time as being distinct from the monetary productions of the rest of Spain. The obverse featured the coat of arms of the city surrounded, according to the denomination, by a crown or holm oak branches. On the reverse of these issues the appearance of the nominal value has pride of place, a value expressed for the first time in pesetas on the gold and silver issues, and in *cuartos* on those of copper. M.C.M.

Felipe IV, trentin from Barcelona

1633

MNAC/GNC 107389

∅ 31 mm

Principality of Catalonia, 5 reales from Vic

1641

MNAC/GNC 3767

∅ 37 mm

French Occupation, 5 pesetas from Barcelona

1812

MNAC/GNC 32382

∅ 40 mm

Going by the name of *pellofes* or leads are different kinds of tokens with a fixed monetary value and equivalence that circulated within various religious communities. The clergymen used to receive them in return for their assistance at certain liturgical acts. In this way they were a control mechanism and at the same time an incentive to participate. Moreover, they were used as a system of payment, given that at the end of a set period the pieces received were exchanged for normal coinage.

In some communities *pellofes* with different values were manufactured and circulated simultaneously. In order to avoid confusion, the different values were engraved on the corresponding *pellofa*, which, furthermore, adopted different measurements and shapes. A good example of this are the *pellofes* proceeding from the community of priests of the church of Santa Maria in Vilafranca del Penedès. The iconography of the *pellofes* is religious and in this instance the eyes allude to St Lucy, patron saint of the above ecclesiastical community. Incuse examples are involved; namely, both the obverse and reverse have the same type, in positive on the obverse and in negative on the reverse. This particularity is due to the fact of having been minted on a fine sheet of gilded brass by the system of hammering a single die-stamp with the design one wishes the *pellofa* to have engraved in negative. A.E.-R.

In 1964 a coffer was found with twenty kilograms of coins in a house situated in the township of Puig-reig (Berguedà). The hoard consisted of 781 coins, of which 730 were of silver and 51 of gold. Of the 730 silver coins, only 16 were examples from Spanish mints. The rest were foreign coins, of which 679 were French 5 franc pieces and 35 examples of other provenances, although of a value equivalent to 5 French francs. The hoard also contained 51 gold coins from Spanish mints—peninsular and from the overseas territories—corresponding to the reigns of Carlos III, Carlos IV, Ferdinand VII and Isabella II.

The Puig-reig hoard, then, demonstrates that in the middle of the nineteenth century the circulation of silver coinage was dominated by foreign currency, and gold coinage by issues from the mints of Spain and its overseas colonies. Other monetary finds also reflect this duality, as does the written documentation. Of especial interest in that respect is an inventory of coinage in the safe of the Bank of Spain undertaken in 1849 by Vicente Vázquez Queipo at the request of the Coinage Board. The gold coinage found consisted of many Carlos IV and Ferdinand VII *onzas*, half *onzas*, above all Ferdinand VI ones, and gold doubloons. As regards silver coinage, there were only French 5 franc pieces, the majority from the reign of Louis XVIII and Louis-Philippe. M.C.

Die-stamp and *pellofa* from the church of Santa Maria in Vilafranca del Penedès

End of the eighteenth century – middle of the nineteenth

MNAC/GNC 78128 and 105915

Hoard from Puig-reig

1855 or shortly afterwards

MNAC/GNC 106001-106781

The Provisional Government, set up after the 1868 Revolution that overthrew Isabella II, promoted a political programme of unificatory, rationalist reforms. In terms of the monetary system, a recent project proposing a rapprochement with the models prevailing in Western Europe was revived. In concrete terms, it took as a model the system agreed upon by France, Belgium, Switzerland and Italy in 1865 in the treaty setting up the Latin Monetary Union. In conformity with this treaty a single monetary system was adopted which revolved, in point of fact, around the French franc. The Spanish reform which established the peseta as the new monetary unit was introduced by Decree on 19 October 1868, signed by the Catalan Laureà Figuerola (1816-1904), Chancellor of the Exchequer at the time.

The minting of the first units in silver took place before the approval of the 1869 Constitution and, given that the reforming of the Government was as yet undecided, the Provisional Government was named as the issuing authority. The iconography chosen for the obverse was a female figure personifying Hispania. This figure, which lies with Gibraltar at her feet and the Pyrenees at her back, wears a mural crown on her brow and holds an olive branch in her hand. In point of fact the model was based on mintings from the reign of the Roman Emperor Adrian with a similar iconography. For the reverse an heraldic motif was chosen designed by the Royal Academy of History, which possessed the novelty of being a coat of arms symbolising the nation and not the arms of the reigning dynasty. A.E.-R.

The Civil War caused many monetary problems. One might especially point to the hoarding of silver currency and the distressing lack of small change. Faced with these shortages, in September 1936 the Generalitat's Finance Ministry decided to create a paper money of legal tender for all of Catalonia. This was a series of issues certified by the treasury of the Generalitat, apart from the system guaranteed by the Bank of Spain, which meant that the Republic would end up rejecting and prohibiting them in 1938.

The aim of the Generalitat's resolution to issue paper money was for Catalonia to have a complete monetary system of its own. Different values were planned, extending from 1 to 1,000 pesetas, although in practice only 2, 5 and 10 peseta notes circulated. The design was entrusted to the *Noucentista* artist Josep Obiols (1894-1967) and they were printed in the famous Institut Gràfic Oliva in Vilanova on special paper. The obverse sides of all values were identical, with the shield of Catalonia and a hammer and ear of corn, which alluded to Industry and Agriculture. The reverses of each denomination, meanwhile, were different, as was the colour. In particular the motif of the 5 peseta note depicts a worker and a peasant working on either side of a kind of military trophy consisting of rifles and machine-gun ammunition belts, which appears to allude to the need of focusing all economic activity on the war. A.E.-R.

Provisional Government, 1 peseta from Madrid
1869

MNAC/GNC 38457

∅ 23 mm

Generalitat de Catalunya, 5 peseta note
1936

MNAC/GNC 38251

168 x 70 mm

The appearance of the Catalan medal in the eighteenth century is directly linked to the traditional artisanal production of silversmiths and engravers. It was not until the second half of the nineteenth century that sculptors began to intervene directly in their manufacture. This step undoubtedly involved a renovation of medallistics and a notable increase in the technical quality of the medal. One of the first works that denotes this change of tendency is the medal dedicated to Mariano Fortuny on the occasion of his death in 1874.

Jacint Morató, the sculptor who modelled it, is a little-known artist to whom other medals are attributed, medals that, however, do not possess the skill of the one dedicated to Fortuny. This is a high-quality piece that denotes the transcending of the conventional, academic language of the official medal and the introduction of a more sculptural conception. Worth emphasising, in that respect, are the modelling of the face appearing on the obverse and especially the rich and painstaking working of the painter's curly hair. Features, all of these, which demonstrate an harmonious knowledge of technique and aesthetics. A.E.-R.

The Catalan medal underwent a genuine flowering during *Modernisme*. The most important artist of the period, for the quantity as well as the quality of his work, was Eusebi Arnau. In fact, he was the sculptor who specialised the most in this typology and the one who best understood its visual possibilities. Arnau's consecration as a medallist took place in the 1888 Barcelona Universal Exhibition, for which he created two official medals. From that moment on he monopolised many of the official assignments.

It was precisely Barcelona City Council which commissioned, among other works, this piece dedicated to the *V Exposición Internacional de Arte* held in 1907. Especially noteworthy in this piece is the obverse with the profile bust of a young woman with flowing hair and a crown on her head, outlined against a background in which the shield of Barcelona is hinted at. The allegory of the city, with its North-European medievalising airs, is based on a sculpture on the same theme created by Arnau in 1897. A.E.-R.

Jacint Morató
To Mariano Fortuny
1874

MNAC/GNC 61033

∅ 75 mm

Eusebi Arnau
(Barcelona, 1864-1933)
V Exposició Internacional d'Art de Barcelona
1907

MNAC/GNC 111566

∅ 60 mm

The figure of Pablo Gargallo stands out among the group of early-twentieth-century sculptors who cultivated the art of medal making at a particular moment. Gargallo was a disciple of the sculptor and medallist Eusebi Arnau and revealed himself in turn to be a artist who was especially sensitive to the sculptural relief. All of this gives us a set of clues as to why he might produce various medals.

Outstanding among the lesser-known pieces by Gargallo is, without a shadow a doubt, the medal put out by the Vallmitjana Company on the occasion of the Barcelona Artistic Circle's 1905 exhibition of medals. This is an artist's proof example which is of special interest in that it shows the idealised figure of an engraver of die-stamps accompanied by an inscription which alludes to the Vallmitjana workshop as the publisher of medals. The execution of the image displays a notable expressive and synthetic ability with an economy of iconographic means. It is worth remembering that in 1903 the artist had obtained a grant in Paris, where he had been impressed by the works of the sculptor Auguste Rodin (1840-1917). This early influence may perhaps be discerned in the expressive strength emanating from this medal. A.E.-R.

Antoni Parera was, along with the sculptor Eusebi Arnau, one of the most prolific Catalan medallists. The inauguration of the new Barcelona Law Courts in 1908 enabled him to produce one of his most successful *Modernista* medals. This is a piece that on the obverse features a monumental vision of the building, and in the exergue, below a crown, the shields of Barcelona and Spain. On the reverse, meanwhile, an allegorical scene is shown in which the personification of Barcelona, with crown and shield, offers the Courthouse to the figure of Justice, who advances with her attributes, the scales and the sword. In the exergue, a number of tablets of the Law complete the symbolic evocation of the Courthouse.

One of Parera's most outstanding merits in the design of this medal resides in the fact that he managed to invest an iconography strongly rooted in the tradition of the official, academic medal with the refined and sinuous language of *Modernisme*. Outstanding in that respect is the marked ornamentalist feeling impregnating the composition as a whole and the undulating etherealness, of Symbolist influence, of the allegorical figures of Barcelona and Justice. A.E.-R.

From the first decade of the twentieth century onwards *Modernisme* was increasingly contested. In France, an immediate cultural reference for Catalonia, it evolved in the interwar period to become what is known as Art Deco. This is a style that adopted a sophisticated, refined and elitist language of highly elaborate forms full of exotic, sensual references.

The sculptor Enric Bassas prepared at least two pieces that can be included within this tendency. One of them is a medallion dedicated in 1919, shortly after the end of the First World War, to Peace; the second, the piece illustrated here, is the corporate medal the Reial Cercle Artístic de Barcelona decided to create in 1917. The iconography of the medal associates beauty and inventive and creative genius as the stimuli of the artist. Hence, a female face is shown on the obverse, representing Beauty, while on the reverse the rider mounting a horse is identified with Icarus, the mythological inventor. As for the aesthetics of the piece, the subtle combination of clearly classical features and a refined exoticism is outstanding. A.E.-R.

Pablo Gargallo
(Maella, 1881 – Reus, 1934)
Círculo Artístico de Barcelona Exhibition
1905
MNAC/GNC 111866

∅ 45 mm

Antoni Parera
(Barcelona, 1868-1946)
Barcelona Law Courts
1908
MNAC/GNC 62769

∅ 70 mm

Enric Bassas
(Tiana, 1890-1975)
Reial Cercle Artístic de Barcelona
1917
MNAC/GNC 111862

∅ 45 mm

Index